READING ROUND-UPS

130 Ready-to-Use Literature Enrichment Activities for Grades 5-8

Barbara Farley Bannister

**THE CENTER FOR APPLIED
RESEARCH IN EDUCATION**
West Nyack, New York 10995

With love to Dan, Bob, Lori,
and Eden

ISBN 0-87628-750-X

THE CENTER FOR APPLIED
RESEARCH IN EDUCATION
BUSINESS & PROFESSIONAL DIVISION
A division of Simon & Schuster
West Nyack, New York 10995

Printed in the United States of America

ABOUT THE AUTHOR

Barbara Farley Bannister has been an elementary library media specialist at Memorial Grade School (K–6) in McMinnville, Oregon for over 13 years. Besides her library/media duties, she teaches library skills to all grades and reading enrichment to grades 2-5. Prior to her present position, she taught kindergarten and grades 2, 3, and 5.

Mrs. Bannister earned her B.A. from Western Michigan University (Kalamazoo) and did graduate work at Portland State and Western Oregon State College. A member of the Oregon Educational Media Association and the National Education Association, she has written several media center activity books, including *Library Media Center Activities for Every Month of the School Year* (The Center for Applied Research in Education, 1986).

ABOUT *READING ROUND-UPS*

Reading Round-Ups: 132 Ready-to-Use Literature Enrichment Activities for Grades 5-8 can be used in both the library media center and the classroom. The book's projects and activities will give the library media specialist an already developed program to broaden the students' interests either by using them in library classes or by recommending them to classroom teachers who want to supplement their regular reading program. The units can be the basis for reading clubs, such as a science fiction reading club or a mystery/adventure reading club. The units also can be used for literature appreciation in small-group library skills classes.

The classroom teacher will find this book useful with students who like to work independently. The ready-to-use activities and projects also can be a literature supplement to the basic text or as a program for children who have finished the basic text and need something else for their reading program. One classroom method is to introduce the unit to the entire class using filmstrips or video programs and then let all the students read books in the field at their own level. Those who are able readers could read the books in the unit, do the activities, and then present the projects to the whole class.

Reading Round-Ups features six different areas of fiction. They are:

- Unit 1: Fantasy and Science Fiction
- Unit 2: Mystery and Adventure
- Unit 3: Boys and Girls of Today
- Unit 4: Humorous Stories
- Unit 5: Historical Fiction
- Unit 6: Animals in Fiction

Each unit focuses on one type of fiction and is probably best used in a four- to-six-week period. Ten book titles, along with two reproducible activity pages for each title, are included in each unit. Suggestions for the teacher are given at the beginning of each unit, offering ways to introduce the unit and to make it interesting. Audio-visual material related to the particular unit is listed as well as a list of additional related books. Summaries of each book also are given so that you can become familiar with the story without having to read all of the books.

Each book title in *Reading Round-Ups* has one activity page that lists several projects connected with the book. The student is to choose a project, do it, and then share the project with the class or group. These projects are usually preceded by general questions about the book's author and/or characters. The second activity page for a book title can be diverse, involving such skills as recall, following directions, analysis, or synthesis. These pages can take the form of such activities as creative writing, mazes, crossword puzzles, or wordsearches.

Each unit also includes two pages of additional activities and projects that can be used with other titles in the particular area of fiction. These can be used when you want the students to read other titles or if there are not enough of the specified titles in your book collection.

The titles in *Reading Round-Ups* are ones that children enjoy but are sometimes not read independently unless encouraged to do so. For this reason, such authors as Beverly Cleary or Judy Blume are not included because these authors are usually discovered, read and loved by children on their own. Newbery gold medal winners also are not included since most of these titles are already being covered in Newbery programs by the teacher or librarian. However, several Newbery honor books are mentioned.

Once the reading group has been formed, you can use several methods to determine which student will read a particular title. If your students are all about equal in ability, you can put the titles in a hat and let the students draw the title they will read. Or you might give a brief book talk about each (using the summaries in each unit) and let each student volunteer for the title he or she thinks is most interesting. If there is great diversity in reading abilities, the level of reading difficulty shown in the Skills Index can help you assign books according to ability if you feel this is necessary. After the students begin to exhibit their projects and tell about the books they have read, the other children will usually want to read these books, too.

A "Student's Record Sheet" is included in *Reading Round-Ups* so that students will have a record of the books they have read in each area. Encourage each student to make or buy a folder in which to keep the record sheet and completed activity pages. A "Teacher's Record Sheet" also is included so that you can have a record of the recreational or independent reading of each child in the group.

Best of all, two other important features are included in *Reading Round-Ups*. The first is the Skills Index that will help you quickly locate all the projects and activities for teaching or reinforcing a particular skill, such as creative writing or making judgments. Second, a complete Answer Key for each activity is included at the end of the book, to provide a quick reference when you want to check the answer to any question.

These projects and activities have been used and enjoyed by many students in my own library enrichment classes. I hope that you, too, will find *Reading Round-Ups* an enrichment to your literature appreciation program.

Barbara Farley Bannister

Name _____ Grade _____

STUDENT'S RECORD SHEET

Write in the date when the title is read and the activity sheets completed. If you have previously read the book, put a checkmark under the "Date Completed" column. In the "Opinion" column, put a "G" if you thought the book was GREAT, an "L" if you LIKED it, and a "D" if you DISLIKED the book.

Date Completed	Title	Opinion
	Unit 1: FANTASY AND SCIENCE FICTION	
_____	1-1 *The Lion, the Witch, and the Wardrobe*	_____
_____	1-2 *The Indian in the Cupboard*	_____
_____	1-3 *The White Mountains*	_____
_____	1-4 *The Great Rescue Operation*	_____
_____	1-5 *The Book of Three*	_____
_____	1-6 *The House with a Clock in Its Wall*	_____
_____	1-7 *Omega Station*	_____
_____	1-8 *The Wonderful Flight to the Mushroom Planet*	_____
_____	1-9 *In the Keep of Time*	_____
_____	1-10 *The Forgotten Door*	_____
_____	1-11 _____	_____
	(Title of your choice of book for Unit 1)	
	Unit 2: MYSTERY AND ADVENTURE	
_____	2-1 *The One-Hundredth Thing about Caroline*	_____
_____	2-2 *The Curse of Camp Gray Owl*	_____
_____	2-3 *The Adventures of Tom Sawyer*	_____
_____	2-4 *The Ghost Next Door*	_____
_____	2-5 *My Side of the Mountain*	_____
_____	2-6 *The Red Room Riddle*	_____
_____	2-7 *The Dollhouse Murders*	_____
_____	2-8 *The Egypt Game*	_____
_____	2-9 *The Callender Papers*	_____
_____	2-10 *The Case of the Baker Street Irregulars*	_____
_____	2-11 _____	_____
	(Title of your choice of book for Unit 2)	

STUDENT'S RECORD SHEET (continued)

Date Completed	*Title*	*Opinion*

Unit 3: BOYS AND GIRLS OF TODAY

Date Completed		*Title*	*Opinion*
_____	3-1	*The Unmaking of Rabbit*	_____
_____	3-2	*Don't Hurt Laurie*	_____
_____	3-3	*Nothing's Fair in Fifth Grade*	_____
_____	3-4	*The Iceberg and Its Shadow*	_____
_____	3-5	*Hideaway*	_____
_____	3-6	*Philip Hall Likes Me. I Reckon Maybe*	_____
_____	3-7	*Cracker Jackson*	_____
_____	3-8	*What Do You Do When Your Mouth Won't Open?*	_____
_____	3-9	*Will the Real Gertrude Hollings Please Stand Up?*	_____
_____	3-10	*Hello, My Name is Scrambled Eggs*	_____
_____	3-11	_____	_____

(Title of your choice of book for Unit 3)

Unit 4: HUMOROUS STORIES

Date Completed		*Title*	*Opinion*
_____	4-1	*Thirteen Ways to Sink a Sub*	_____
_____	4-2	*Me and the Terrible Two*	_____
_____	4-3	*The Great Brain*	_____
_____	4-4	*The Kids' Candidate*	_____
_____	4-5	*The Cybil War*	_____
_____	4-6	*Anastasia on Her Own*	_____
_____	4-7	*Alvin Fernald, TV Anchorman*	_____
_____	4-8	*Mysteriously Yours, Maggie Marmelstein*	_____
_____	4-9	*Buddies*	_____
_____	4-10	*Soup on Wheels*	_____
_____	4-11	_____	_____

(Title of your choice of book for Unit 4)

Unit 5: HISTORICAL FICTION

Date Completed		*Title*	*Opinion*
_____	5-1	*The Sign of the Beaver*	_____
_____	5-2	*The Terrible Wave*	_____

Name _____ Grade _____

STUDENT'S RECORD SHEET (continued)

Date Completed		Title	Opinion
_____	5-3	*Wait for Me, Watch for Me, Eula Bee*	_____
_____	5-4	*Journey to Topaz*	_____
_____	5-5	*My Brother Sam Is Dead*	_____
_____	5-6	*An Orphan for Nebraska*	_____
_____	5-7	*Snow Treasure*	_____
_____	5-8	*Fire in the Wind*	_____
_____	5-9	*Three Knocks on the Wall*	_____
_____	5-10	*When Hitler Stole Pink Rabbit*	_____
_____	5-11	_____	_____
		(Title of your choice of book for Unit 5)	

Unit 6: ANIMALS IN FICTION

Date Completed		Title	Opinion
_____	6-1	*Sasha, My Friend*	_____
_____	6-2	*Runaway Stallion*	_____
_____	6-3	*Rascal*	_____
_____	6-4	*Where the Red Fern Grows*	_____
_____	6-5	*A Morgan for Melinda*	_____
_____	6-6	*Old Yeller*	_____
_____	6-7	*Lassie Come Home*	_____
_____	6-8	*The Black Stallion*	_____
_____	6-9	*Misty of Chincoteague*	_____
_____	6-10	*Incident at Hawk's Hill*	_____
_____	6-11	_____	_____
		(Title of your choice of book for Unit 6)	

My favorite book in all of the units was _____

_____

My favorite area of fiction was _____

My favorite type of activity page was _____

Student's Name _____

TEACHER'S RECORD SHEET

Titles Read	*Date*	*Grade*

Unit 1: FANTASY AND SCIENCE FICTION

_____	_____	_____
_____	_____	_____
_____	_____	_____
_____	_____	_____

Unit 2: MYSTERY AND ADVENTURE

_____	_____	_____
_____	_____	_____
_____	_____	_____
_____	_____	_____

Unit 3: BOYS AND GIRLS OF TODAY

_____	_____	_____
_____	_____	_____
_____	_____	_____
_____	_____	_____

Unit 4: HUMOROUS STORIES

_____	_____	_____
_____	_____	_____
_____	_____	_____
_____	_____	_____

Student's Name _____

TEACHER'S RECORD SHEET (continued)

Titles Read   *Date*   *Grade*

Unit 5: HISTORICAL FICTION

_____   ____   ____

_____   ____   ____

_____   ____   ____

_____   ____   ____

_____   ____   ____

Unit 6: ANIMALS IN FICTION

_____   ____   ____

_____   ____   ____

_____   ____   ____

_____   ____   ____

NOTES AND COMMENTS:

CONTENTS

Activity Sheets:

Unit 3 BOYS AND GIRLS OF TODAY   61

Activity Sheets:

Unit 4   HUMOROUS STORIES   91

Suggestions for the Teacher • *92*

Audio-Visual Aids and Related Book Titles • *92*

Summaries of Unit 4 Books • *93*

Activity Sheets:

Unit 5   HISTORICAL FICTION   121

Suggestions for the Teacher • *122*

Audio-Visual Aids and Related Book Titles • *122*

Summaries of Unit 5 Books • *123*

Activity Sheets:

Unit 6   ANIMALS IN FICTION   155

Activity Sheets:

ANSWER KEYS 181

SKILLS INDEX

(Note: The reading difficulty is based on the ability of good readers in intermediate grades. The following key is used: E for EASY, A for AVERAGE, and D for DIFFICULT.)

	RESEARCH SKILLS	LITERATURE APPRECIATION	CREATIVE WRITING	THINKING SKILLS	RECALL/COMPREHENSION	FOLLOWING DIRECTIONS	CREATIVITY/ART	MAKING JUDGMENTS	CREATIVITY/DRAMA	EXPOSITORY WRITING
1-1 *The Lion, the Witch, and the Wardrobe* (D)										
Projects			•	•		•	•		•	
Activities	•				•	•				
1-2 *The Indian in the Cupboard* (A)										
Projects	•	•	•				•			
Activities			•					•		
1-3 *The White Mountains* (D)										
Projects	•		•				•			
Activities	•				•	•				
1-4 *The Great Rescue Operation* (E)										
Projects	•		•				•			
Activities	•			•	•	•				
1-5 *The Book of Three* (D)										
Projects					•		•			
Activities					•	•	•	•		
1-6 *The House with a Clock in Its Wall* (D)										
Projects	•		•				•			
Activities	•				•	•				
1-7 *Omega Station* (E)										
Projects	•		•				•			
Activities	•				•	•				
1-8 *The Wonderful Flight to the Mushroom Planet* (A)										
Projects			•	•			•		•	
Activities			•	•	•					
1-9 *In the Keep of Time* (D)										
Projects	•	•	•				•			
Activities	•				•	•				
1-10 *The Forgotten Door* (E)										
Projects	•									
Activities	•		•		•			•		
1-11 Additional Projects			•	•	•				•	
Additional Activities	•				•	•		•		

SKILLS INDEX

	RESEARCH SKILLS	LITERATURE APPRECIATION	CREATIVE WRITING	THINKING SKILLS	RECALL/COMPREHENSION	FOLLOWING DIRECTIONS	CREATIVITY/ART	MAKING JUDGMENTS	CREATIVITY/DRAMA	EXPOSITORY WRITING
2-1 The One-Hundredth Thing about Caroline (E)										
Projects	•		•				•			•
Activities				•	•	•		•		
2-2 The Curse of Camp Gray Owl (A)										
Projects	•			•						
Activities	•			•	•			•		
2-3 The Adventures of Tom Sawyer (D)										
Projects	•							•	•	
Activities				•	•			•		
2-4 The Ghost Next Door (E)										
Projects	•		•				•			
Activities				•	•			•		
2-5 My Side of the Mountain (D)										
Projects	•		•	•			•	•		•
Activities	•		•	•				•		
2-6 The Red Room Riddle (D)										
Projects	•		•	•						
Activities	•				•	•				
2-7 The Dollhouse Murders (A)										
Projects			•				•		•	
Activities					•	•		•		
2-8 The Egypt Game (D)										
Projects	•			•			•			
Activities	•					•		•		
2-9 The Callender Papers (D)										
Projects	•								•	•
Activities				•	•			•		
2-10 The Case of the Baker Street Irregulars (D)										
Projects	•			•			•			
Activities	•			•	•	•		•		
2-11 Additional Projects	•		•	•					•	
Additional Activities	•			•	•					

SKILLS INDEX

		RESEARCH SKILLS	LITERATURE APPRECIATION	CREATIVE WRITING	THINKING SKILLS	RECALL/COMPREHENSION	FOLLOWING DIRECTIONS	CREATIVITY/ART	MAKING JUDGMENTS	CREATIVITY/DRAMA	EXPOSITORY WRITING
3-1	*The Unmaking of Rabbit* (A)										
	Projects	•		•				•			•
	Activities	•			•	•			•		
3-2	*Don't Hurt Laurie* (A)										
	Projects	•	•	•							•
	Activities	•				•	•				
3-3	*Nothing's Fair in Fifth Grade* (E)										
	Projects	•	•	•					•	•	•
	Activities	•			•	•					
3-4	*The Iceberg and Its Shadow* (A)										
	Projects				•	•		•			
	Activities					•	•				
3-5	*Hideaway* (D)										
	Projects	•		•				•	•	•	•
	Activities					•	•	•	•		
3-6	*Philip Hall Likes Me. I Reckon Maybe* (D)										
	Projects	•						•	•	•	•
	Activities	•				•	•		•		
3-7	*Cracker Jackson* (A)										
	Projects	•				•			•		•
	Activities	•		•	•				•		
3-8	*What Do You Do When Your Mouth Won't Open?* (E)										
	Projects			•	•					•	
	Activities	•									•
3-9	*Will the Real Gertrude P. Hollings Please Stand Up?* (D)										
	Projects	•		•				•			•
	Activities	•				•	•		•		
3-10	*Hello, My Name Is Scrambled Eggs* (A)										
	Projects		•	•							•
	Activities	•		•		•			•		

SKILLS INDEX

	RESEARCH SKILLS	LITERATURE APPRECIATION	CREATIVE WRITING	THINKING SKILLS	RECALL/COMPREHENSION	FOLLOWING DIRECTIONS	CREATIVITY/ART	MAKING JUDGMENTS	CREATIVITY/DRAMA	EXPOSITORY WRITING
3-11 Additional Projects	•						•		•	•
Additional Activities			•		•	•		•		
4-1 *Thirteen Ways to Sink a Sub* (E)										
Projects		•	•	•			•			
Activities	•					•		•		
4-2 *Me and the Terrible Two* (A)										
Projects			•	•						
Activities	•		•	•	•			•		
4-3 *The Great Brain* (D)										
Projects	•	•		•				•		
Activities	•			•	•	•				
4-4 *The Kids' Candidate* (A)										
Projects			•				•		•	
Activities	•				•	•				
4-5 *The Cybil War* (A)										
Projects	•	•	•						•	
Activities	•			•	•	•		•		
4-6 *Anastasia on Her Own* (A)										
Projects			•	•		•				
Activities	•			•	•			•		
4-7 *Alvin Fernald, TV Anchorman* (A)										
Projects	•	•	•					•		
Activities	•			•	•					
4-8 *Mysteriously Yours, Maggie Marmelstein* (A)										
Projects	•		•			•	•			
Activities	•		•		•			•		
4-9 *Buddies* (A)										
Projects			•	•				•	•	
Activities	•				•	•		•		
4-10 *Soup on Wheels* (A)										
Projects	•		•	•				•	•	
Activities	•			•	•			•		

SKILLS INDEX

	RESEARCH SKILLS	LITERATURE APPRECIATION	CREATIVE WRITING	THINKING SKILLS	RECALL/COMPREHENSION	FOLLOWING DIRECTIONS	CREATIVITY/ART	MAKING JUDGMENTS	CREATIVITY/DRAMA	EXPOSITORY WRITING
4-11 Additional Projects	•		•	•				•		
Additional Activities				•	•					
5-1 *The Sign of the Beaver* (D)										
Projects			•				•			•
Activities	•		•	•	•					
5-2 *The Terrible Wave* (A)										
Projects	•		•				•			•
Activities	•			•	•	•				
5-3 *Wait for Me, Watch for Me, Eula Bee* (D)										
Projects	•						•			•
Activities				•	•	•		•		
5-4 *Journey to Topaz* (A)										
Projects	•		•	•						•
Activities	•			•	•			•		
5-5 *My Brother Sam Is Dead* (D)										
Projects	•						•			•
Activities	•			•	•	•		•		
5-6 *An Orphan for Nebraska* (D)										
Projects	•		•			•	•			
Activities	•			•	•	•		•		
5-7 *Snow Treasure* (A)										
Projects	•		•				•			•
Activities	•			•	•	•		•		
5-8 *Fire in the Wind* (A)										
Projects	•						•		•	
Activities	•			•	•	•				
5-9 *Three Knocks on the Wall* (D)										
Projects	•						•			•
Activities	•			•	•	•		•		
5-10 *When Hitler Stole Pink Rabbit* (A)										
Projects		•	•				•			
Activities				•	•			•		

SKILLS INDEX

	RESEARCH SKILLS	LITERATURE APPRECIATION	CREATIVE WRITING	THINKING SKILLS	RECALL/COMPREHENSION	FOLLOWING DIRECTIONS	CREATIVITY/ART	MAKING JUDGMENTS	CREATIVITY/DRAMA	EXPOSITORY WRITING
5-11 Additional Projects	•			•			•			•
Additional Activities	•			•	•	•				
6-1 *Sasha, My Friend* (A)										
Projects	•		•				•	•		•
Activities	•		•		•					
6-2 *Runaway Stallion* (A)										
Projects			•				•		•	
Activities	•		•		•					
6-3 *Rascal* (D)										
Projects	•			•			•			•
Activities	•		•	•		•				
6-4 *Where the Red Fern Grows* (D)										
Projects	•						•			•
Activities				•	•					
6-5 *A Morgan for Melinda* (E)										
Projects	•						•			•
Activities			•	•				•		
6-6 *Old Yeller* (D)										
Projects	•		•				•			
Activities	•			•	•	•		•		
6-7 *Lassie Come Home* (D)										
Projects	•	•					•			•
Activities	•			•	•	•				
6-8 *The Black Stallion* (A)										
Projects	•		•				•			•
Activities	•		•		•			•		
6-9 *Misty of Chincoteague* (A)										
Projects	•						•			•
Activities	•			•	•	•				
6-10 *Incident at Hawk's Hill* (D)										
Projects	•			•			•		•	•
Activities	•		•		•			•		

SKILLS INDEX

	RESEARCH SKILLS	LITERATURE APPRECIATION	CREATIVE WRITING	THINKING SKILLS	RECALL/COMPREHENSION	FOLLOWING DIRECTIONS	CREATIVITY/ART	MAKING JUDGMENTS	CREATIVITY/DRAMA	EXPOSITORY WRITING
6-11 Additional Projects	●			●			●		●	●
Additional Activities					●					

FANTASY AND SCIENCE FICTION

SUGGESTIONS FOR THE TEACHER

Fantasy and Science Fiction are so closely related that it is often difficult to determine into which category a book will fit. Children of today seem to enjoy both fantasy and science fiction if encouraged to read them.

Starting children in a fantasy and science fiction unit could be begun by introducing students to the type of books they will read with a sound filmstrip such as *Fantasy* by Pied Piper Productions. Other sound filmstrips available that help to introduce this type of book are *Science Fiction*, also by Pied Piper Productions, and *Reading in Science Fiction* by Random House. Showing one or more of these sound filmstrips will familiarize them with the type of books they will be reading and also help them to realize that science fiction is not necessarily just books about outer space and that fantasy is not always just about talking animals.

After introducing the students to the type of books they will be reading, show them the books in this unit by exhibiting them and giving a book talk about each. If you feel uncomfortable giving book talks, read the summary of each book given with this unit or read the blurb on the book jacket. If you want your introduction to the books to be more exciting, you could prepare a prop for each book such as a piece of Turkish Delight candy for *The Lion, the Witch, and the Wardrobe*, a toy plastic Indian for *The Indian in the Cupboard*, a wire mesh cap for *The White Mountains*, some tiny stuffed mice for *The Great Rescue Operation*, etc.

After the introduction to each book, whether elaborate or simple, let the children choose their own book as much as possible. If you feel you need to guide them, *The Great Rescue Operation, The Forgotten Door, Omega Station, The Indian in the Cupboard*, and *The Wonderful Flight to the Mushroom Planet* are easier for most children and could be given to the children who have not shown much enthusiasm for this type of fiction or who need material that is easier. *The Book of Three, The White Mountains*, and *In the Keep of Time* are more difficult and could be given to those children who are excellent readers or have already read in this field and are enthusiastic about it. If you need more guidance on the difficulty of the books, see the "Difficulty Chart" at the beginning of this book.

After the children have each picked a book, explain the recordkeeping procedures and tell them about the activity sheets to be done after the reading of their book. Read them some of the possible projects and tell students that they will be asked to do a project for their book and to show it to the class.

When the first student has completed his or her book and has done the activity sheets, you may want to help with choosing a project. After the student has completed the project, be sure to allow class time for each student to exhibit the project and to explain it in relation to the book he or she has read. These projects do much to excite the other children about the titles in the unit and to encourage them to read some of the books.

At the end of the allotted time for this unit, you will find that some children may have read only one or two books and completed activities and projects while others have finished five or six. This is not important as long as each child has had a good introduction to fantasy and science fiction and has had an enjoyable experience reading in this area.

AUDIO-VISUAL AIDS
AND RELATED BOOK TITLES

Here are a few of the many audio-visual items and book titles that can be used with this fantasy and science fiction unit.

Sound Filmstrips

The following filmstrips are accompanied by cassettes:

Science Fiction (Pied Piper Productions)
Fantasy (Pied Piper Productions)
Reading Science Fiction (Random House)
A Wrinkle in Time (Random House)
A Wind in the Door (Random House)
The Time Machine (Random House)
War of the Worlds (Random House)
The Cricket in Times Square (Random House)
Harry Cat's Pet Puppy (Random House)
The Hero and the Crown (Random House)
The Blue Sword (Random House)

Related Book Titles

Anderson, Margaret. *In the Mists of Time.*
Baum, L. Frank. *The Wizard of Oz.*
Bellairs, John. *The Figure in the Shadows.*
Christopher, John. *The City of Gold and Lead* and *The Pool of Fire.*
Cross, John. *The Angry Planet.*
Key, Alexander. *Escape to Witch Mountain.*
L'Engle, Madeleine. *A Wrinkle in Time.*
Lewis, C. S. All the books in *The Chronicles of Narnia.*
McKinley, Robin. *The Blue Sword.*
Norton, André. *The Cat from Outer Space.*
Norton, Mary. *The Borrowers.*
Seldon, George. *Harry Cat's Pet Puppy.*
Slote, Alfred. *The Trouble on Janus.*
White, E. B. *Stuart Little.*

SUMMARIES OF UNIT 1 BOOKS

1-1 *The Lion, the Witch, and the Wardrobe* by C. S. Lewis (New York: Macmillan, 1950. 154 pages). Lucy, Edmund, Peter, and Susan are sent to live with an old professor in the country because of the bombings in London during World War II. While exploring the professor's strange house, Lucy opens a large wardrobe, steps inside, and soon finds herself in the strange land of Narnia. Her brothers and sister will not believe her story of Narnia until they, too, find themselves in this land of eternal winter but where Christmas never comes. The children's struggles to help Aslan, the good lion, defeat the White Witch and bring Christmas and springtime back to Narnia is an exciting story that most children greatly enjoy.

1-2 *The Indian in the Cupboard* by Lynne Banks (New York: Doubleday, 1980. 181 pages). For his birthday, Omri receives a white cupboard from his brother. He wishes that it had a key so he could lock it, so his mother gives him a boxful of keys—and he finds a key that fits. When Omri puts a small plastic Indian inside the cupboard that night, he hears strange noises. Opening the cupboard's door, he finds that the plastic Indian has turned into a tiny—but real—Indian! Omri isn't sure if it's the key or the cupboard that's magic, but he experiments and finds that only plastic items become real when placed in the cupboard. Omri cannot resist telling his friend, Patrick, about the tiny Indian, whose name is Little Bear. Patrick demands that Omri make him a live tiny cowboy. Omri realizes the responsibility of caring for a living being and refuses, but while Omri is out of the room, Patrick changes a plastic cowboy and horse into a live cowboy and his tiny horse. The cowboy and Little Bear do not get along, so Omri's troubles really begin. Omri also has trouble trying to keep the tiny creatures a secret both at home and at school. This is an engrossing story that will be enjoyed by all students.

1-3 *The White Mountains* by John Christopher (New York: Macmillan, 1967. 184 pages). The distant future is the setting for this story. The world as we know it today has been destroyed long ago and the world of the future seems to be ruled by Tripods who control the people by "capping" them as they reach the age of thirteen. This "capping" makes the people docile and receptive to all orders given to them through the cap. Will, a 12-year-old boy, is upset when he sees his fun-loving cousin, Jack, changed by the "capping." Will meets Ozymandias, who has evaded capping by trickery. He tells Will that there is a place, the White Mountains, where there are no Tripods and where people can be free. The story of Will's trip to the White Mountains with two others boys, Henry and Beanpole, is exciting reading and most students will want to read the other two books in the trilogy—*The City of Gold and Lead* and *The Pool of Fire*. While the trilogy is often suggested as reading for gifted students, other students who are good readers but not necessarily "gifted" will enjoy the books for their fast-paced stories.

1-4 *The Great Rescue Operation* by Jean Van Leeuwen (New York: Dial Press, 1982. 167 pages). Marvin the Magnificent, Raymond, and Fats are three contented mice who live a comfortable life in the toy department of Macy's. There is always plenty for them to eat and things for them to play with. Things begin to get boring, however, when there are no more Christmas shoppers. The clerks and customers all seem quiet and bored now that the Christmas rush is over. Marvin tries to add spice to their lives by doing a tightwire circus act. He falls and then everyone notices him and chases him all over the store. When he returns to the dollhouse, which is the home of the three mice, Marvin finds that Fats has disappeared. The last time Raymond saw Fats was when he was taking a nap in a doll carriage that has apparently been sold! Marvin and Raymond find the address of the purchaser by looking through the sales slips and set out to rescue Fats. The ensuing rescue mission involves subway rides, bus trips, bruises, and setbacks as Marvin and Raymond make many plans and try to carry them out. At last they locate Fats living a contented life in the luxurious room of lonely but rich Emily. Now Raymond and Marvin must not only persuade Fats to leave this pampered life, but they must also try to find a friend for the lonely little Emily. The way they manage to complete the great rescue operation is fun-filled reading.

1-5 *The Book of Three* by Lloyd Alexander (New York: Holt, Rinehart & Winston, 1964. 224 pages). Taran, an assistant pigkeeper at Cair Dallben, begins an exciting adventure when he tries to catch Hen Wen, the oracular pig, who has escaped from her pen. In the process of trying to catch the frightened Hen Wen, Taran meets an interesting bard who turns out to be a former king; Eilonwy, a young girl who is in training to be an enchantress; and Gurgi, an odd but loyal creature. These strange friends work together to help defeat the Horned King, who is an evil follower of Arawn, the wicked ruler of Annuvin. They manage to catch the runaway Hen Wen while still helping Lord Gwydion, Prince of Cair Dathyl, to defeat the evil Horned King. In the process of doing all this, Taran, who wishes to be a hero like Lord Gwydion, needs much help but proves himself to be brave and resourceful. This book is exciting but is long and involved and is best enjoyed by readers who already enjoy science fiction and fantasy.

1-6 *The House with a Clock in Its Walls* by John Bellairs (New York: Dial Press, 1973. 179 pages). This is an exciting book for most good readers in the fifth or sixth grades. Lewis lives with his Uncle Jonathan in a strange house whose stained-glass windows have pictures that move and where the fireplace flames can show you any event in history. The unusual is commonplace in this strange house. It's the kind of house Lewis always wanted to live in except for the ticking clock hidden somewhere in the walls. The magic of Uncle Jonathan and his neighbor, Mrs. Zimmerman, always seems to turn out well, but when Lewis tries to impress a friend by using magic in a graveyard on Halloween night, the consequences are almost fatal. This book usually inspires students to read other books about Lewis, such as *The Figure in the Shadows* and *The Letter, the Witch, and the Ring*.

1-7 *Omega Station* by Alfred Slote (New York: Lippincott, 1983. 147 pages). Jack Jameson and his robot Danny One Jameson agree to help Dr. Atkins find out how the evil and dangerous Otto Drago is robot-napping the Atkins' robots from the planet C.O.L.A.R. Jack agrees to pretend to be a robot on C.O.L.A.R. and Danny One is to replace him if it becomes dangerous. The plan works because Jack (as the robot) is robot-napped by Otto Drago himself and taken to Omega Station. Jeff, Anne, Carl, and Danny One, four of Dr. Atkins' robots, are supposed to follow Jack to help him if necessary. Unfortunately, Omega Station has an impenetrable shield that keeps them away. Jack must now not only discover how Otto Drago is robot-napping the robots but also why he is doing it, keep Otto from discovering he is not a robot, and find out the combination that will open the shield so his robot friends can come into Omega Station to help him. The combination is finally deciphered just in time because Jack was about to enter a deadly pool to arm some outlawed plutonium bombs for Dr. Drago. This book is one of a series about Jack Jameson and Danny One, which begins with *My Robot Buddy*.

1-8 *The Wonderful Flight to the Mushroom Planet* by Eleanor Cameron (Boston: Little, Brown and Company, 1954. 214 pages). David and Chuck build a spaceship in answer to a newspaper ad. They are chosen by the mysterious placer of the ad, Mr. Bass, to make the trip to the Mushroom Planet to rescue the people there from death. The people on the Mushroom Planet are slowly dying because their food supply, a particular kind of mushroom, is dying out, so David and Chuck's mission is to try to save the people from starvation. At Mr. Bass' insistence, David and Chuck take along a mascot—David's hen, Mrs. Pennyfeather. This choice of a mascot proves to be a lucky one for the boys because they discover that the particular substance the Mushroom people need in order to live is also found in eggs—the substance being sulphur. So, because of Mrs. Pennyfeather, David and Chuck are able to introduce eggs into the diet of the Mushroom people and save them. The Great Ta, King of the Mushroom People, thanks them by giving the boys a strange necklace of glowing stones. When David and Chuck return to earth, they find that Mr. Bass has disappeared, but he leaves a message and a legacy for them. This book has withstood the test of time and is still enjoyed by even the more sophisticated children of today.

1-9 *In the Keep of Time* by Margaret Anderson (New York: Alfred A. Knopf, 1977. 149 pages). The four Elliot children—Elinor, Andrew, Ian, and Ollie—are sent to Smailholm cottage to spend the summer with their great aunt Grace. They think it will be a boring summer, but it turns out to be more exciting than they could ever imagine! Behind Aunt Grace's cottage is a real castle. The castle belongs to the government, but Aunt Grace keeps the key so tourists can visit it. One day Aunt Grace suggests that the children visit the castle. On their first visit, a large crow falls dead at their feet and makes them feel that there is something strange about the castle. The second time they visit, the key appears to glow luminously and when they turn it in the lock of the castle and go inside, they find themselves in an ancient time with Ollie, the youngest Elliot child, mysteriously trapped in that time as the daughter of Muckle-Mooth Meg. After some exciting adventures, the children manage to return to the present—only to find that little Ollie is still the daughter of the strange woman of the past. Now they must try to return to the past to regain Ollie and in the meantime they must educate the daughter to the present time so that Aunt Grace will not know what has happened. This story should hold the interest of most readers.

1-10 *The Forgotten Door* by Alexander Key (Philadelphia: Westminster Press, 1965. 126 pages). Little Jon is watching the stars one night when he falls through a door into a new and strange country. His memory disappears, but he knows that everything here is strange and that he, too, is a stranger in this unknown land. He first meets people who try to catch him and whom he recognizes as mean-spirited and dangerous. His next encounter is with the Bean family—Thomas, his wife Mary, his daughter Sally, and his son Brooks. The Bean family befriend Little Jon and try to understand who he is and where he came from. They must also defend him from accusations of thievery and try to keep him from being turned over to the Welfare Department of the United States Government. As Little Jon gradually remembers his past life, he realizes that he will cause trouble for the Beans if he stays with them or if he leaves. In the end, Little Jon invites the Beans to return with him to his own planet where people can communicate with their minds both to each other and to animals, where there are no wars, no need for money, and where life is peaceful and beautiful. This book is easy to read for most intermediate students.

PROJECTS FOR
THE LION, THE WITCH,
AND THE WARDROBE

1. C. S. Lewis, the author of *The Lion, the Witch, and the Wardrobe,* was born in Belfast.

   Where is Belfast? _____

2. What do the initials "C" and "S" stand for in this author's name?

   _____

3. Before writing books for children, C. S. Lewis was a well-known theologian. What is a

   theologian? _____

4. What was the first book C. S. Lewis wrote for children?

   _____

5. When was it published? _____

CHOOSE ONE OF THE FOLLOWING PROJECTS:

1. **Prepare Turkish Delight** and share it with the class. Combine and let stand for at least five minutes: ⅓ cup lemon or lime juice, 3 tbsp. cold water, grated rind of one lemon, and 2 tbsp. gelatin. In a large heavy pan over moderate heat, put ⅔ cup water and 2 cups sugar. Stir until sugar dissolves. When boiling, cover pot and boil 2 or 3 minutes. Uncover and cook to a soft ball stage, 234°F, without stirring. Remove pot from heat and add the gelatin mixture. Return to heat and stir until candy thermometer says 224°F. Add food coloring if desired. Pour mixture into lightly oiled 8″ × 8″ pan in which you have sprinkled 1 cup chopped nuts. Let stand for 12 hours. Sprinkle with powdered sugar and then cut with a buttered or sugared knife into small pieces. Dust the pieces with sugar. You might want to dip the pieces in chocolate if desired.
2. **Prepare a diorama** or a painting of Narnia.
3. **Make clothespin characters** of the main characters in Narnia.
4. **Write another adventure** of Peter, Susan, Edmund, and Lucy. Be sure to tell how they get to Narnia, since the Professor told them not to try to use the same route to Narnia (through the Wardrobe).
5. **Make your own wordsearch** using characters or places from the story.
6. **Prepare a television commercial** for the book. Pattern it after commercials you have seen on television. Make your commercial at least one minute long. Then present it to the class.

SAVE LUCY

Lucy is in the castle of the White Witch. Can you rescue her by following the directions below.

1. Go the same number of spaces south as the number of Lucy's brothers and sisters.
2. Go as many spaces west as there were thrones in the Great Hall of Cair Paravel.
3. Go as many spaces south as the number of times Lucy went to Narnia.
4. If Edmund was angry with Lucy, go seven spaces east. If he was angry at Peter, go eleven spaces east.
5. Go as many spaces north as the number of times that Edmund went to Narnia.
6. If Lucy is the youngest in the family, go thirteen spaces east. If Edmund is the youngest, go four spaces east.
7. If Turkish Delight is small cakes, go six spaces south. If it is candy, go eight spaces south.
8. If Lucy's friend Mr. Tumnus had a hollow tree for a home, go five spaces west. If his home was a cave, go eleven spaces west.
9. If Mr. Tumnus cried because he was afraid of the White Witch, go four spaces north. If Mr. Tumnus cried because he tricked Lucy, go three spaces north.
10. Go the same number of spaces west as there were beavers in the story.
11. Go thirteen squares south if Christmas finally comes to Narnia. Go ten spaces south if it never comes.
12. If you look for two lamp posts to find the White Witch's house, go six squares east. If you look for two hills to find it, go eight spaces east.
13. If the wicked Dwarf tied Edmund to a tree, go two spaces north. If he tied him to the sledge, go five spaces north.
14. If Rumblebuffin was a dwarf, go five spaces east. If he was a giant, go three spaces east.

© 1988 by The Center for Applied Research in Education, Inc.

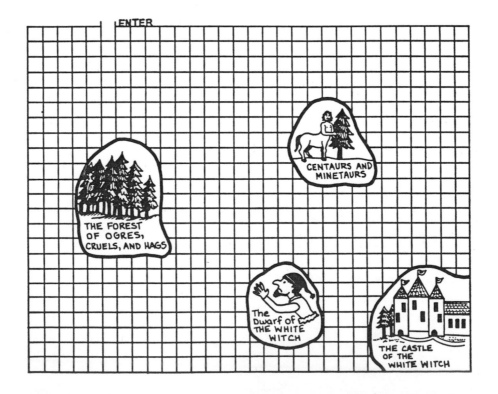

PROJECTS FOR
THE INDIAN IN THE CUPBOARD

1. Would you have liked Omri for a friend? _____

   Why or why not? _____

   _____

2. Would you like to have Patrick as a friend?

   _____ Why or why not? _____

   _____

   _____

   _____

3. Would you have sent Little Bear, Bright Stars, and Boone back to their own time as Omri did, or would you have kept them in the present time? (Tell why you would do this.) _____

   _____

   _____

   _____

CHOOSE ONE OF THE FOLLOWING PROJECTS:

1. Build a longhouse like the one Little Bear made. Make it as much like the one in the story as you can. Include Little Bear and his horse in your construction, if possible. Be ready to show it to the class and tell the class about it and the book *The Indian in the Cupboard*.
2. *The Borrowers* by Mary Norton also is about little people. Read the book *The Borrowers* and then tell the class about this book.
3. Write a new adventure for Omri and his magic cupboard. Let him put a different plastic item in the cupboard and then tell what happens to the item and to Omri.
4. Paint or draw an illustration from *The Indian in the Cupboard*. Be ready to show your illustration to the class and to tell the class about the book.
5. Little Bear said he was an Iroquois brave. Research the Iroquois Indians and write a report on how they lived.
6. Write a story of a girl and a magic cupboard. What kind of a toy might she put into the cupboard? What could happen to the toy and to the girl?

THE MAGIC BOX

Finish the following story by writing your own fantasy. Draw in the picture frame what is in the magic box.

Kelly had found the carved wooden box in the dump. It was caked with dirt and one leg was chipped, but when Kelly cleaned it the box looked very nice on the nightstand in Kelly's room.

It was hard to decide what to keep in the box, but at last Kelly decided to put _____ in the box. After closing the lid Kelly turned out the light and jumped into bed. "Who could have thrown away such a beautiful box?" Kelly thought.

Suddenly there was a strange noise. Kelly turned on the light and looked at the radio…No, it was turned off! The noise seemed to be coming from the carved box. Slowly, Kelly

opened the lid and then blinked in astonishment for there was _____

_____

_____

_____

_____

_____

_____

_____

_____

_____

_____

(If you need more space to write, use the back of this sheet.)

PROJECTS FOR
THE WHITE MOUNTAINS

1. Where was John Christopher born?

_____

2. In what year was he born? _____

3. "John Christopher" is a pseudonym. What is the author's real name?

_____

4. The White Mountains talked about in the story are not called the White Mountains today.

What do you think is the name of these mountains today? _____

5. Are there any mountains called the White Mountains today? Use a geographical dictionary to find out. If there are any, write their locations below.

_____

_____

6. Who do you think the "Ancients" were? _____

What makes you think so? _____

_____

CHOOSE ONE OF THE FOLLOWING PROJECTS:

1. Make a map of Will's journey. Try to figure out where he was by using a present-day map. Show your map to the class and explain it by telling some of the story of *The White Mountains*.
2. Write a television or radio script for this story. You will need to choose just one incident to dramatize. Read your script to the class or choose some friends to help you read or dramatize it.
3. Paint or draw an illustration for this book. Make your illustration at least 12″ × 18″. Show your illustration to the class and explain the part of the story which it illustrates.
4. Write a story of the adventures of a boy and girl who escape the "capping." You might have them meet Will and try to join him or you could have them find their own escape from the Tripods.

CAN YOU FIND THE WHITE MOUNTAINS?

After you have read *The White Mountains*, you should be able to follow the directions below and reach the White Mountains.

1. Go as many spaces south as the number of friends who tried to reach the White Mountains.
2. Go 5 spaces east if Eloise had been capped. If she had not been capped, go 3 spaces west.
3. If the boys wanted to reach the White Mountains because they thought there were no cappings or Tripods there, go 5 spaces east. If they wanted to get to the White Mountains because Henry's father was there, go 5 spaces south.
4. If the cappings took place in a Tripod, go 6 spaces south. If the cappings took place in a church, go 2 spaces south.
5. If Will received the map with the route to the White Mountains from Beanpole, go 5 spaces west. If he received the map from Ozymandias, go 5 spaces east.
6. Eloise's prize for being chosen "Queen of the Tournament" was to serve the Tripods forever. If Eloise was happy about this, go 2 spaces south. If she was sad, go 4 spaces south.
7. If Will got away from the Castle of the Red Tower on foot, go 2 spaces east. If he escaped on horseback, go 8 spaces west.
8. If the Tripods could follow the boys because of the metal button under Will's arm, go 7 spaces south. If they followed them because of a searchlight, go 8 spaces south.
9. If the boys got away from the Tripods by hiding in a cave, go 3 spaces south. If they got away by throwing "metal eggs" and destroying it, go 3 spaces east.

© 1988 by The Center for Applied Research in Education, Inc.

ENTER HERE

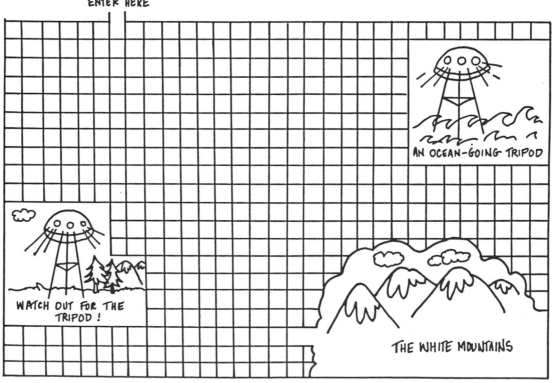

AN OCEAN-GOING TRIPOD

WATCH OUT FOR THE TRIPOD!

THE WHITE MOUNTAINS

PROJECTS FOR
THE GREAT RESCUE OPERATION

Raymond, Fats, and Marvin the Magnificent
are very different. Put the name of the mouse
most likely to do the thing described on the lines below.

1. _____ Swing on a chandelier

2. _____ Keep a diary of his daily activities

3. _____ Tickle a sleeping guard at Macy's Department Store

4. _____ Go to the kitchen at midnight in search of a chocolate cupcake

5. _____ Sleep on a soft pillow

6. _____ Discuss a plan of action carefully before acting

7. _____ Rush into action without a plan

8. _____ Be very brave (but sometimes not very wise!)

CHOOSE ONE OF THE FOLLOWING PROJECTS:

1. Make a two-story dollhouse like the one Raymond and Marvin lived in at Macy's or at Emily's house.

2. Prepare a bibliography of mouse books that are available in your library. Include both fiction and nonfiction. Be sure to include at least ten titles.

3. Write a new adventure for Marvin, Raymond, and Fats.

4. Marvin is certainly a "city mouse." Read the fable of the country mouse and the city mouse. Write a new fable with Marvin as the city mouse. Tell what happens to him when his cousin invites him to the country. Then tell what Marvin shows his country cousin when the cousin visits the city.

5. Write a 5-day diary for Marvin. Remember, he is an adventuresome mouse, so be sure to have many adventures for him. Perhaps he could visit the Empire State Building or the Statue of Liberty. Perhaps he could get lost in Central Park or on the subway.

6. Make clay replicas of Marvin, Fats, and Raymond. Be ready to show the figures to the class and tell about each one.

CAN YOU RESCUE FATS?

By knowing your mouse facts and using the card catalog, *Junior Book of Authors,* a dictionary, and an encyclopedia, you can find your way through the spaces to rescue Fats. Follow the directions exactly!

1. If the copyright date for *The Mouse and the Motorcycle* is 1965, go 2 spaces east. If the copyright is 1980, go 5 spaces east.
2. If a mouse is a type of chamois, go 4 spaces north. If it is a type of rodent, go 3 spaces north.
3. If *Mousekin's Golden House* is by Mercer Mayer, go 4 spaces east. If it is by Edna Miller, go 3 spaces east.
4. If Jean Van Leeuwen was born in 1937, go 7 spaces south. If she was born in 1942, go 9 spaces south.
5. If Jean Van Leeuwen's book *The Great Cheese Conspiracy* has a copyright date of 1978, go 4 spaces west. If the copyright date is 1969, go 2 spaces west.
6. If a dormouse is a real mouse, go 2 spaces south. If a dormouse is a doorstop shaped like a mouse, go 4 spaces south.
7. If the Mouse Tower is a ride in Disneyland, go 3 spaces east. If it is a tower on an island in Germany, go 5 spaces east.
8. If the word "mouse" comes from an old Sanskrit word meaning "thief," go 1 space south. If it comes from a German word meaning "quiet one," go 5 spaces south.
9. If house mice have 10 to 12 babies at one time, go 6 spaces east. If house mice have 4 to 7 babies at a time, go 9 spaces east.
10. If people are the mouse's worst enemy, go 9 spaces north. If cats are the mouse's worst enemy, go 7 spaces north.
11. If grasshopper mice got their names because they eat grasshoppers, go 4 spaces west. If they got their names because they hop and jump, go 2 spaces west.
12. If *The Great Rescue Operation* is Jean Van Leeuwen's third book about Fats, Marvin, and Raymond, go 2 spaces south. If it is her first book about them, go 1 space south.

© 1988 by The Center for Applied Research in Education, Inc.

ENTER →

PROJECTS FOR
THE BOOK OF THREE

There are many unfamiliar names of people, places, and things in *The Book of Three*. Match the names below to the description of each by putting the number on the blank next to the correct description.

1. Prydain
2. Medwyn
3. Gwydion
4. Coll
5. Arawn
6. Hen Wen
7. Taran
8. Gurgi
9. Caer Dallben
10. The Horned King
11. Achren
12. Eilonwy
13. Flewddur Fflam
14. Melyngar
15. Dallben

_____ A brave warrior who rescues Hen Wen from Arawn
_____ A silver-haired wicked woman who lives in the Spiral Castle
_____ A wise old man—keeper of *The Book of Three*
_____ The beautiful white horse of Gwydion
_____ The wicked ruler of Annuvain
_____ The beloved country of Taran
_____ A protector of animals who lives in a beautiful hidden valley
_____ A pig with magical powers
_____ A prince of Cair Dathyl
_____ An evil follower of Arawn
_____ A strange creature who loves "Munchies"
_____ A bard whose harp strings break whenever he lies
_____ The niece of Achren who is learning her magical powers
_____ The home of Taran, Coll, and Dallben
_____ An assistant pig-keeper who wants to be a hero

CHOOSE ONE OF THE FOLLOWING PROJECTS:

1. Use the names of the above characters and make a word-search with them.
2. Illustrate a scene from *The Book of Three*.
3. Make a clay model of Hen Wen, the oracular pig.
4. Make a clay model or a painting of the beautiful white horse of Gwydion.

A REAL PUZZLER

Cross out the letters that spell the answer to each question in the puzzle below. The letters that remain will spell out a message. (The blackened square stands for a period.)

1. The one who had a lighted golden sphere was _____.

2. The home of Achren was the _____ _____.

3. The one who could not lie without breaking the strings of his harp was _____.

4. The home of Lord Gwydion was _____ _____.

5. Taran was named an assistant _____.

6. An injured bird who was helped by Taran and who later helped him was a _____.

7. The one Eilonwy allowed to use the mighty sword of Dyrnwyn was _____ _____.

8. The home of Taran, Coll, and Hen Wen was _____ _____.

9. Eilonwy was learning to be an _____ in the Spiral Castle.

R	E	I	L	E	O	N	A	D	W	T	H	Y	E	B
L	S	P	I	A	R	A	L	C	A	C	S	T	L	E
K	F	C	F	A	L	E	W	U	D	D	U	L	D	R
R	C	A	O	I	R	D	A	N	T	H	N	Y	E	L
X	P	I	T	G	■	K	E	E	I	T	P	E	I	R
G	S	W	A	Y	N	T	H	A	E	I	N	X	T	C
L	I	O	R	T	D	I	G	W	Y	D	N	I	O	N
G	C	B	A	I	R	D	O	A	L	L	B	O	E	N
E	K	N	C	H	T	A	N	T	O	R	E	S	O	S

THE MESSAGE IS:

_____

_____

_____

© 1988 by The Center for Applied Research in Education, Inc.

PROJECTS FOR
THE HOUSE WITH A
CLOCK IN ITS WALLS

1. In what year was John Bellairs born? _____

2. Where did he grow up? _____

3. His first book for children was _____.

4. List three things which John Bellairs says he likes. _____

   _____   _____

5. Were any of these things in the book *The House with a Clock in Its Walls?*

   _____ What? _____

6. List two other books by John Bellairs. Give their publisher and copyright.

Title	Publisher	Copyright date
Title	Publisher	Copyright date

CHOOSE ONE OF THE FOLLOWING PROJECTS:

1. Uncle Jonathan called himself a "parlor magician" which means an amateur magician. Harry Houdini was a famous professional magician. Read about Houdini and then give a report to the class about him.
2. Prepare a bibliography of at least ten books about magic or magic tricks. Use your library's card catalog to find the books and then prepare the bibliography using the form suggested by your teacher.
3. Make a diorama of *The House with a Clock in Its Walls*. Include Lewis, Uncle Jonathan, and Mrs. Zimmerman in the diorama. (You may include others if you wish.) Show the diorama to the class and talk about the book.
4. Write a new adventure for Lewis. Include his new friend, Rose, in the story. Describe Rose and then tell an adventure that she and Lewis could have. It could be an adventure involving finding a secret room in Uncle Jonathan's strange house or they could discover a hidden treasure there. Think of your own ideas for the adventure, too.

FIND THE WORDS

Find the words listed below in the wordsearch. The words can be found forwards, backwards, horizontally, vertically, and diagonally.

```
C A L J I N Z S R X Y M B C H M
B H C M H O A T L L A B E S A B
D I O I N S T R U C T I O N S E
K L E C F G P W Q U V H D E L E
O L M I O I T E U E T R Q R S D
R A P G A L S B E T I O U K T E
T B V S E T A R B Y C D C E H B
P T O G I L C T K Y S O F A U E
M H U W A P I M E F L I R E Z Z
S G T W U P S K S C T M T G P W
G I O A L H N Q O A H R G E A E
N E R A S T O U R L S I W U H N
R M O I A F N O R E K O P R S K
T C N R N T I W L T V S E Z O L
A L T S R S I W E L I M N K O J
```

NEW ZEBEDEE   CLOCKS   NITWITS
CHOCOLATE CHIP   ORGAN   EIGHT BALL
TARBY   KEY   COAL PIT
ARM   INSTRUCTIONS   LEWIS
BASEBALL   POKER   ROSE

PROJECTS FOR
OMEGA STATION

Omega Station is science fiction. Answer the following science FACT questions about space travel.

1. When did the first astronaut land on the moon? _____

2. What were the names of the two astronauts who first walked on the moon?

   _____ and _____

3. What was the name of their lunar module? _____

4. Name four other astronauts who have landed on the moon. _____

   _____

5. Astronauts from the United States were the first to land on the moon, but they were not

   the first to enter space. Who was the first to orbit the earth, from which country was he,

   when did he first orbit the earth, and how long was his flight? _____

   _____

   _____

CHOOSE ONE OF THE FOLLOWING PROJECTS:

1. Make a miniature space station. It may be in the form of a diorama or a model. Show it to the class and tell how it relates to the book *Omega Station*.

2. Read a book about an actual space station, such as Skylab. Compare the factual space station with the one in *Omega Station*. Write your comparison of the two in a written report and read it to the class.

3. Jack Jameson and his robot friend, Danny One, have had many adventures. Write a new space adventure for them.

4. Prepare a science fiction bibliography of books available in your library. Make an attractive science fiction booklet for this bibliography. Use the bibliography form recommended by your teacher or librarian.

HOW TO REACH OMEGA STATION

Follow the directions exactly and you will be able to reach Omega Station.

1. Go 3 spaces south if Otto Drago was once a designer of robots. Go 4 spaces south if he was not.
2. If C.O.L.A.R. is a space station, go 10 spaces west. If it is a planet, go 4 spaces west.
3. If Jack's mother made him take hay fever pills with him because C.O.L.A.R. was three months ahead in time of Earth, go 3 spaces south. If she made him take the pills because it was hay fever season on Earth, go 1 space south.
4. If Otto Drago realized that Jack was not a robot because he forgot to walk stiff-kneed, go 10 spaces west. If he discovered that Jack was not a robot because he forgot to use a robot-like voice, go 6 spaces west.
5. If the shield to Omega Station opened by reciting a rhyme, go 2 spaces south. If it opened by a code of musical notes, go 5 spaces south.
6. If Danny One and Jack changed places on Omega Station when the lights were out, go 3 spaces west. If they changed places when Otto Drago went into his laboratory, go 5 spaces west.
7. Go as many spaces south as there were nuclear bombs in Otto Drago's pool.
8. Go as many spaces east as the number of seconds during which humans could stay alive in Otto Drago's pool.
9. Go as many spaces north as the number of robots on the C.O.L.A.R. spaceship that was following Jack and Otto Drago.
10. Go 8 spaces east if Otto Drago thought Jack (really Danny One) was saved by Alpha pills. Go 6 spaces east if he thought there was something wrong with the water.
11. Go 4 spaces south if Otto Drago was taken back to Dr. Atkins by Jack and Danny One. Go 2 spaces south if he was dissolved by the plutonium water.

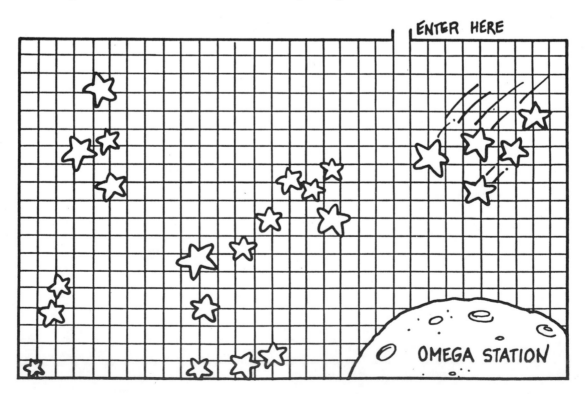

ENTER HERE

OMEGA STATION

PROJECTS FOR
THE WONDERFUL FLIGHT TO THE MUSHROOM PLANET

1. What did David take with him on his trip to the Mushroom Planet? _____
   _____
   _____

2. If you had to make a sudden trip to an unknown place and you could take only one suitcase, what would you bring? _____
   _____
   _____
   _____

3. Try to match these characters, places, and things from the *The Wonderful Flight to the Mushroom Planet* with their descriptions:

   A. Basidium-X   ____ one of Ta's wise men
   B. Mrs. Pennyfeather ____ the earth
   C. The Great Ta   ____ the Mushroom Planet
   D. The Great Protector ____ a strange animal creature
   E. Morunbend or Morabun ____ King of the Mushroom Planet
   F. Mebe   ____ a chicken mascot

CHOOSE ONE OF THE FOLLOWING PROJECTS:

1. Make a painting of how you think the Mushroom Planet looked.
2. Make a model of a space ship. This model may be of a real or an imaginary ship. Be ready to show it to the class.
3. Write a television newscaster's description of the boys' trip to the Mushroom Planet. This newscast can be as an interview with the two boys or as a television news description of the flight. (Remember that good news articles whether in the newspaper, on radio, or on television must tell who, where, why, and when!) When you have written your newscast pretend to be the newscaster and present your newscast to the class.
4. Make a wordsearch of your own using words, characters, places, or things found in the book *The Wonderful Flight to the Mushroom Planet*. If possible, make copies of your wordsearch so that other members of the class can do the wordsearch.

READ ALL ABOUT IT!

In *The Wonderful Flight to the Mushroom Planet,* two boys answer an ad in a newspaper and begin a wonderful adventure. Suppose you saw this ad in your local newspaper:

WANTED: A boy and a girl to train with the astronauts for a future trip to the moon. Interested children ages 10-13 apply in writing by stating your reasons for wanting to make a space trip and why you feel you would be the best candidate. Send applications to: ASTRONAUT PROGRAM, Box 64, My Town.

Answer the above ad, giving your reasons why you would like to train with the astronauts and be part of a moon trip. Be sure to tell about yourself and why you think you would be a good candidate for a future trip to the moon. If you need more space to write, use the back of this sheet.

_____

_____

_____

_____

_____

_____

_____

_____

_____

_____

_____

_____

_____

PROJECTS FOR
IN THE KEEP OF TIME

All of the words below have something to do with castles. Look each one up in a book about castles or in a dictionary and match the word to its proper meaning.

1. palisade
2. moat
3. portcullis
4. battlement
5. manor
6. keep

_____ a gate of iron or wood that could be raised or lowered

_____ the main tower of a castle

_____ the estate of a lord consisting of a castle and the land around it

_____ a deep ditch dug around the castle for protection, usually filled with water

_____ a parapet on top of a wall with low places where shots could be fired during a battle

_____ a fence made of wooden stakes used for the defense of the castle

CHOOSE ONE OF THE FOLLOWING PROJECTS:

1. Build a replica of a castle using sugar cubes, clay, or whatever else you want to use. Consult a book about castles, such as David Macauley's *Castle,* to be sure you build it correctly. Show the castle to the class and explain the different parts of the castle.

2. Read *Castle* by David Macauley and make several drawings of a castle, labeling each part.

3. Write a story of another adventure of the Elliot children. Perhaps they could go into the castle again and be taken to another time period, such as the 1800s. Describe how people were dressed and what they thought about the children's clothes. Describe how the children would explain television, space flights, etc. Tell an adventure the children could have before they find their way home again.

4. Read another book where the characters are put into another time, such as *Fireball* by John Christopher or *Danny Dunn and the Time Machine* by Jay Williams. Write a report comparing the book you read with *In the Keep of Time.*

A "TIMELESS" WORDSEARCH

Write the answers in the blanks below, then find those answers in the wordsearch.

1. The oldest Elliot child was _____.

2. The castle's name was _____.

3. Andrew hid the key in a _____ _____.

4. The boy who played with Andrew and who wanted to help drive the English from Roxburgh castle was _____.

5. The one who was lost in time was _____.

6. The town the children visited in the future was _____.

7. Mae's mother was called _____-_____ _____.

8. The one who helped Mae become Ollie again was _____.

9. The children thought that Vianah looked just like _____ _____.

10. The one who did not want to spend his money to buy a book to teach Mae to read was _____.

```
P B H I K D L F E M N A C G M
E C M L O H L I A M S O E N O
I A U E V G E A W H I M D Y L
L F G P S H I N S R H I R J K
L A L L M N N O V T P K I Z E
O E W B K E L S O N O L C P L
B C R O M E D O U R S T M R O
D A S T S T M M A R S T U W H
C R E B A E H A N A I V Y A T
A G O N L E D C D H V B A I I
A T A K R B C D R G U N O J B
Y N C R E F E E E F I P M K B
B U A F H O P Q W R S W Z L A
M A G E L L T H A M H A I S R
```

PROJECTS FOR
THE FORGOTTEN DOOR

1. What things about Little Jon convinced Mr. and Mrs. Bean that he had come from another planet? _____

   _____

2. Why did so many people, reporters, and government agencies become interested in Little Jon? _____

   _____

3. Look in your card catalog and see if your library has any other books by Alexander Key. If so, list two titles with their copyright dates and publishers.

TITLE	PUBLISHER	COPYRIGHT DATE
_____	_____	_____
_____	_____	_____

CHOOSE ONE OF THE FOLLOWING PROJECTS:

1. Make a clay replica of the doe which Little Jon followed when he tried to find help. Be ready to show it to the class and explain what part the deer played in the story.
2. Read a nonfiction book about space travel. Try to find any references to planets in other galaxies which might be inhabited. Tell the class about the book or write a brief report on the book telling at least ten interesting facts which you learned. Write the facts in paragraph form—not as 10 sentence statements.
3. How do you think Little Jon's real home looked. Make a painting or drawing to show to the class and then describe it for them.
4. The Bean family went with Little Jon when he returned to his home on another planet. Imagine that later, one or all of the family wishes to return to Earth. Write a story describing why they want to return, how they manage to return, and what they find on Earth.

IF YOU FOUND LITTLE JON

Suppose Little Jon wandered into your city or town. Would he have found the same kind of people as he found in *The Forgotten Door?* Pretend you were the one to find Little Jon. Write a story telling where you found him, where you would take him, what you would show him, and how you would help him. Write your story in the first person, but write it as a story—not as statements such as, "I would do this." If you need more space to write your story, use the back of this sheet.

PROJECTS FOR YOUR CHOICE OF FANTASY OR SCIENCE FICTION

1. What is the title of your book? _____

2. Who is the author? _____

3. Name two or three of the main characters: _____

   _____   _____

4. The fantasy in the story is: _____

   _____

   _____

5. Do you consider this book to be more fantasy or more science fiction? _____

6. Use the back of this page to write a paragraph or more about the plot of this book.

CHOOSE ONE OF THE FOLLOWING PROJECTS:

1. Make a wordsearch using characters and places from the book you just read.
2. Make a diorama of a scene from your story. Be ready to tell the class about your diorama and about the book.
3. Make clothespin dolls of four characters from your book. Attach the dolls to a cardboard backing. Put the name of the characters and the title of the book on the cardboard. (Using real cloth and yarn or other materials make your clothespin characters more attractive.) Be ready to show the characters to the class and to tell them about the book from which the characters are taken.
4. Make a large drawing or painting of something that happened in the book. Exhibit your art work to the class and tell them about the picture and about the book which you have read.
5. Write a radio script for one chapter or scene from the book you have read. Remember that a radio script must be mostly dialogue. Ask a friend or friends to help you to record the script. Then play your radio program to the class.

Name _____ Date _____

FANTASY AND SCIENCE FICTION WORDSEARCH

Use the card catalog to find the authors' names in each of the questions below. Then cross out the letters in each row that spell the name of the author of the book given. The remaining letters will spell out a message.

1. What is the last name of the author of *The White Mountains*?
2. What is the last name of the author of *The Wonderful Flight to the Mushroom Planet*?
3. What are the first and last names of the author of *The House with a Clock in Its Walls*?
4. What are the first and last names of the author of *Escape to Witch Mountain*?
5. What are the first and last names of the author of *The Indian in the Cupboard*?
6. What are the first and last names of the author of *My Robot Buddy*?
7. What is the last name of the author of *The Great Cheese Conspiracy*?
8. What are the first and last names of the author of *The Book of Three*?
9. What is the first name of the author of *A Wrinkle in Time*?
10. What are the first and last names of the author of *Alice in Wonderland*?
11. What are the first and last names of the author of *A Cricket in Times Square*?
12. What is the last name of the author of *The Phantom Tollbooth*?

THE MESSAGE IS: _____

_____

_____

F	C	A	H	R	I	S	T	N	O	P	H	E	T	R
A	C	A	M	S	Y	A	E	N	R	D	S	O	N	C
J	O	H	I	N	B	E	L	L	E	A	I	R	S	N
A	L	E	C	X	A	N	D	E	E	R	K	F	E	Y
I	L	V	C	N	N	E	T	B	A	I	N	K	O	S
N	A	L	F	A	R	E	D	R	S	L	E	O	T	E
V	A	N	F	L	E	V	E	U	N	T	W	O	E	N
L	L	O	R	Y	D	A	L	E	X	A	N	D	E	R
M	A	D	E	E	L	A	E	D	I	N	E	■	Y	
O	L	E	W	U	I	S	C	A	W	R	R	O	L	L
I	G	E	O	R	L	G	E	S	E	L	D	O	L	N
L	J	I	U	S	K	E	T	E	T	H	R	E	M	■

MYSTERY AND ADVENTURE

SUGGESTIONS FOR THE TEACHER

Many books fall into the mystery/adventure classification. In the mystery category are the detective-type mysteries as well as the atmosphere-type mysteries. In the adventure category are such high adventure stories as *Treasure Island* as well as the less dramatic, but more realistic type of stories such as *My Side of the Mountain*.

Unit 2 can be introduced by showing one or more of the sound filmstrips, films, or videos that are available in this classification. Some possible choices are *Mysteries* or *Adventures*, both published by Pied Piper Productions. You also could choose audio-visual material that focuses on a specific book title such as *Julie of the Wolves*, a video from Random House, or *The House of Dies Drear*, a sound filmstrip from Pied Piper.

After the introduction, discuss with the students the types of books they will be reading in this unit and then give a brief book talk on each specific title using the summary given in the unit, the jacket blurb, or a summary of your own. Since the unit spotlights mystery, it might be fun to let the title of the book each child will read be a mystery by letting the students pick the title out of a hat. If you feel that the students comprise too wide a range of ability, however, you may want to guide them into choices that they will enjoy and that will be appropriate to their reading level. *The Callender Papers, The Adventures of Tom Sawyer, The Case of the Baker Street Irregulars*, and *My Side of the Mountain* are probably the most difficult while *The One-Hundredth Thing about Caroline* and *The Ghost Next Door* are the most easy to read.

Add interest and fun to Unit 2 by having an activity associated with a mystery each day. These activities could take up part of the class time, with the rest of the time used by the students reading the books, and doing the activity pages and projects. An example is to have students write their own mystery one day of the week. *The Mysteries of Harris Burdick* by Chris Van Allsburg is a great book to use to get children excited about writing their own mystery story. On another day of the week, you might have a research mystery such as a Student Detective Mystery (Quailridge Media). On another day, it might be fun to use a Sherlock Holmes Cliffhanger sound filmstrip (Spoken Arts Multimedia) and stop the filmstrip in time to let the students try to solve the mystery.

An activity based on *The Egypt Game* is to show a film or filmstrip about the Egyptian pyramids and discuss how it has been a mystery of the ages as to how the pyramids were able to preserve things for such a long time. If you have access to a model pyramid (available from such science companies as Edmunds Scientific), you might let the children try to solve the mystery with an experiment. Place half an apple, half a banana, or half an orange in the model pyramid and seal it. Place the other half of the fruit in a glass jar and seal it. Put both the jar and the pyramid where the children can observe them but not move them. Let the children make daily observations of the changes in the fruit and let them determine for themselves if the shape of the pyramid is the key to the mystery of the pyramid's preserving powers.

Another thinking activity that fits in with this unit is to put an object in a box and let the students ask questions about it that can be answered with a yes or no. At the end of the guessing time (perhaps 15 to 20 questions), each student writes on a piece of paper what he or she thinks is in the box. At the end of the class time, the object is revealed and the students who correctly identified the objects are named the day's super detectives.

The preceding activities are but a few of the many things that can be done to increase the students' enjoyment of mystery and adventure books.

AUDIO-VISUAL AIDS
AND RELATED BOOK TITLES

Here are a few of the many audio-visual items and book titles that can be used with this mystery and adventure unit.

Audio-Visual Items

Adventures, a sound filmstrip (Pied Piper Productions)

Mysteries, a sound filmstrip (Pied Piper Productions)

The House of Dies Drear, a sound filmstrip (Pied Piper Productions)

Sherlock Holmes Cliffhangers, a sound filmstrip (Spoken Arts Multimedia)

The Student Detective, an activity book (Quailridge Media)

Julie of the Wolves, a video (Random House)

Related Book Titles

Avi. *Who Stole the Wizard of Oz?*

Christopher, Matt. *Stranded.*

Clapp, Patricia. *Jane-Emily.*

Doyle, Sir Arthur Conan. *The Adventures of Sherlock Holmes.*

Hamilton, Virginia. *The House of Dies Drear.*

Platt, Kin. *Sinbad and Me.*

Roberts, Willo. *The View from the Cherry Tree.*

Sperry, Armstrong. *Call It Courage.*

Wright, Betty Ren. *Christina's Ghost.*

SUMMARIES OF UNIT 2 BOOKS

2-1 *The One-Hundredth Thing about Caroline* by Lois Lowry (Boston: Houghton Mifflin, 1983. 150 pages). Caroline loves studying dinosaurs so much that she spends every spare moment at the Museum of Natural History learning all she can about them. Caroline knows that some day she will be a paleontologist. Stacy, Caroline's best friend, is equally determined to be an investigative journalist when she grows up. In the meantime, both girls like to be detectives and try to investigate the other tenants in the apartment houses they live in. While Stacy is investigating the love life of a tenant in her building, Caroline thinks she has discovered a murderer in her apartment house because she finds a note in the trash basket that reads in part, "...The woman's terrific. But the kids, frankly, seem more and more of a problem. Eliminate the kids..." The note had been written to Frederick Fiske, a tenant of the apartment house. When Caroline finds out that Mr. Fiske is dating her mother, Caroline is sure that Mr. Fiske plans to murder her and her brother. When Caroline's mother plans a dinner party and invites Mr. Fiske as well as Stacy and Mr. Keretsky, Caroline and her brother J.P. plan a surprise and an unveiling of Mr. Fiske as a murderer. Instead, Caroline and J.P. are surprised! Students will like this humorous mystery. It is not difficult, so it would be a good one for children who are not avid readers.

2-2   *The Curse of Camp Gray Owl* by Patricia Edwards Clyne (New York: Dodd, Mead and Company, 1981. 174 pages). Sue, Andy, Alana, and Chad hope they can help Roy get back enough enthusiasm and self-confidence after his leg injury to continue in school. They think they can interest him in exploring an abandoned army camp that is supposedly haunted by an old Indian who had cursed it for disturbing an old Indian burial ground. While exploring the abandoned tunnels, tower, and command post, the five youngsters encounter enough excitement and unexplained happenings to make them half believe that Camp Gray Owl really *is* haunted! With some unexpected help, Roy regains his self-confidence and the mystery of Camp Gray Owl is solved. This is a book most students will read quickly and enjoy.

2-3   *The Adventures of Tom Sawyer* by Mark Twain (there are many fine editions of this book). This classic has been made into films and seen so often by both children and adults that the book itself is often overlooked. Tom Sawyer is living with his Aunt Polly, his sister Mary, and half-brother Sid in a little town on the Mississippi. Sid and Mary are always doing what they are supposed to do, but Tom is always in trouble. He plays hooky from school, feeds the cat his own cough medicine, gets into numerous fights, and drives his poor aunt to distraction. His best friends are Joe Harper and Huckleberry Finn, son of the town drunkard. The many adventures of Tom Sawyer and his friends could fill more than one book as he and Huck solve a murder, he and Becky Thatcher are lost in a cave, he and his friends run away and then attend their own funeral, and he and Huck find a wonderful treasure. His adventures are the stuff of which a boy's dreams are made! There are some prejudices and superstitions common to the time in the book, but these can be discussed and explained in relation to the times. The story itself is too good not to be read and enjoyed today just as it was in the many years since it was first written.

2-4   *The Ghost Next Door* by Wylly Folk St. John (New York: Harper & Row, 1971. 178 pages). Miss Judith's niece, Miranda, drowned in a fish pond a long time ago, but because Miss Judith believed in the occult, she had tried to get in touch with Miranda through a spiritualist group. Lindsey and her best friend Tammy listen to Miss Judith talk about her niece and become interested in her. They are especially interested in the story of how Miranda had made her aunt a cement owl with "love in its eyes" and had then hidden it before she could give it to her aunt. Aunt Judith had searched for it, but could not find it. Miss Judith tells the two girls that Miranda's mother and father had been divorced and that Miranda's father has remarried and has another daughter, Sherry, who is ten years old. Sherry and her parents are coming to visit Miss Judith, who cautions the two girls to say nothing about Miranda since Sherry's father had never told Sherry nor his wife about his first daughter. When Sherry arrives, the girls find her a difficult child to like. She seems to have an imaginary playmate that knows about things that only Miranda could have known. The girls and Aunt Judith begin to wonder if the imaginary playmate is the ghost of a long-dead Miranda! Lindsey and Tammy finally decide that Sherry must have found Miranda's diary somewhere and that is how she has found out about the girl. They are certain that Sherry is jealous of Miranda and wants Miss Judith to love her more than she loved Miranda. After some exciting adventures, including Lindsey's brother falling in an unused well and the girls attending a seance, the long-lost cement owl with "love in its eyes" is found and Sherry finds out that Miss Judith loves her as much as she did her first niece. Lindsey and Tammy are not sure if Sherry had known all about Miranda because she had found the diary or if there really was a "ghost next door." This is an easily read mystery with a lot of action.

2-5   *My Side of the Mountain* by Jean Craighead George (New York: E. P. Dutton, 1959. 166 pages). Sam Gribley leaves New York in May with only a knife, a ball of cord, and forty dollars. He also has some flint and steel for starting a fire. He is only a boy but he is determined to go to the Old Gribley farm in the Catskill Mountains and live for a year on only things he can find on the land. He knows there are no farmhouse and living quarters, but he is tired of the cramped New York City apartment where he lives with his parents and eight brothers and sisters. After Sam finally locates the Gribley land, he has the summer and autumn to learn how to make a warm waterproof shelter, how to live on the food from the land, and even how to sew some of his own clothes from deerskin. At times lonesome, Sam makes friends with some of the animals and tames and trains a falcon to help him catch food and to be his companion. Sam tries to avoid any contact with other humans, but he does meet a young man who is camping near him. Because he had heard a police siren just before meeting the man, Sam decides the man is a criminal and names him Bando, nickname for Bandit. He later finds out that the man is not a criminal, but a teacher on vacation. Bando teaches Sam to make and fire clay pots for eating and cooking. He promises to visit Sam during his Christmas vacation—and does. Although Sam receives help from several people during the year he spends alone, this is a story of his personal triumph over nature. Written in a diary style and with diagrams of some of Sam's accomplishments, this book appeals to both boys and girls.

2-6 *The Red Room Riddle* by Scott Corbett (Boston: Little, Brown and Company, 1972. 104 pages). Bruce and Bill Slocum are interested in haunted houses and in ghosts. They don't believe Jamie, however, when he says he lives with ghosts and would introduce them to the boys. On Halloween night, the two boys wait for Jamie to take them to the haunted house in which he supposedly lives. Jamie is late, but when he finally appears, the boys follow him to a door in the wall that leads through a tunnel-like arbor. Bruce begins to get frightened when something ice cold swishes past him and hits Bill. The appearance of the large house Jamie leads them to is also frightening. Since they have given up their other Halloween fun, the boys are determined not to back out even though they are uneasy about entering the house lit only by gas and oil lamps. No grownups seem to be around in the frightening mansion and before the boys' visit is completed, they meet a strange old woman in a maid's uniform who seems to neither hear nor see them, a strange blood-red room, and a spiral secret staircase where they are chased by Roman soldiers carrying broad swords. When the strange night is over, Bruce is convinced that they had not only seen ghosts but also that Jamie himself was a ghost. Bill, however, is convinced that there are no ghosts and that Jamie had hypnotized them. The real answer is not revealed by the author who has Bruce end the story with the words, "I was the one who met the boy who lived with ghosts and I still don't know what to think about it."

2-7 *The Dollhouse Murders* by Betty Ren Wright (New York: Holiday House, 1983. 149 pages). Amy loves her younger sister Louann, who is "different," but she wishes her mother would not always expect her to watch Louann every minute and have her always tagging along with her and her friends. Amy felt that her friends did not like it when Louann was with them because it embarrassed them when Louann behaved more like a two-year-old than a bigger-than-average eleven-year-old. After a particularly embarrassing day with Louann at the shopping mall, Amy runs away to her Aunt Clare, who is staying at the old Treloar house, which belonged years ago to Amy's great-grandparents. Aunt Clare welcomes Amy and invites her to stay awhile and keep her company while she goes through the house getting it ready to sell. Amy welcomes the chance to get away from Louann and to have some time to get better acquainted with both her aunt and with her new friend Ellen. Amy finds a wonderful dollhouse in the attic of the old house. Her aunt tells Amy that the dollhouse was a long-ago present from the Treloars and that it is an exact replica of the house they are in. Even the dolls in the house represent Grandma and Grandpa Treloar, Aunt Clare as a girl, and Amy's own father as a little boy. The rooms and the furniture of the dollhouse are exact replicas of the rooms and furniture of the house they are in. Amy is fascinated but soon realizes that Aunt Clare does not like the dollhouse. One morning Amy discovers the positions of the dolls in the house are changed and she becomes frightened. One night she actually sees a light in the dollhouse and the tiny figures moving. Then Amy realizes that the dollhouse is trying to tell her something! When Amy reads in a back issue of a long-ago newspaper that Grandma and Grandpa Treloar were murdered and not killed in an accident, she begins to wonder if the strange happenings in the dollhouse have anything to do with these long-ago murders. How the mystery is solved and how Amy comes to appreciate her sister make a story that students in the fifth and sixth grades will be asking for again and again.

2-8   *The Egypt Game* by Zilpha Snyder (New York: Atheneum, 1976. 215 pages). April, a strange, lonely little girl, lives with her grandmother. Her mother, who lives in Hollywood and is trying to become a movie star, has sent April to stay with her grandmother but promises to send for her soon. April meets Melanie and finds that they both have good imaginations. When they see an unused yard behind an old antique shop, they decide to change it into the "land of Egypt." They change the yard into "Egypt" and develop an elaborate "Egypt Game" in which they each play a part with costumes and impressive rituals. Melanie's little brother, Marshall, becomes the young pharaoh Marshmosis, and a new friend Elizabeth becomes the beautiful Nefertiti. A murderer loose in the neighborhood adds excitement to the story. One night, April and Marshall go to "Egypt" to try to find Marshall's beloved stuffed octopus when suddenly a hand reaches out and grabs April. This story is exciting and involves the fun of the Egypt Game, the danger of a murderer at large, and the development of April from an insecure, strange child to a more loving and self-confident person.

2-9   *The Callender Papers* by Cynthia Voigt (New York: Atheneum, 1983. 214 pages). Jean Wainwright lives with her aunt, who is the headmistress of a school for girls, and is offered the job of sorting through the papers of Irene Callender Thiel. Irene Callender is dead and her husband, Mr. Thiel, hires Jean although she is only twelve-years-old. Jean is apprehensive about undertaking such a task, which also involves going to Mr. Thiel's home in Marlborough and living in his home. She decides to accept the job, however, because she knows the money will be helpful to her and to her aunt. Mr. Thiel, a taciturn and rather unapproachable man, has a housekeeper who is also frightening at first. Jean finds the job of sorting the papers tedious but interesting as they unfold the past of Mr. Thiel, his dead wife Irene, and Irene's brother, Enoch Callender. Meeting Mac, a local boy, makes the job more bearable but she and Mac begin to suspect that there may be a mystery involved in Irene's death. When Jean is poisoned one night, she becomes frightened for her own safety. The mystery of Irene's death and the disappearance of her child and the child's nurse is eventually solved through Jean's determination. This book will be enjoyed by some of the better readers in your class.

2-10 *The Case of the Baker Street Irregulars* by Robert Newman (New York: Atheneum, 1978. 216 pages). Andrew wonders why Mr. Dennison, his tutor, has brought him to London after his aunt dies. He would much rather have stayed in Cornwall with his friend, the blacksmith, but he had to go with Mr. Dennison since his aunt had made him Andrew's guardian. Andrew's wonder changes to fright when he sees Mr. Dennison apparently being kidnapped and Andrew is left alone in a strange, frightening city. He is befriended by Screamer, a little girl from a poor family. Screamer's brother, Sam, is a Baker Street Irregular, a group of poor children who sometimes work for the great Sherlock Holmes. Andrew also gets the chance to work for Holmes, although he is unaware of it and believes he is being employed by a blind beggar. Before the story ends, Andrew has helped Sherlock Holmes solve cases involving bombings, art thefts, and murder. In the process, Sherlock Holmes helps Andrew to discover that he is not an orphan but the illegitimate child of a famous woman star of the theater. This exciting book will be enjoyed by the better readers in your class.

PROJECTS FOR
THE ONE-HUNDREDTH THING ABOUT CAROLINE

Some of the things that J.P., Caroline, and Stacy did might be considered a crime. Below are some crimes. Write the things which the children did next to the crime that is most like their actions.

1. attempted murder _____

_____

2. breaking and entering _____

_____

3. invasion of privacy _____

_____

4. theft _____

_____

CHOOSE ONE OF THE FOLLOWING PROJECTS:

1. *The One-Hundredth Thing about Caroline* ends without telling us what happens when Caroline's mother finds the galoshes full of evidence including the cannolis and the dead mouse. Write a story about what might happen. Make your story at least 300 words long.

2. Make a model of a dinosaur out of clay, papier-mâché, or any other material you feel is suitable. Show the model to the class and tell which dinosaur your model represents. Then tell the class what dinosaurs have to do with *The One-Hundredth Thing about Caroline*.

3. Research the career of a paleontologist, which is what Caroline wanted to be when she grew up. Tell the education requirements, the work a paleontologist would do, job opportunities, and the probable salary range. (If your school library does not have a reference book on careers, go to the public library.) Read your job description to the class and tell how this project relates to the book.

4. Lois Lowry, the author of *The One-Hundredth Thing about Caroline,* is a favorite author of many children. Look up Lois Lowry in *The Junior Book of Authors* (or another reference source) and prepare a report on her and her books. Present your report to the class.

DO YOU REMEMBER?

1. If Caroline's father was dead, color three of the spines on the dinosaur green. If he was still alive, color three of the spines red.
2. If Mr. Fiske was a college professor, color three more of the spines on the dinosaur blue. If he was a marine biologist, color three spines yellow.
3. On the dinosaur's back, write the number of envelopes of evidence that J.P. brought back from Mr. Fiske's apartment.
4. Color three more of the dinosaur spines purple if Mr. Keretsky could not tell who was winning a basketball game because he was from a foreign country. Color them orange if he could not tell who was winning because he was color blind.
5. What household job did Caroline love doing? Write the name of that job on the dinosaur's tail.
6. What did Stacy want to do when she grew up? Write that job on the dinosaur's neck.
7. Put the name of Caroline's favorite dinosaur under the number you wrote on the dinosaur's back.
8. Put the titles of two other books by Lois Lowry beneath the dinosaur.
9. Subtract the number of pages in this book from the copyright date of the book and then put that number on the dinosaur's right front leg.
10. Put your name in the lower left-hand corner of this sheet.

PROJECTS FOR
THE CURSE OF CAMP GRAY OWL

1. Why was Roy planning to quit school? _____

_____

_____

2. What reason was given to Roy about why they were exploring Camp Gray Owl? _____

_____

3. Describe Sue. Tell about her personality as well as her appearance. _____

_____

_____

4. Why didn't Longbow reveal his presence to the children when they first began to explore Camp Gray Owl? _____

_____

CHOOSE ONE OF THE FOLLOWING PROJECTS:

1. Make a large map of Camp Gray Owl. Show it to the class and tell about a few of the things that happened at the different places on the map.
2. Many states have abandoned military camps or installations. Do some research to find out if your state has any such camps or installations. Research one or more of these abandoned places and write a report on the history of the place, why it was abandoned, and how it is being used at the present time.
3. Camp Gray Owl was an old Indian burial ground. Research the Indians who lived or live in your area. Give a report on them and on their customs, art work, and how they lived before white men came. Include some pictures, if possible.
4. A map played an important part in this book. Make a map of your school and schoolyard. Make it large enough to show to the class. Label it and be sure it is right according to direction. Include a directional box and a key to the symbols you use on the map.

RESEARCHING OTHER CAMPS

Part One: Patricia Clyne has written many books for children. Check in the card catalog and see if your library has any other books written by her. If so, write the titles and copyright dates below.

TITLE _____

_____

COPYRIGHT DATE _____

TITLE _____

COPYRIGHT DATE _____

Part Two: The setting for *The Curse of Camp Gray Owl* was an abandoned military camp. Many camps have been abandoned but there are still some training camps in many states in the United States. Use an almanac to see if you can find the name of the state in which each of the following training camps is located.

1. Fort Belvoir _____

2. Fort Bragg _____

3. Fort Dix _____

4. Fort Gordon _____

5. Fort Huachuca _____

6. Fort Jackson _____

7. Fort Lee _____

8. Fort Sill _____

Part Three: Most (but not all) of these Army Training Camps are located in southern states. Can you think of a reason for this? _____

_____

_____

Part Four: What use could be made of an old military camp that was no longer needed? Give two possible uses and try to be as descriptive and specific as possible. Write your answers on the back of this sheet.

PROJECTS FOR
THE ADVENTURES OF TOM SAWYER

1 Describe Tom. Use complete sentences and don't forget to tell both his good points and his bad points. (If you need more space to write, use the back of this sheet.)

_____

_____

_____

_____

2. Was there anything likeable about Sid? _____ Describe him. _____

_____

_____

3. Tom had several exciting adventures in this book. Which adventure was your favorite? Tell about this adventure on another sheet of paper.

CHOOSE ONE OF THE FOLLOWING PROJECTS:

1. Read a biography of Mark Twain or do some research on him in the encyclopedia and one other reference source. Make a written report on him and then read it to the class.
2. Mark Twain was fascinated by the Mississippi River and the riverboats that traveled along it. Research riverboats and steamships and make a report on them to the class. Use drawings and pictures to make your report more interesting and then be sure to tell the class what the report has to do with the book.
3. Write a radio script or a play about one incident in the book, such as the trial of Muff Potter, the finding of the treasure, or being lost with Becky in the cave. (You may choose another incident if you prefer.) Ask some friends to help you present the radio skit or play to the class.
4. Draw a large, colorful illustration of something that happened in this book. Show it to the class and explain what your picture illustrates.

REMEMBERING AND CATEGORIZING

Below are some categories of parts that Tom might have played if this were a movie or play. Decide which adventure of Tom's fits each category. (You might be able to think of more than one for some categories.)

1. Tom Sawyer, the Veterinarian: _____

_____

_____

2. Tom Sawyer, Hero: _____

_____

_____

3. Tom Sawyer, Good Friend: _____

_____

_____

4. Tom Sawyer, Treasure Hunter: _____

_____

_____

_____

5. Tom Sawyer, Trial Witness: _____

_____

_____

6. Tom Sawyer, Con Man: _____

_____

_____

7. Tom Sawyer, the Pirate: _____

_____

_____

The book about Tom Sawyer was written long ago. Do you think a boy or girl of the present time could have adventures such as Tom had? _____ Use the back of this sheet to tell why or why not.

PROJECTS FOR
THE GHOST NEXT DOOR

1. How did the two girls know that the owl that Sherry dug up was not the right owl? _____

_____

2. Why did Sherry want to be the one to find the owl and give it to Miss Judith? _____

_____

3. Why hadn't Dr. Alston told his wife and daughter about Miranda? _____

_____

4. How did Sherry find out about Miranda? _____

_____

5. Do you think the author wants you to believe that there really was a "ghost next door"? _____ Why or why not? _____

_____

CHOOSE ONE OF THE FOLLOWING PROJECTS:

1. Make a cement owl (use plaster of Paris, hardening clay, or papier-mâché) like the one Miranda made.
2. Write a diary as if you were Miranda. Tell in it the things that Sherry read that made Aunt Judith think she talked to Miranda's ghost.
3. Write a ghost story of your own.
4. Prepare an oral book report about this book to present to the class. Be sure you do not tell the ending, but make it so exciting that other students will want to read the book.
5. Try to find out something about the author by using reference sources or the biography on the jacket of one of her books. If you cannot find out anything about this author, write to her in care of the publisher of her books and ask her to tell you about herself.

A "GHOSTLY" CROSSWORD PUZZLE

ACROSS

1. Lindsey's best friend
4. Miranda and Aunt Judith made one from cement
6. The fake owl was dug up out of this
8. The highest valued card
10. Opposite of "begin"
11. Dame Pythia held this at Greenfield's house
14. Homonym for "two"
15. Present tense of "was"
17. Homonym for "scene"
18. An exclamation when one is hurt
19. Opposite of "smart"
21. A small city is a _____
23. Homonym for "meat"
25. If you go ahead, you are in the _____
27. Dinner is your evening _____
28. Lindsey's six-year-old brother
32. Aunt Judith's niece who died
34. Lindsey thought Sherry had read Miranda's _____
35. Homonym for "sew"
37. Lindsey's nine-year-old brother
39. The one who wanted her aunt to love her
42. Fish eggs
44. An exclamation
46. To get away from
47. "Old Maid" is a card _____

DOWN

1. The real cement owl was found in a _____
2. Dame Pythia was one
3. Opposite of "no"
5. A decoration on clothes, tablecloths, etc.
6. Opposite of "you"
7. Miranda _____ in the pond
9. A penny is a _____
12. Fat _____ a pig
13. A salamander looks like a _____
14. To pull
16. An odor
20. A "honey" of an insect
22. Opposite of "forget"
24. Roads and roofs might be coated with this
26. Opposite of "cruel"
29. Your _____ is between your thigh and your calf
30. Opposite of "fail" a grade
31. A kind of grain
33. He _____ a bicycle
36. An exclamation
38. A female deer
40. This might cover a floor
41. A sweet potato
43. Opposite of "down"
45. Opposite of "she"

PROJECTS FOR
MY SIDE OF THE MOUNTAIN

1. *My Side of the Mountain* by Jean Craighead George is the story of a boy's survival through a year's four seasons. Below are some other fiction books about survival. Look them up in your card catalog and write the authors' names and the copyright dates.

   a. *Robinson Crusoe* by _____

      Copyright date _____

   b. *Canyon Winter* by _____

      Copyright date _____

   c. *Swiss Family Robinson* by _____

      Copyright date _____

   d. *Climb a Lonely Hill* by _____

      Copyright date _____

   e. *Julie of the Wolves* by _____

      Copyright date _____

2. Do you think most parents would let their child leave home and be gone for a year without trying to find him or her? ____ What would most parents have done to find their child? _____

   _____

   _____

3. Do you think the ending of this book was probable? ____ Use the back of this sheet to tell why or why not.

CHOOSE ONE OF THE FOLLOWING PROJECTS:

1. Pretend you are lost in the woods or mountains for a week. Keep a diary of what you do each day and how you manage to survive. Think carefully about what you would do each day based on such things as the weather, the environment, and the time of year.
2. Sam cooked many wild plants in *My Side of the Mountain*. Cook something using edible wild plants. Bring a sample of your cooking to the class with the recipe and the ingredients.
3. Make a booklet with drawings and information on your state's edible plants. Be sure to tell where each plant can be found, how to cook it if necessary, and what time of year it is available.
4. Study the types of shelters used by native Americans and also the early settlers. Build a model shelter of a type used by the native Americans or by the early settlers. Use only materials such as they might have used.

ON YOUR OWN

Finish the stories below by telling what you would do if you were lost in the following situations. Remember some of the things Sam did which might help you to survive. However, in your case, you want to be found so you also must think of ways to attract the attention of someone who can help you find your way back to civilization.

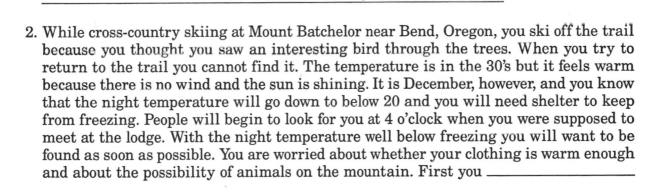

1. While exploring the forest on Larch Mountain, you become separated from your friends. It is in July and the temperature is hot during the day and in the low forties at night. You know that everyone will begin looking for you at five o'clock when you were supposed to meet. You also know that people have been lost for many days on this rugged mountain and you do not want that to happen to

   you. You decide to _____

   _____

   _____

   _____

   _____

   _____

   _____

2. While cross-country skiing at Mount Batchelor near Bend, Oregon, you ski off the trail because you thought you saw an interesting bird through the trees. When you try to return to the trail you cannot find it. The temperature is in the 30's but it feels warm because there is no wind and the sun is shining. It is December, however, and you know that the night temperature will go down to below 20 and you will need shelter to keep from freezing. People will begin to look for you at 4 o'clock when you were supposed to meet at the lodge. With the night temperature well below freezing you will want to be found as soon as possible. You are worried about whether your clothing is warm enough and about the possibility of animals on the mountain. First you _____

   _____

   _____

   _____

(Use the back of this paper if you need more room.)

PROJECTS FOR
THE RED ROOM RIDDLE

Check the card catalog to see if the following ghost stories are in your school library. If they are, write the copyright date and call number of each. If they are not in your library, write "no" on the call number line.

	Call Number	Copyright Date
The Ghost Belonged to Me by Richard Peck	_____	_____
The Ghost of Follensbee Folly by Florence Hightower	_____	_____
The Ghost of Windy Hill by Clyde Bulla	_____	_____
The Ghost on Saturday Night by Sid Fleischman	_____	_____
Footsteps on the Stairs by Carole Adler	_____	_____
Behind the Attic Wall by Sylvia Cassedy	_____	_____
A Dream of Ghosts by Frank Bonham	_____	_____
Georgie's Halloween by Robert Bright	_____	_____
The Thing at the Foot of the Stairs by Maria Leach	_____	_____
Gus Was a Gorgeous Ghost by Jane Thayer	_____	_____
The Ghost with the Halloween Hiccups by Stephen Mooser	_____	_____
The Gray Ghost of Taylor Ridge by Mary Shura	_____	_____
Ghosts and Ghastlies by Helen Hoke	_____	_____
The Haunting of America by Jean Anderson	_____	_____
Mischievous Ghosts by Larry Kettlekamp	_____	_____

WHAT'S YOUR OPINION? Do you think the author of *The Red Room Riddle* wanted the readers to believe this is a REAL ghost story? _____ What makes you think so? Use the back of this sheet for your answer.

CHOOSE ONE OF THE FOLLOWING PROJECTS:

1. Make a bibliography of ghost stories available in your library. Include at least 12 books. Put them in the bibliography form recommended by your teacher or librarian.
2. Make a wordsearch using titles from books by Scott Corbett.
3. Write a ghost story of your own. Be ready to read it to the class.

FIND YOUR WAY OUT OF THE HAUNTED HOUSE

1. If Bruce's best friend was named Bob Sterrett move 5 spaces south, but if his name was Bill Slocum move 4 spaces south.
2. If the boys got directions to the haunted house from a mailman go 7 spaces west, but if they got directions from a policeman go 5 spaces south.
3. If the copyright date of *The Red Room Riddle* was 1972 go 2 spaces south, but if the copyright date was 1970 go 5 spaces south.
4. If the first strange sound the boys heard at the haunted house was a moan go 10 spaces east. If the first strange sound they heard was sniffing and padding go 16 spaces east.
5. If Jamie Bly's dog's name was "Mister" go 5 spaces south. If his name was "Major" go 3 spaces south.
6. If the caretaker at the haunted house was described by Jamie as being half blind and hard of hearing go 5 spaces west. If Jamie said the caretaker was almost eighty years old go 8 spaces west.
7. If the boys were to meet Jamie on Halloween night go 8 spaces south. If they met Jamie on the night before Halloween go 5 spaces south.
8. If the haunted house had no lights at all go 10 spaces west. If it had gaslight and oil lamps go 14 spaces west.
9. If Bruce was scratched on the face going into the haunted house go 9 spaces south. If Bill was the one whose face was scratched go 12 spaces south.
10. If the old woman who walked through the haunted house lighting lamps was the maid go 13 spaces east. If the old woman was Jamie's grandma go 8 spaces east.
11. If the boys got locked in the red room go 5 spaces north. If they wanted to stay in the red room go 8 spaces north.
12. If the boys found Jamie again by talking to the caretaker of the haunted house go 5 spaces east. If they could not talk to him because he had been dead for over a year go 7 spaces east.

ARE YOU OUT OF THE HAUNTED HOUSE? YOU SHOULD BE BY NOW. IF NOT, GO BACK AND TRY AGAIN!

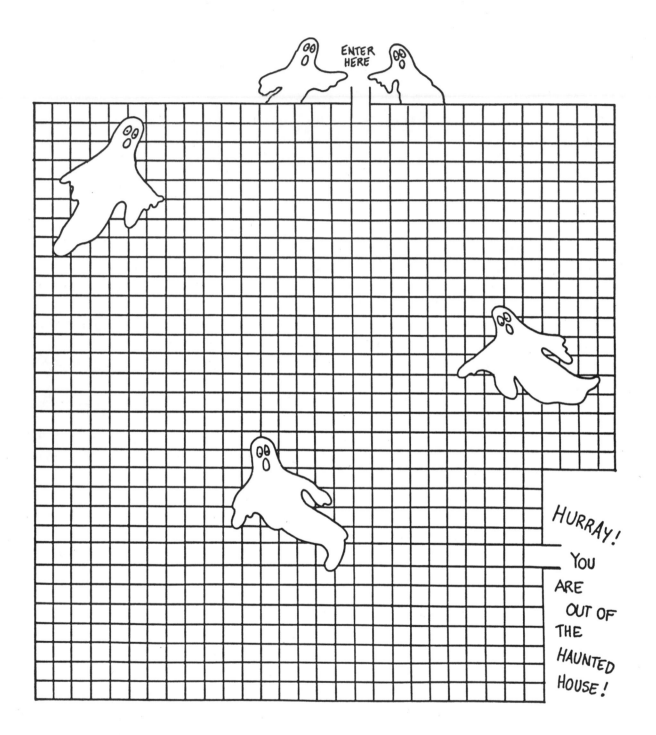

PROJECTS FOR
THE DOLLHOUSE MURDERS

1. Which character in the story did you like best? _____

   Describe this character and tell why you liked the character. _____

   _____

   _____

   _____

2. Which character did you like least? _____

   DESCRIBE THIS CHARACTER AND TELL WHY YOU DISLIKED THE

   CHARACTER. _____

   _____

   _____

   _____

3. Did you like the way the story ended? ____ Can you think of an ending you would have

   enjoyed more? Write it here and on the back of this paper if you need more room. ____

   _____

4. Do you think it was right that Louann was given the dollhouse or do you think that Amy

   should have received it? (Tell why you think so.) _____

   _____

CHOOSE ONE OF THE FOLLOWING PROJECTS:

1. Make a dollhouse like the one in *The Dollhouse Murders*. Perhaps you could tape shoeboxes together for the different rooms or use your imagination to think of other possibilities. Use the dollhouse to help tell the class about the book.
2. Prepare a television commercial for this book. Make the commercial as exciting as you can. Try to borrow the school's video equipment and film your commercial to show the class.
3. Pretend you are Amy and write a diary for one week during the time she was staying with Aunt Clare.

THE SECRET MESSAGE

$\overline{1}$ $\overline{2}$ $\overline{3}$ $\overline{4}$ $\overline{5}$ $\overline{6}$ $\overline{7}$ $\overline{8}$ $\overline{9}$ $\overline{10}$ $\overline{11}$ $\overline{12}$ $\overline{13}$ $\overline{14}$ $\overline{15}$ $\overline{16}$ $\overline{17}$ $\overline{18}$ $\overline{19}$ $\overline{20}$ $\overline{21}$ $\overline{22}$

1. What is the name of the town where Amy and her family live? _____ Put the 5th letter of that word in space 15.

2. Who is Amy's new friend? ____ Write the first letter of the friend's name in spaces 7 and 13.

3. When Louann got lost at the shopping mall, Amy found her watching a show. What kind of a show was it? _____ show. Put the fifth letter of the word you wrote in spaces 3 and 16. Put the second letter of the word you wrote in space 14.

4. Louann made a shop-keeper in the mall angry when she picked a flower. What kind of flower was it? ____ Put the 4th letter of that word in space 21.

5. How old was Louann? ____ Put the last letter of the word you wrote in space 17.

6. What food did Aunt Clare plan to make and serve at the birthday party for Amy and her friend? ____ Put the second letter of the name of the food in space 10 and space 19.

7. How old were Amy and her friend on their birthday? ____ Put the second letter of that word in space 2.

8. Amy's great-grandparents' last name was ____. Put the first letter of their name in spaces 1, 6, and 22.

9. Amy found out her great-grandparents had been murdered when she read an article in an old ____. Put the first letter of that word in space 4. Put the 6th letter in space 9.

10. Aunt Clare was angry because she thought Amy had moved the ____ in the dollhouse. Put the second letter of the word you wrote in space 5. Put the last letter of the word in space 8.

11. What was the title of the book in which Amy's great-grandmother hid the note? _____ Write the first letter of the 2nd word of that title in spaces 11, 18, and 20.

12. What was the name of Amy's great-grandparents' handyman? ____ Put the 1st letter of his name in space 12.

THE MESSAGE: _____

PROJECTS FOR
THE EGYPT GAME

1. What is the date of Zilpha Keatley Snyder's birth? _____

2. Where did she grow up? _____

3. What were her main interests as a child? _____

4. When did she first decide to be an author? _____

5. What was her first published book? _____

6. One of Zilpha Snyder's books won a Newbery award. What is the title of that book?

_____

7. Look in the card catalog and, on the back of this sheet, write the titles of three books by Zilpha Keatley Snyder which can be found in your library.

CHOOSE ONE OF THE FOLLOWING PROJECTS:

1. Make a diorama of the junkyard after the children made it into the "land of Egypt."
2. Read about pyramids and build a model of one to show the class. Be prepared to tell the class about the construction of the pyramid and also what was inside the pyramids.
3. Read about Egyptian hieroglyphics and write a sentence using Egyptian hieroglyphics. Be sure the sentence is written large enough so it can be seen by the class. Explain to the class about hieroglyphics and explain the meaning of each one in your sentence.
4. Make up an alphabet using your own hieroglyphics.
5. At the end of the story April and Melanie decide that they are tired of the Egypt game. They decide that they are going to make up a new game. Make up a new game for them. Tell what costumes they can wear, where they can play the game, what parts each one will play, and what things they can do in their new game.

FIND OUT ABOUT EGYPT

1. Who was Nefertiti? _____

2. When did Nefertiti live? _____

3. Why do we remember Nefertiti when we do not remember many other Egyptian queens?

_____

_____

_____

4. Who was Isis? _____

_____

_____

5. What was a "Pharaoh"? _____

6. What does the word "Pharaoh" mean? _____

_____

In the space below, draw a picture of how you might have looked as a queen or king of Egypt.

PROJECTS FOR
THE CALLENDER PAPERS

1. Describe the main character, Jean Wainwright. Be sure to describe her character as well as her appearance.

   _____

   _____

2. Do you think this was a good book? (Be sure to tell why or why not you like the book.)

   _____

   _____

   _____

3. Did you guess the ending of the book? _____ Do you think this was the right ending?

   _____

   _____

CHOOSE ONE OF THE FOLLOWING PROJECTS:

1. Write a television commercial for this book. Make it exciting by giving a short scene from the book. You may use a classmate or classmates to help you.
2. Research the author of this book, Cynthia Voigt, and then prepare an interview with her by writing questions an interviewer might ask. Present the interview to the class by having a friend be the interviewer and you pretend to be the author.
3. If you liked this book, write a letter to the author in care of her publisher. Tell her what you liked about the book. Be polite and use the accepted form for letters, remembering the heading, salutation, body, and closing correct forms.
4. Cynthia Voigt, the author of *The Callender Papers,* won a Newbery medal for her book, *Dicey's Song.* Research the Newbery medal and write a report on what it is and how it is won. Include in the report some other books which have won the medal. When you read your report to the class tell what your report has to do with *The Callender Papers.*

A CALLENDER CROSSWORD PUZZLE

ACROSS

1. The first name of the girl who sorted the Callender papers
3. The first name of Jean Wainwright's aunt
9. The name of the boy who tried to help Jean
11. An article (part of speech)
13. Something one buys to put a house on
14. A big jump
15. What Irene and Enoch fell from
17. An area surrounding a building
19. The number of categories in the Dewey Decimal Classification system
21. Opposite of "me"
24. The last name of the one who hired Jean
26. Where Jean went on the train
31. Adhesive or masking _____
32. The symbol for the element rhenium
33. A pentagon is a five-_____ shape
34. Mrs. Bywall stole six of these
36. To peek
37. To compete
38. To fit, a shoe must be the right _____
40. Neither this _____ that
43. Opposite of "ill"
44. Write on the _____
46. Opposite of "out"
47. Mac was a _____ of Jean when they studied Latin
49. A negative
52. Opposite of "awake"
53. Opposite of "subtract"
54. Past tense of drive

DOWN

1. Poke
2. Mr. Callender's first name
4. Opposite of "young"
5. A negative answer
6. Where a pig might live
7. If you mean "yes," you _____ your head
8. A tiny magical creature
9. You might wipe your feet on one
10. A large monkey-like creature
12. Some people worship one of these
16. "Sing a song of sixpence, a pocketful of _____"
18. Opposite of "none"
20. Opposite of "yes"
22. What Jean had to sort
23. Mrs. Bywall was sent to one
24. How old Jean was in this book
25. The lady who fell from a board and died
26. Created
27. Scarlet
28. Opposite of "cowardly"
29. To moan in pain
30. A female chicken
31. A man might wear this around his neck
33. The planets are far out in _____
35. Odd
39. A pronoun
41. Opposite of "tame"
42. Past tense of "is"
44. Put this on top of a pot
45. Opposite of "begin"
48. Opposite of "Ma"
50. He will do it _____ he won't
51. Homonym of "two"

PROJECTS FOR
THE CASE OF THE BAKER STREET IRREGULARS

1. What was the real name of Andrew's friend Screamer? _____

2. Mrs. Harker pretended that she wanted Sherlock Holmes to find her daughter. Why did she tell Sherlock Holmes this story?

   _____

3. Do you think Andrew will be happy living with his newly-found mother? Why or why not? _____

   _____

4. How do you think Andrew's mother could help Screamer and her family? _____

   _____

CHOOSE ONE OF THE FOLLOWING PROJECTS:

1. Detectives sometimes must disguise themselves when they are solving a mystery. Sherlock Holmes was a master of disguise. Check out a book about disguises and then prepare a disguise for yourself. Wear it to show the class. Tell the class what a disguise has to do with this book and also explain to them why a disguise for a child is more difficult than one for an adult.

2. Detectives sometimes need to solve codes. Read a book on different codes and then choose one of the types of codes to use to write a message. Write the message large enough for the class to see it. Let the class try to figure out the message and then explain the code to them.

3. Sherlock Holmes is a famous adult detective. Make an alphabetical list of child detectives or detective clubs made up of children that can be found in books in your library. Be sure there are at least 10 names on your list. Read it to the class and tell how it relates to the book.

4. Test the observation talents of the class. You or a friend do something in front of the class and then prepare a test to give to the students to see how well they observed. Do not tell the class they are going to be tested on their observations. Then tell them good detectives must be observant and tell how this test related to *The Case of the Baker Street Irregulars*.

BE A SHERLOCK HOLMES

The name of "Sherlock Holmes" has become almost synonomous for "detective." While Sherlock Holmes is probably the most famous detective in the world, everyone who has learned to use reference sources can be a detective, too. Be a good detective and figure out the message by using the clues below.

$\overline{}$ $\overline{}$ $\overline{}$ $\overline{}$ $\overline{}$ $\overline{}$ $\overline{}$ $\overline{}$ $\overline{}$ $\overline{}$ $\overline{}$ $\overline{}$ $\overline{}$ $\overline{}$ $\overline{}$ $\overline{}$ $\overline{}$ $\overline{}$ $\overline{}$ $\overline{}$ $\overline{}$ $\overline{}$ $\overline{}$ $\overline{}$ $\overline{}$ $\overline{}$ $\overline{}$
1   2   3   4   5   6   7   8   9 10 11 12 13 14 15 16 17 18 19 20 21 22 23 24 25 26 27

$\overline{}$ $\overline{}$ $\overline{}$ $\overline{}$ $\overline{}$ $\overline{}$ $\overline{}$ $\overline{}$ $\overline{}$ $\overline{}$
28 29 30 31 32 33 34 35 36 37

1. If Sherlock Holmes was a fictional detective, put a "G" in space 1. If he was a real detective, put a "G" in space 4.
2. If *The Case of the Baker Street Irregulars* has a copyright date of 1976, put an "L" in spaces 4 and 5. If the copyright date is 1978, put an "L" in spaces 36 and 37.
3. If London's 1980 population was more than 6,000,000 people, put an "F" in space 20. If it was less than 6,000,000 people, put a "P" in space 20.
4. Put the first letter of the last name of the man who wrote Sherlock Holmes books in spaces 9, 25, and 31.
5. Put the first letter of the middle name of the author of the Sherlock Holmes books in spaces 9, 25, and 31.
6. Alan Pinkerton was a famous real detective. If his detective agency was in the United States, put a "T" in spaces 7 and 10. If it was in England, put an "M" in spaces 7 and 10.
7. Scotland Yard is a famous detective agency. If it is in England, put an "R" in spaces 18, 22, and 30. If it is in the United States, put an "N" in spaces 18, 22, and 30.
8. Put the first letter of the first name of the queen of England from 1837-1901 in space 12.
9. England is a part of the United Kingdom. If its flag is blue and white, put an "R" in space 24. If it is red, white, and blue, put an "N" in space 24.
10. Put the first letter of the nickname of the little girl who helped Andrew in spaces 14, 16, 27, and 33.
11. If Mrs. Harker was Andrew's real mother, put a "U" in spaces 15 and 29. If she was not Andrew's mother, put an "A" in spaces 15 and 29.
12. Put a "B" in space 24 if Sam was a Baker's assistant. If he did jobs for Sherlock Holmes, put a "W" in space 34.
13. If there is a dedication in this book, put an "I" in space 11. If there is no dedication, put an "A" in space 11.
14. If "hansom" is an adjective meaning "good looking," put an "O" in spaces 6, 8, 13, 17, 19, 21, 23, 26, 32, and 35. If it is a noun meaning a two-wheeled horse-drawn carriage, put an "E" in those spaces.
15. If Sherlock Holmes used a disguise in this book, put an "O" in spaces 2, 3, and 28. If he used no disguise in this book, put an "E" in spaces 2, 3, and 28.

THE MESSAGE IS:

_____

PROJECTS FOR
YOUR CHOICE OF MYSTERY OR ADVENTURE

1. What is the title and author of your book? _____

   by _____.

2. Do you feel your book is best classified as a mystery or an adventure book? _____

3. Describe your favorite character in this book. (Both the character's appearance and

   personality) _____

   _____

   _____

4. What is the mystery or adventure in this book? (Use the back of this paper if you need

   more room.) _____

   _____

   _____

   _____

© 1988 by The Center for Applied Research in Education, Inc.

CHOOSE ONE OF THE FOLLOWING PROJECTS:

1. Make a bibliography of mystery books available in your library. (Use the accepted bibliographic form recommended by your teacher or librarian.) Include at least fifteen titles.
2. Make a secret message puzzle which can be solved by using reference sources.
3. Finish this mystery: Jim was frantic. His parents had trusted him to watch his four-year-old sister, Kim, and now where was she? He had left her watching her favorite cartoon on T.V. and had gone into the kitchen to fix lunch. When he came back only fifteen minutes later she was gone! Jim didn't know what to do. Finally he---
4. Prepare a three or four minute television commercial for the mystery or adventure book which you have just read. Act out a scene from the book (you may use a friend or friends to help you) and then try to "sell" the book. If your school has video equipment ask your teacher if you can videotape or have someone else videotape your commercial to show to the class.

TITLE RIDDLES

Can you figure out the titles of these mystery and adventure books?

1. a personal pronoun + homonym for "sighed" + rhymes with "dove" + THE + a very high hill =

   _____

2. THE + spooked + home = _____

3. THE + a spirit + nearest to something + opening to a building =

   _____

4. THE + home for a girl's toy + homicides =

   _____

5. an alphabetized reference source usually containing several volumes + a dark color + lad + sleuth =

   _____

6. great riches + land surrounded by water =

   _____

7. child + slept briefly = _____

8. antonym for "young" + screamer = _____

9. THE + scarlet + part of a house + a conundrum =

   _____

10. land surrounded by water + preposition rhyming with "dove" + THE + a sky color + porpoise =

   _____

BOYS AND GIRLS OF TODAY

SUGGESTIONS FOR THE TEACHER

The books about the children of today are already vastly popular. Books such as those by Judy Blume, Betsy Byars, and Ellen Conford are eagerly read by students. However, a unit such as this will give you the opportunity to get students to read other authors who write about the children of today—their lives, problems, and fun.

As an introduction to Unit 3, you might want to show a sound filmstrip such as *Realistic Fiction* from Pied Piper Productions, *Meet the Newbery Author, Betsy Byars* produced by Random House, or *The Great Gilly Hopkins* also from Random House. These filmstrips will help explain and illustrate the realistic fiction your students will be reading.

It is important to let your students select their own books from this unit as it could be possible that some of the students may already have read several of the titles. Exhibit each book mentioned in this unit and several others of this type that students could read and use with the additional activity sheets. Give a short book talk about each and let the students choose the one they want to read first. If you feel you need to assign the books because of obvious differences in the students' reading abilities, then *What Do You Do When Your Mouth Won't Open?*, *Nothing's Fair in Fifth Grade*, and *Hello, My Name Is Scrambled Eggs* are probably the easiest of the selections. None of the others are especially difficult, although *Hideaway* and *Will the Real Gertrude Hollings Please Stand Up?* may be a little more difficult.

If you want to make your book talks more appealing, use some props such as a goldfish in a bowl for *The Iceberg and Its Shadow;* classroom items labeled with "hello"-type labels for *Hello, My Name Is Scrambled Eggs;* a seashell for *Hideaway;* and a homemade cookie for each class member for *Don't Hurt Laurie.*

As the students finish their projects, don't forget to reserve time at the beginning of each session for students to show and explain the projects to the class.

AUDIO-VISUAL AIDS
AND RELATED BOOK TITLES

Here are a few of the many audio-visual items and book titles that can be used with this unit on books for children of today.

Audio-Visual Items

Realistic Fiction, sound filmstrip (Pied Piper Productions)

Dear Mr. Henshaw, sound filmstrip (Random House)

The Summer of the Swans, listening cassette (Random House)

Philip Hall Likes Me. I Reckon Maybe, sound filmstrip (Random House)

The Planet of Junior Brown, sound filmstrip (Random House)

The Great Gilly Hopkins, sound filmstrip (Random House)

The Noonday Friends, sound filmstrip (Random House)

Related Book Titles

Blume, Judy. *Hello, God, My Name Is Margaret* and *Blubber.*

Byars, Betsy. *The Pinballs* and *The Night Swimmers.*

Fox, Paula. *One-Eyed Cat.*

Greene, Constance. *I Know You, Al.*

Hamilton, Virginia. *The Planet of Junior Brown.*
Hunt, Irene. *The Lottery Rose.*
Lowry, Lois. *A Summer to Die.*
Paterson, Katherine. *The Great Gilly Hopkins.*
Perl, Lila. *Me and Fat Glenda.*
Smith, Doris. *A Taste of Blackberries.*
Stolz, Mary. *The Noonday Friends.*

SUMMARIES OF UNIT 3 BOOKS

3-1 *The Unmaking of Rabbit* by Constance Greene (New York: Viking Press, 1972. 125 pages). Paul's father left when the boy was two, and his mother brings him to live with his grandmother because she can't "cope" with him anymore. Paul is smaller than the average eleven-year-old and feels that he has no friends of his own age. Freddy, the leader of a gang of boys, calls Paul "Rabbit" with disdain and the other boys follow suit. Paul is therefore a little suspicious when Freddy tries to be friendly to him and promises him a "sleep out" with the gang if Paul helps them on Saturday. Paul wants to stay away from Freddy and the gang on Saturday but is afraid to, so he goes with them. When they arrive in a particular neighborhood, Paul learns that his "help" is to crawl in a small upstairs window in a rich-looking home and then open the door for the rest of the boys so that they can rob the house. The window is too small for any of the other boys to climb through. At first, Paul is hopeful that the window is locked, then he hopes that it is too high, but when these hopes are dashed Paul is afraid he'll have to go through with it. Then one of the boys yells, "Atta boy, Rab." If they'd called him Paul instead of Rabbit, he might have gone through with the robbery, but when he hears the hated name of Rabbit, Paul's mind hardens and he remembers a bigger boy once telling him that he could get out of anything by threatening to be sick. Paul tells Freddy that he has to get down or he will be sick all over them. At last the gang believes him and Paul escapes. Through the friendship of a visiting boy, Gordon, Paul begins to appreciate himself, to recognize that his mother is never going to take him back to live with her, and that he really wants to stay where he is—with his grandmother who loves and needs him.

3-2 *Don't Hurt Laurie* by Willo Roberts (New York: Atheneum, 1977. 166 pages). Laurie calls her mother "Annabelle" because she doesn't seem like a *real* mother—the kind who loves you, bakes cookies for you, and tucks you into bed at night. Annabelle is unpredictable, but Laurie has learned to stay away from her if she has a headache, for then she often hurts Laurie by hitting her with anything handy...once with a butcher knife! Laurie also knows that after she has been to the hospital emergency room for stitches after one of these episodes, the family will probably be moving because Annabelle doesn't want anyone to get curious about Laurie's many "accidents." Annabelle has remarried and Laurie likes her stepfather's two children, who are younger than Laurie. Tim is understanding, and Shelly, though too young to be of any help to Laurie, is a lovable child. Even her stepfather, Jack, seems kind but he is seldom home because of his job. Laurie desperately wants to tell someone about how afraid she is of being really hurt by her mother, but she isn't sure who to tell. Laurie finds a friend in her stepbrother Tim, and also in Gerald, a crippled boy who lives in the duplex next door. They have fun down in a ravine near their home until the fun comes to an end because of Annabelle. How Laurie eventually finds help is an absorbing story that fifth and sixth graders enjoy and one that might be of help to a child concerned with child abuse.

3-3 *Nothing's Fair in Fifth Grade* by Barthe DeClements (New York: Viking Press, 1981. 137 pages). Jennifer, Diane, and Sharon are best friends. When the new girl appears in the fifth grade, Jennifer is not happy to have to show her around the school and miss recess with her friends. Besides, the new girl, Elsie, is "gross." She is the fattest child any of the class has ever seen. Then when lunch money begins to disappear from the fifth grade classroom, the students really begin to be mean to Elsie. Jennifer begins to be sorry for Elsie—the girl whose mother wouldn't take her to a movie because she was taking her little sister and there was only room for two in the sports car; the girl whose mother seemed to always be criticizing and never loving. When Jennifer's mother hires Elsie, who is very bright in math, to tutor Jennifer after school, Jennifer begins to see Elsie in a different way. She slowly becomes a friend to Elsie, the first friend that Elsie has ever had. When Elsie's mother threatens to send her away to boarding school, Jennifer, Diane, and Sharon begin to try to help Elsie with her overeating and problems at school. This story of the changes in Elsie and in Jennifer makes the book a favorite with fourth- through sixth-grade girls.

3-4 *The Iceberg and Its Shadow* by Jan Greenberg (New York: Farrar, Straus and Giroux, 1980. 119 pages). Anabeth and Rachel are best friends. Anabeth is good at stories and poetry, while Rachel is great at drawing and painting. They made a great pair until Mindy comes to the sixth grade. Anabeth is selected to be Mindy's buddy along with Tracy and Carolyn, but Mindy seems to dislike Rachel and ignores her, leaving her out of all the activities and calling her "Toadeye." Anabeth feels sorry for Rachel, but does not stand up for her. She is afraid of Mindy and justifies her treatment of Rachel by telling herself that Rachel is being "stubborn" and "impossible." Anabeth finally gets tired of Mindy's bossy attitude and realizes that she and Mindy do not enjoy the same things. When Anabeth dares to criticize Mindy's attitude toward her father, Mindy's anger turns toward Anabeth. At a party, Anabeth finds herself ostracized, ignored, and humiliated by Mindy, Tracy, and Carolyn. For the remainder of the school year, Anabeth is made the object of Mindy's wrath. Anabeth realizes that she is now experiencing what Rachel has but she is afraid and ashamed to try to be Rachel's friend again. When the creative but unorthodox teacher of their sixth grade is fired by the conservative principal, Anabeth is determined to try to help her by circulating a petition protesting the firing. Anabeth is afraid of the taunts she knows Mindy will lead, but she faces the class and persuades everyone—except Mindy, Tracy, and Carolyn—to sign the petition. After she gradually regains her self-respect and no longer fears Mindy, Anabeth finally gains the courage to call Rachel, ready to apologize and ask for another chance to be her friend. This is a book with characters similar to many in an average sixth grade class. Most fifth and sixth grade girls will relate to the story and enjoy reading it.

3-5 *Hideaway* by Eloise McGraw (New York: Atheneum, 1983. 217 pages). Jerry is not happy that his mother has remarried and that he will be living with Vicky, Jeanne, and Tom, the children of his new stepfather Walter Fox. To make matters even worse, Jerry's dad, who was supposed to pick Jerry up after the wedding and take him on vacation while Jerry's mother was on her honeymoon, had not shown up. Jerry knows his father has forgotten again, as he so often did. Jerry decides to take what money he has and catch a bus to the Oregon coast to stay in his grandparent's house. He knows they are not home, but they would not mind him staying there. When Jerry arrives at their house, he manages to get in through a door his grandfather had made for a dog, but gradually Jerry begins to feel that things do not seem right. Could his grandparents have moved without telling him? He knows they love him, but they are his father's parents and since he lives with his mother, he had not been to see them except once in the last five years. Jerry finally realizes that he is in the home of strangers and, when he hears someone coming, he hides outdoors. Later, during a violent storm when he tries to return to the house, he twists his ankle and can barely drag himself to cover in the shelter of the house. Luckily, he finds help from Hanna, a sixteen-year-old foster child who is watching the house for the owners. She helps him and brings him food and companionship. Jerry wants to run away to California with her and, even though Hanna wants to keep her housesitting job and is afraid someone will find out that Jerry is staying in the house, she is tempted to go. Together they work out their problems and decide what is best for each of them.

3-6 *Philip Hall Likes Me. I Reckon Maybe* by Bette Greene (New York: Dial Press, 1974. 135 pages). Elizabeth Lorraine Lambert, Beth for short, is the second smartest kid in her class. Philip Hall is the smartest. Beth sometimes wonders if she is, perhaps, the smartest in the class; she suspects that sometimes she lets Philip beat her in grades because she's afraid he wouldn't like her if she outdid him. Besides being smart, Beth is spunky. Once she saved the family turkey from being stolen by threatening the thieves with what they thought was a rifle, but was really a BB gun. Another time she got a skinflint store owner to refund the club's money when their newly purchased T-shirts shrunk. Once she rescued her friend Philip from a mountain where he had gotten lost. Beth organizes her friends into a club called the Pretty Pennies; they are usually trying to defeat the boys, who organized their own club called the Tiger Hunters. Beth defeats Philip at the calf-raising contest at the county fair when her calf receives the blue first place ribbon and Philip's calf receives the red second place ribbon. Beth is sure that Philip is mad about it, but when she says to him, "I should've let you win," Philip answers that he doesn't want to be "let won." He said he wasn't used to losing, and losing takes getting used to. When Beth invites him to enter the square-dance contest as a team, Philip agrees and says, "Sometimes I like you, Beth Lambert," as they run off together to the contest. While this book is about black children, it is not about racial differences or problems. Rather, it is a book about children everywhere and the problems Beth has are problems any girl might have. Most students will relate to the competitive feelings between boys and girls.

3-7 *Cracker Jackson* by Betsy Byars (New York: Viking, 1985. 147 pages). Alma is Cracker Jackson's babysitter, but now she is in trouble. Alma's husband no longer lets Cracker visit her. Although she denies it, Cracker is sure Alma's husband is beating her. There are constant and varied bruises on her body that she cannot hide. One day, Cracker gets a desperate phone call from Alma. She admits that her husband beats her, but this time her husband also hit their baby, Nicole, and Alma cannot stand that. Cracker tells her about a place where people like Alma can go for help. It is in Avondale, a nearby town, but Alma says she has no way to get there. Cracker's mother is out of town and he is with a young babysitter, but he does not know where the keys to the car are kept. Although he is underage and not even old enough to be learning to drive, he offers to drive her to Avondale. First, he calls his best friend, Goat, and together they take the car. The ride is hair-raising. They are almost to the outskirts of Avondale when Alma changes her mind and demands to be taken home. Cracker and Goat manage to get her back home and the car in the garage without any damage, but Cracker is so worried about Alma and Nicole that when his mother comes home she could tell that something is wrong. She finally persuades Cracker to tell her his worries and she immediately calls Alma and talks to her. They make an appointment for Alma to see her, but when Alma misses the appointment, Cracker is sure something is terribly wrong. Cracker's mother leaves the house and drives off hurriedly without telling Cracker where she is going, but Cracker knows it has something to do with Alma. He goes to Alma's house as fast as he can and learns from the neighbors that Alma and the baby have been taken to the hospital. The book ends on a note of hope that things will be better for Alma, Nicole, and for Cracker, too. This is an absorbing, well-written book that reflects some of the concerns children of today might have.

3-8   *What Do You Do When Your Mouth Won't Open?* by Susan Beth Pfeffer (New York: Delacorte Press, 1981. 114 pages). Reesa has a problem—she has a phobia about public speaking. In fact, she cannot even read aloud in class. She is a good writer, however, and is delighted when told that her essay on "What I Like Best about America" had won the school essay contest and will now be entered in the county-wide contest. Her delight turns to dismay, however, when her older sister Robby tells her that she'll have to read her essay for the county-wide contest—probably in front of about 500 people! Reesa decides to fight her phobia by going to a psychologist. Dr. Marks is not very enthusiastic about trying to cure Reesa of her phobia when she learns there are only two weeks before the county contest. In fact, Dr. Marks tells Reese that it is impossible and sends her home. Latr, Dr. Marks calls Reesa and says she would try to help her by teaching her a relaxation technique. Between Dr. Marks' coaching and reading a book called *Stand Up and Speak Out,* Reesa works hard to overcome her fear of public speaking. The night of the contest Reesa feels confident until she looks at the audience. She tries to find her mother's friendly face, but instead finds her sister. What her sister does helps Reesa through the ordeal. This is a readable book that should not be difficult for most students.

3-9   *Will the Real Gertrude Hollings Please Stand Up?* by Sheila Greenwald (Boston: Little, Brown and Company, 1983. 162 pages). Gertrude Hollings is labeled "learning disabled." Her cousin Albert is a "superachiever." When Gertrude finds out that she is going to spend three weeks with her super-organized aunt and uncle and the superachiever while her parents are away, she is very unhappy. How could she, a "dyslexic," unmotivated, learning disabled child stand to spend three weeks with a compulsive winner and his family? Then she decides that maybe she could teach Albert something about coping with a sibling in the family, because Albert's mother is going to have a baby soon. Gertrude's aunt hopes, too, that being with Gertrude will help Albert adjust to the coming birth of a brother or sister, but instead, the imaginative Gertrude scares Albert by pretending to be an oracle from ancient Egypt who tells him to beware of the "babe." To Gertrude's disbelief, Albert believes almost all of her play-acting and actually becomes sick with worry about the impending arrival of a baby in the household. Albert's overprotective mother decides that Gertrude is a bad influence on Albert and arranges to send Gertrude to spend the remainder of the time with Gertrude's girlfriend. After Gertrude leaves, Albert decides he misses having the creative and imaginative Gertrude around so he runs away from home. Gertrude knows where to find him. She and Albert's parents go to Gertrude's family apartment where Albert wants to hide out. But a neighbor, seeing lights, thought a burglary was in progress and had called the police. Gertrude's parents arrive home just in time. Gertrude is congratulating herself on helping Albert adjust to another child in the family when she discovers that she, too, will be having a brother or sister soon. This book is amusing while still making the point that labeling people is damaging and often promotes misjudging children and their talents and abilities.

3-10   *Hello, My Name Is Scrambled Eggs* by Jamie Gilson (New York: Lothrop, Lee, and Shepard, 1985. 159 pages). Harvey Trumble's family is asked by their church minister to host a family from Viet Nam for a short time until their house is completed. The family has a boy about Harvey's age and Harvey feels it is his responsibility to turn the boy, Tuan Nguyen, into an all-American kid. Harvey attempts to teach Tuan English, but he is often frustrated and the results are often mixed-up and amusing. His friend, Quint, is no help for he seems to be undermining Harvey's efforts. For example, on the first day at a church welcoming dinner for the Nguyen, Harvey tries to teach Tuan the word "fork" while Quint is calling it "porcupine." Quint seems to resent the Nguyens, perhaps because Mr. Nguyen has a job at a gas station where Quint's uncle hopes to work. Harvey is very serious about teaching Tuan English and American ways. In fact, he is perhaps too serious for it isn't much fun for Tuan.

He even changes Tuan's name to Tom Win and Tuan is not sure that he wants the new name. In fact, Tuan at times seems to prefer to be with Quint who could be cruel but who sometimes has fun with him. When Tuan begins to call Harvey "Zilch," which is what the self-proclaimed genius Quint calls Harvey, Harvey is jealous and upset. Quint seems to be trying to cause trouble for Harvey and one night eggs him on to go with Tuan and decorate the town statue with toilet paper. Harvey and Tuan are caught by the police and, even though the police do not report it to their parents, Harvey knows that Tuan is upset by the incident. Tuan's family, homesick for friends they can talk to, decide to leave and go to Chicago where there are many more Vietnamese. Before they leave, however, a new family moves into town from Viet Nam. This family also has a boy Tuan's age and since there are now other Vietnamese in the city, the Nguyen family decides to stay. Tuan also decides that he'll be an American kid but keep his name and Vietnamese customs. Most students enjoy this amusing story. It, like most of Jamie Gilson's books, is especially enjoyed by boys.

PROJECTS FOR
THE UNMAKING OF RABBIT

1. Describe Paul's grandmother. Tell how she looked and something about her character. _____

_____

2. Do you think Paul's mother loved him and really wanted him to live with her? Why or why not? _____

_____

3. Why do you think Paul at last got the courage to stand up to Freddy and tell him, "My name is Paul. It's not Rabbit. It's Paul. And don't you forget it."?

_____

_____

4. Do you think *The Unmaking of Rabbit* is a good title for this book? _____

Explain what you think the author meant by this title. _____

_____

_____

CHOOSE ONE OF THE FOLLOWING PROJECTS:

1. Research the author, Constance Greene in the *Junior Book of Authors* or another reference book. Write a report on her and read it to the class. Show them several other books which she has written.
2. If you liked this book, write a letter to the author, Constance Greene, telling her why you liked the book. Be sure to use the proper letter-writing form and your best penmanship. Get the address of her publisher from an almanac or other reference source and address the letter to the author in care of her publisher.
3. The book *The Unmaking of Rabbit* has no illustrations. Take an incident from the story and illustrate it. Use paint or ink or felt tip pens so that it can be seen by the class. Show the illustration to the class and tell them about the incident in the book which you illustrated.
4. When the story ends Paul has Gordon as a friend but Gordon does not live where Paul does. Write a story about how Paul makes a friend in his own school or neighborhood. Think about how they could meet and what each one did that made the other like them. Read your story to the class and explain how it relates to *The Unmaking of Rabbit*.

A CONSTANCE GREENE WORDSEARCH

Constance Greene has written many books for children. Find out if your library has each of the following books. Write the copyright date beside the book if your library has it. Write "No" beside the title if the book is not in your library. Then find each title in the wordsearch.

_____ *Isabelle the Itch*
_____ *I Know You, Al*
_____ *The Ears of Louis*
_____ *I and Sproggy*
_____ *The Unmaking of Rabbit*

_____ *A Girl Called Al*
_____ *Your Old Pal, Al*
_____ *Beat the Turtle Drum*
_____ *Dotty's Suitcase*

```
A S T S I U O L F O S R A E E H T O R
B R O C O D A T R M O D P S E A H L A
E M N A V I E C O K R A T T H E S F
A B O M D L N I O L P C C R C E U M O
T C P X Y Z I S L T N I T O M N I D
T S L N O F I N B I C A I E Y O M N E
H Y E N E E P W U H Y E U A O U A K A
E G O Y S E H S L L H S O C H R K O K
T G O R L D S C I T E Y E H O L I I L
U O T N W Y M O E W O S T I B S N W A
R R O O T O E L T E H K H I O N G C A
T P T T L A L A P D L O R U O Y O U T
L S O O T E H W O O N E E E M I F W Y
E D O G B W O T O N W X T K W L R C O
D N T A G I R L C A L L E D A L A S D
R A S S T A N I N A P L E N B L B N D
U I K N O W Y O U A L O S I E F B S C
M T S A T Y A Y N H I N G A T A I N C
E N M O T I S H T T U A B O L L T R H
```

PROJECTS FOR
DON'T HURT LAURIE

The following titles are other books about child abuse. Check the card catalog in your library to see if they are part of your library's collection. If the book is in the card catalog, write the year of its copyright.

The Lottery Rose by Irene Hunt   COPYRIGHT _____

Boy Wanted by Ruth Fennisong   COPYRIGHT _____

The Summer of My German Soldier by Bette Greene   COPYRIGHT _____

The Pinballs by Betsy Byars   COPYRIGHT _____

CHOOSE ONE OF THE FOLLOWING PROJECTS:

1. Read one of the books listed above. Show it to the class and tell them about it.

2. Amigo was a golden retriever. Look up dogs in a reference source and give a report on them to the class. You may report on the history of dogs, the various breeds of dogs, or the care and training of dogs. Your report should be interesting and with pictures or charts if possible.

3. Write a GOOD letter to Willo Roberts in care of her publisher. Tell her what you liked about *Don't Hurt Laurie,* ask her questions about her writing, and ask about any other books she might have written. Be sure your letter is interesting, legible, and in the correct letter form.

4. There was a time when some children had to work in factories and fields. They had to work long hours and were often mistreated. See if you can find some information on the child labor laws and why it was necessary to have these laws. Give a report to the class about the abuses of children in the work force of several years ago and about the child labor laws today.

WHAT'S THE MESSAGE?

Fill in the statements with answers from the book *Don't Hurt Laurie* by Willo Roberts. Each answer is then to be crossed off in the puzzle below. The remaining letters will spell out a message.

1. The one who gave Laurie a seashell was _____.

2. The one who had to have another operation on his legs was _____.

3. The one who wouldn't let the police take the children home was _____.

4. The one who was afraid to go to the ravine was _____.

5. The one who yelled at Annabelle, "Don't hurt Laurie!" was _____.

6. The one who was afraid of dogs was _____.

7. The one who was missing was _____.

8. The one who wanted to tell the school nurse about Annabelle was _____.

9. The one who baked bread and gave it to Laurie was _____.

10. The children hid Amigo from Annabelle by tying him in the _____.

1.	J	R	E	A	A	D	I	C	N	K	G	I
2.	S	G	F	E	O	U	N	R	G	E	R	E
3.	A	N	D	E	I	N	L	G	L	I	S	I
4.	S	N	F	H	E	O	L	R	L	M	Y	A
5.	T	T	I	I	V	M	E	K	E	E	P	R
6.	A	N	N	E	A	A	B	E	D	L	L	E
7.	I	A	M	N	G	I	A	N	G	D	O	Y
8.	O	U	W	L	I	A	L	U	R	L	I	E
9.	M	H	R	S	G	E	R	R	A	O	L	D
10.	V	E	R	A	F	U	V	I	N	N	E	

PLEASE HELP LAURIE!

THE MESSAGE IS: _____

_____

_____

PROJECTS FOR
NOTHING'S FAIR IN FIFTH GRADE

1. How many public school districts are there operating in the United States?

   _____

2. How many classroom teachers are there in the United States? _____

3. How many classroom teachers were there in 1900? _____

4. What was the average classroom teacher's salary in 1900? _____

5. What was the average teacher's salary in 1981? _____

CHOOSE ONE AND DO IT AND THEN SHOW IT TO YOUR CLASS:

1. Read *Blubber* by Judy Blume or *Me and Fat Glenda* by Lila Perl. Compare this book with *Nothing's Fair in Fifth Grade.* Give a book talk to the class on the book you chose compared with *Nothing's Fair in Fifth Grade.*

2. Make a television commercial advertising the book *Nothing's Fair in Fifth Grade.* Watch television and see how commercials for books or movies are done. Then write a good commercial for your book. You or you and a friend or friends film the commercial with your school's video equipment and show it to the class.

3. People are often concerned about their weight. Some are worried that they are too fat and others worry about being too thin. Read *Beanpole* by Barbara Parks and compare the problems of being too thin with that of being too fat. Show the two books to the class and compare them.

4. Research good nutrition. Make a report on the basic foods children need to grow and be strong. Make a plan for a week of good meals and snacks for children of your age. You may make your report as a written one or as a poster using pictures you have found or drawn yourself.

5. Write a story about what happens to Elsie next year when she comes back to school. Will she still have a weight problem and a problem with taking things or will she become an accepted member of her class?

GOOD BOOKS TO READ ABOUT KIDS AND SCHOOL

Nothing's Fair in Fifth Grade by Barthe DeClements is just one of many good books to read about kids and school. Shown below are the titles of several of the books. Write the author's first and last names beside each title.

1. *4B Goes Wild* by _____

2. *The Beast in Mrs. Rooney's Room* by _____

3. *Nothing's Fair in Fifth Grade* by _____

4. *The Wheel on the School* by _____

5. *The Great Brain at the Academy* by _____

6. *The Iceberg and Its Shadow* by _____

7. *Tales of a Fourth Grade Nothing* by _____

8. *Miss Nelson Is Missing* by _____

9. *The Snake That Went to School* by _____

10. *Schoolhouse in the Woods* by _____

11. *Schoolhouse Mystery* by _____

12. *17 Gerbils of Class 4A* by _____

Now cross out the author's name in the matching line of the puzzle below. The remaining letters in the puzzle will spell out a message. (The blackened squares are periods.)

J	A	T	M	I	E	H	E	G	R	I	L	E	S	A	O	R	N	E	M	A
N	P	A	Y	T	R	G	I	O	C	I	A	O	D	G	I	B	F	O	O	F
B	K	A	R	S	T	H	A	E	D	B	E	C	L	E	O	M	E	N	T	S
U	M	E	I	N	T	D	E	K	R	T	D	I	E	D	J	O	S	N	A	G
N	J	O	D	H	N	F	S	I	T	Z	C	G	E	R	H	A	O	O	L	D
J	L	A	N	S	■	G	R	E	U	E	S	N	E	T	B	H	E	E	R	G
C	A	R	J	U	D	D	C	Y	A	B	L	T	U	A	L	M	O	G	E	T
H	O	A	F	R	R	I	Y	N	D	A	O	L	L	N	A	E	■	R	C	D
H	L	E	I	C	L	I	K	A	N	I	T	O	M	U	O	T	O	A	R	E
R	N	E	B	D	E	C	T	C	A	H	C	A	E	U	D	N	I	H	L	L
A	G	E	V	R	T	R	E	U	D	F	E	W	U	A	R	N	N	E	R	R
E	A	W	D	I	I	L	L	N	I	A	M	G	H	I	O	O	T	K	S	■

THE MESSAGE IS: _____

PROJECTS FOR
THE ICEBERG AND ITS SHADOW

1. Describe Mindy. In your description, tell what you think she looked like as well as

   something about her character, abilities, and bad points. _____

   _____

   _____

   _____

2. What do you think about the way Anabeth treated Rachel? Why do you think Anabeth

   acted as she did? _____

   _____

   _____

   _____

3. Do you think anything like what happened in this book could happen in your classroom?

   Why or why not? _____

   _____

   _____

   _____

CHOOSE ONE OF THE FOLLOWING PROJECTS:

1. Make an "Iceberg and Its Shadow" sculpture like the one described in this book. Think about what you can use for the sculpture...glass, plastic, or cellophane?
2. Make up an activity for the class to do such as Anabeth did with her "Fish Tale" or Rachel did with her mouse-house collage. Before letting the class do the activity tell how this activity relates to this book.
3. The author does not say what happens after Anabeth calls Rachel. Write a story about how Rachel and Anabeth become friends again. Then write about something that happens to them when they begin Junior High.
4. Draw or paint an illustration for this story. Show your illustration to the class and tell them something about the book.

A "FISHY" PUZZLE

Fill in the correct words in the sentences. Then cross off your answers in the appropriate lines of the letter grid below. The remaining letters will spell out a message. HINT: Use first *and* last names in numbers 1, 2, 3, 5, 6, 8, and 10.

1. The one who set off the fire alarm in school one rainy day was _____.

2. The one who got to go to France and was a walking encyclopedia of famous quotations was _____.

3. The one who cooked the best chili and won a chili contest was _____.

4. The one who got in trouble with Dr. Munch because of polegars was _____.

5. The one who gave a report called "Fish Tale" and taught her goldfish to nip her finger was _____.

6. The one whose house was the scene of the Monster Bash party was _____.

7. The place where Anabeth and her friends lived was _____.

8. The one who was called "Toadeye" was _____.

9. The only goldfish to survive the great fish-tale experiment was _____.

10. The one with a pet boa constrictor named Julius Squeezer was _____.

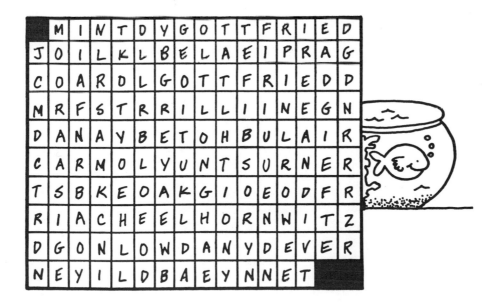

THE MESSAGE IS: _____

PROJECTS FOR
HIDEAWAY

1. Did you like Hanna in this story? _____ Would you like her

   as a friend? _____ Why? _____

   _____

   Describe Hanna's appearance and her character. _____

   _____

   _____

2. Why did no one look for Jerry after he left his home in Portland?

   _____

   _____

3. If you had gone to a house you thought was your grandparents and then found out it wasn't as Jerry did, what would you have done? Would you have stayed in the house as he did or would you have tried to find your grandparents? If you would try to find them,

   how would you look for them? _____

   _____

4. How did Hanna try to make Jerry decide for himself that he wanted to go home?

   _____

   _____

CHOOSE ONE OF THE FOLLOWING PROJECTS:

1. Hanna and Jerry decided not to take Jerry's money and go live in California. Write a story about their adventures if they had decided to go.
2. Jerry lived in Portland, Oregon. Research Portland and write a report on the city. Read your report to the class and tell how this report relates to *Hideaway*.
3. At first Hanna helped Jerry because she thought he was a runaway Polish boy who did not want to return to Poland with his parents. Prepare a T.V. interview with Jerry, the polish boy. Ask him about himself, why he wants to stay in the United States, where he has been hiding, and any other questions which you think are interesting. Then ask a friend to help you present the interview to the class.
4. This book has no illustrations. Make a good illustration for the book. Make it large enough that the class will be able to see it. Show it to the class and tell which part of the story it represents.

JERRY'S MISSING

We have all seen many missing children posters. If Jerry's mother had returned and found Jerry gone, she would probably have wanted a missing child poster circulated to help find him.

In the poster below draw a picture of Jerry or find one in a magazine or newspaper to represent him. Then give his name, describe him, and tell when and where he disappeared.

PROJECTS FOR
PHILIP HALL LIKES ME. I RECKON MAYBE

1. This book is set in the state of Arkansas. Answer these questions about that state:

   a. What is the population of Arkansas? _____

   b. What is the state motto? _____

   c. What is the state capital? _____

   d. What is the ZIP code for the capital of Arkansas? _____

2. Beth's father raised turkeys for a living. How many turkeys were eaten per capita (per person) in the United States in 1982? _____ in 1984? _____.

3. How did the Pretty Pennies get Mr. Putterham to refund the money for the shrinking T-shirts? _____

4. This book is about a smart girl who wasn't sure she wanted to do her best because she might beat the boy she liked. Do you think most girls feel like this? _____ Why or why not? Use the back of this sheet for your answer.

CHOOSE ONE OF THE FOLLOWING PROJECTS:

1. Raising turkeys was the way Beth's father made his living. Some people think that turkeys are among the most stupid of animals. Research turkeys and make a report on them to the class. In your report include the history of turkeys, problems in raising them, and production numbers, if possible. In your report consider whether you feel that turkeys are stupid and why. After giving your report to the class show them *Philip Hall Likes Me. I Reckon Maybe* and tell them what a report on turkeys has to do with this book.

2. Beth Lambert was not only smart, she was also an achiever. Look up some famous women achievers and make a wordsearch with their names. Have at least ten women achievers in your wordsearch.

3. Make a television commercial for *Philip Hall Likes Me. I Reckon Maybe*. Choose a scene to dramatize with a friend or friends and then use it to advertise the book. Use the school's video equipment to televise it if your teacher agrees.

4. Make a large poster advertising this book. Use magazine cut-outs, cut out letters from construction paper, paint, or felt-tip pens to make your poster as eye-catching and attractive as possible. Show your poster to the class and tell them a little about the book.

DO YOU REMEMBER?

If you remember the story of *Philip Hall Likes Me. I Reckon Maybe,* you will be able to figure out the message below. Cross out the answers in each line of the word grid. The remaining letters will spell out a message. (A blackened square indicates a period.)

1. The girl who caught turkey thieves with a BB gun.
2. The Lamberts' new baby.
3. The Lamberts' pretty older daughter.
4. The turkey thief.
5. The last name of the owner of the Busy Bee Bargain Store.
6. The Pretty Penny who talked most of the time.
7. Philip Hall's best friend.
8. The boy who got lost on a mountain.
9. The Lamberts' oldest child.
10. The preacher from the Old Rugged Cross Church.
11. The name of the boys' club.
12. The name of the girls' club.
13. Philip Hall's calf.
14. Beth Lambert's calf.

1.	B	B	E	O	T	H	Y	L	A	S	M	B	E	A	R	T
2.	N	B	A	B	D	Y	G	B	E	N	I	J	A	M	I	N
3.	A	N	R	N	I	L	E	L	A	M	B	S	E	W	R	T
4.	I	L	C	L	A	L	L	V	I	I	N	C	K	O	O	K
5.	E	P	U	T	T	H	I	E	R	S	H	B	A	O	M	
6.	B	O	O	N	N	K	I	A	E	B	L	B	A	O	K	E
7.	U	G	O	T	R	D	B	E	T	O	H	N	L	A	M	B
8.	E	R	T	P	H	A	I	L	N	I	P	H	D	A	L	L
9.	L	U	T	P	H	E	R	L	H	A	M	B	E	I	R	T
10.	L	R	E	I	V	E	R	E	P	N	D	R	O	H	S	S
11.	T	A	I	G	E	L	R	H	U	L	N	T	E	■	R	S
12.	P	R	E	I	T	T	Y	P	R	E	N	E	N	I	E	S
13.	C	K	L	E	O	O	N	N	A	M	A	R	D	Y	B	E
14.	■	M	D	A	D	I	E	D	L	Y	I	O	N	U	E	?

THE MESSAGE IS: _____

_____

PROJECTS FOR
CRACKER JACKSON

1. Cracker Jackson felt that he was afraid of too many things. How do you feel about Cracker? Do you think he was brave or cowardly? Describe Cracker and what you think

   about him. _____

   _____

   _____

2. Do you think that Goat was a good friend to Cracker? Why or why not? _____

   _____

   _____

3. Betsy Byars is a famous author of children's books. One of her books won the Newbery

   Medal. Which one was it? _____

   In which year did it win the medal? _____

4. Look in the card catalog, and on the back of this sheet, write the titles of three other books by Betsy Byars that are in your library.

HELP ME, CRACKER!

CHOOSE ONE OF THE FOLLOWING PROJECTS:

1. Make a bibliography of all the books in your library by Betsy Byars. Use the accepted bibliography form recommended by your teacher or librarian. Include at least ten books in your bibliography. Show the class one or two of the books which you included and tell them a little about the book you just read, *Cracker Jackson*.
2. Look up Betsy Byars in *The Junior Book of Authors* or another reference source. Make a report on her to the class and show them several of her many books.
3. This book is not illustrated. Make a large illustration for an incident that happened in the book. Show your illustration to the class and explain the incident to them.
4. See if your city or town has a place which helps battered or abused people. If so, see if someone from the shelter will come and speak to your class about their agency and how it helps people.
5. Prepare five mixed-up nursery rhymes like the ones on the page "Mixed-Up Nursery Rhymes." Read them to the class and see if they can give the right words to the rhymes.

MIXED-UP NURSERY RHYMES

Cracker Jackson's dad would never read a story the way it was written. He always changed the words, usually making it sound like a television commercial. Cracker didn't like it very much and always tried to make his dad read the story right. Below are some nursery rhymes written like a televsion commercial might be. See if you can write the nursery rhyme the way it should be beside each one.

1. Mary, Mary quite contrary,
   How does your garden grow?
   With Vigoro, and Weed and Feed,
   And Alaska Fish in the row.

2. Little Jack Horner
      Sat in a corner
   Eating a Sara Lee Pie.
   He reached in his sack
   For just one more snack
   And said, What a smart boy am I!

3. Old Mother Goose when she
      Wanted to roam
   Would swish all around
   In an Oldsmobile brougham.

4. I had a little mustang
   And it was white and gray.
   I lent it to a lady
   Who rode a hundred miles away.
   She raced it and she braked it
   And she drove it through the snow.
   I would not lend my mustang now,
   For all that lady's dough!

5. Diddle, Diddle dumpling, my son John
   Went to bed with his Levi's on.
   One Florsheim off, one Florsheim on,
   Diddle, diddle dumpling, my son John.

Now see if you can change a favorite nursery rhyme into a commercial using your own words but keeping the rhythm of the rhyme. Use the back of this page for your rhyme.

PROJECTS FOR
WHAT DO YOU DO WHEN YOUR
MOUTH WON'T OPEN?

Reesa had a phobia about speaking in public. A phobia is an exaggerated fear of something. Below are several phobias and what the phobia is. Match the phobia to the fear by using a dictionary.

1. hydrophobia   _____ A. fear of heights

2. claustrophobia   _____ B. fear of cats

3. acrophobia   _____ C. fear of open places

4. pedophobia   _____ D. fear of crowds

5. photophobia   _____ E. fear of water

6. pyrophobia   _____ F. fear of being enclosed in a small space

7. ailurophobia   _____ G. fear of fire

8. hemophobia   _____ H. fear of light

9. ochlophobia   _____ I. fear of blood

10. agoraphobia   _____ J. fear of children

© 1988 by The Center for Applied Research in Education, Inc.

CHOOSE ONE OF THE FOLLOWING PROJECTS:

1. Reesa won an essay contest on "What I Like Best About America." Write an essay of your own on this topic. Make it at least two hundred words in length. Read it to the class and explain to them how it relates to this book.

2. Give a speech to the class on how to get over a fear of public speaking. Make a chart of the activities recommended in this book. Show the chart during your speech and explain each activity.

3. Choose one of the phobias in the list above and write a fictional story about someone who has this phobia. In the story tell how the main character overcomes the phobia.

4. Make an alphabetical list of at least twenty things that people are afraid of. Read your list to the class and explain what it has to do with this book.

HELP, DR. MARKS!

OUR FEARS

In this book Reesa was afraid of public speaking. She is not alone in having fears. Most of us do not have a phobia such as Reesa had but all of us are afraid of something. Many famous people have spoken or written about fears. Use a book of quotations to find out who said the following. (Remember to use the KEY word when looking up the quotation.)

1. "The only thing we have to fear is fear itself." _____

2. "The only thing I am afraid of is fear." _____

3. "Fear cannot be without hope nor hope without fear." _____

4. "We must get rid of fear." _____

All people are afraid of something. On the lines below write about something you are afraid of or about some fear that someone you know has. Tell how you or the person with the fear tries to overcome that fear.

_____

_____

_____

_____

_____

_____

_____

_____

_____

_____

_____

_____

_____

_____

PROJECTS FOR
WILL THE REAL GERTRUDE HOLLINGS PLEASE STAND UP?

1. To do your best is admirable but Albert went too far. Describe Albert and tell some of the things which he did which made Gertrude dislike him rather than admire him.

_____

_____

2. Why did Albert act the way he did? _____

_____

_____

3. Do you think Gertrude was really "learning disabled"? _____ Why or why not? _____

_____

_____

4. Do you think putting labels on people is good or bad? _____ Why? _____

_____

CHOOSE ONE OF THE FOLLOWING PROJECTS:

1. Everyone has talents. One might be talented in being a friend, another in writing, speaking, math, art, music, cooking, or many other fields. Interview five of your classmates and write a paragraph about each one telling of their abilities, good points, and talents.
2. This book is not illustrated. Make a large, *good* illustration of Albert and Gertrude lost in the woods, or choose another incident to illustrate. Show your illustration to the class and explain it in relation to this book.
3. Gertrude was good at using her imagination. Use your imagination and write a story about Oliver and Olivia, Gertrude's stuffed toy owls. If you like to draw, make your story for young readers and illustrate it.
4. Mrs. Hollings told Gertrude that many famous people found school difficult. She mentioned Albert Einstein, Winston Churchill, and Woodrow Wilson. Choose one of these men and do some research on him. Then write a report to read to the class, explaining what the report has to do with this book.

BEWARE OF THE BABE !

NORTH, SOUTH, EAST, WEST

In the book *Will the Real Gertrude Hollings Please Stand Up?* Albert and Gertrude get lost in the woods when Gertrude forgets to follow the compass. Do you think you know your directions and can read a map? Help Gertrude and Albert get out of the woods below by knowing your way around a map.

1. Go four spaces south if Grand Island, Nebraska is southwest from Minneapolis, Minnesota. If it is southeast of Minneapolis, go 2 spaces south.
2. Go 3 spaces in the direction you would go if you went from Nashville, Tennessee to Knoxville, Tennessee.
3. Go 3 spaces in the direction you would go if you went from Salina, Kansas to Wichita, Kansas.
4. Go 10 spaces in the direction you would go if you went from the Canadian province of Ontario to the province of Saskatchewan.
5. Go 5 spaces in the direction you would go from Cleveland, Ohio to Akron, Ohio.
6. Go 7 spaces in the direction you would go to get from Poland to Great Britain.
7. Go 2 spaces in the direction you would go to get from Frankfurt, Germany to Stuttgart, Germany.
8. Lines of latitude and longitude help us to go the right direction when using a map. If Portland, Oregon has an approximate latitude of 45° N and a longitude of 123° W then go 15 spaces east. If it has an approximate latitude of 25° N and 11° E, go 8 spaces east.
9. If Omaha, Nebraska has an approximate latitude of 55° N and a longitude of 45° W, go 2 spaces south. If it has an approximate latitude of 41° N and a longitude of 95° W, go 3 spaces south.
10. Go 7 spaces west if Washington, D.C. has an approximate latitude of 62° N and 50° W. Go 13 spaces west if it has an approximate latitude of 38° N and 77° W.

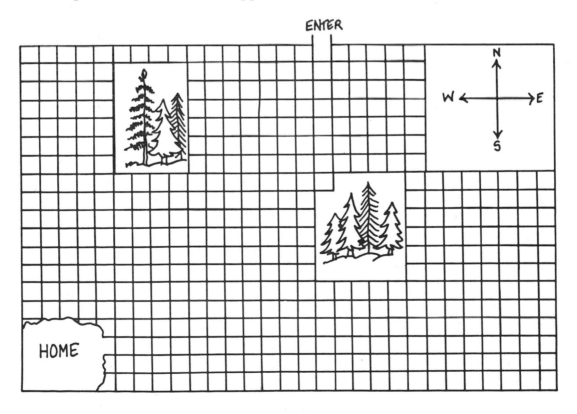

PROJECTS FOR
HELLO, MY NAME IS SCRAMBLED EGGS

1. Did you like the character of Harvey in this book? _____ Describe Harvey.

_____

_____

2. Think of two other things Harvey might have done to help Tuan and write them below:

_____

_____

3. Did you think Quint was a good friend? _____ Describe him below: _____

_____

_____

_____

4. Jamie Gilson has written several books for children. Look in the card catalog and write the titles and copyright dates for two other books written by her.

TITLE	COPYRIGHT DATE
_____	_____
_____	_____

PORCUPINE

CHOOSE ONE OF THE FOLLOWING PROJECTS:

1. Read another book by Jamie Gilson. Report on this book to the class and compare it to *Hello, My Name Is Scrambled Eggs*.

2. If you know about or can find anyone who has come here to live from a non-English speaking country, interview that person and then read your interview to the class. Be sure to ask them about their problems in understanding their new country, who helped them, and ways that people in this country could help new citizens. Explain to the class how this project relates to this book.

3. If your teacher agrees, invite someone who has come to live here from a non-English speaking country to come to the class and talk to the class about the problems of newcomers. Introduce the person to the class and to the teacher and explain why you asked the person to come. Write a thank you note to the person for coming and speaking.

4. Write a letter to Jamie Gilson telling her what you liked about her book. Before you mail the letter show it to your teacher to be sure it is in the correct letter form. Mail the letter to Jamie Gilson in care of her publisher. The publisher's address can be found in a dictionary of addresses or in an almanac.

YOUR OWN STORY

In *Hello, My Name Is Scrambled Eggs,* Tuan is in a country where he knows very little of the language. Choose a non-English speaking country and pretend you are lost there. Write a story about how you got lost and what you did to find your way back to your family. Remember that you **cannot** read or speak the language. (If you need more space to write your story, use the back of this sheet.)

LOST IN _____

_____

_____

_____

_____

_____

_____

_____

_____

_____

_____

_____

_____

_____

_____

_____

_____

_____

_____

_____

PROJECTS FOR YOUR CHOICE OF A BOOK ABOUT BOYS AND GIRLS OF TODAY

1. What is the title of your book? _____

2. Who is the author of your book? _____

3. Who are the main characters? _____

   Describe them briefly. _____

   _____

   _____

4. What is the problem that these characters face? (Tell what it is and how they solve it. You may use the back of this page if you need more space.)

   _____

   _____

   _____

   _____

   _____

WE LIKE BOOKS ABOUT KIDS LIKE US!

CHOOSE ONE OF THE FOLLOWING PROJECTS:

1. Prepare a good bibliography of at least fifteen realistic fiction books about the children of today. Use the accepted bibliographic form recommended by your teacher or librarian.
2. Make a poster advertising the book you have read. Use paint, felt-tip pens, or cut-out construction paper so your poster will be highly visible and attractive. Make it at least 12″ × 18″.
3. Prepare a television commercial for your book. Ask a friend or friends to help you present your commercial to the class or film the commercial with the school's video equipment if your teacher agrees. Then show the video to the class.
4. The students of today have many problems but so did the children of the past. Do some research on the problems which children had in earlier years and then write a report contrasting the problems of today with those of the past. (Researching child labor laws, the diseases of the past, or the schooling of the past might give you a start.)

BOOK TITLE RIDDLES

Below are some riddles for the titles of some fiction books about the boys and girls of today. Try to figure out each title. When you have finished, go to the card catalog and find out who is the author. (If you are REALLY stumped, ask your teacher and he or she will give you the author's name to help you figure out the title. But try to figure each one out by yourself first.)

1. a spice beginning with "G" + what Little Jack Horner stuck his thumb into =

_____ by _____

2. an article + television + child = _____ by

_____

3. homonym for "dew" + yellow fruit + masticate Wrigley's or Dentine =

_____ by _____

4. an article + opposite of midnight night + opposite of enemies =

_____ by _____

5. an article + opposite of fake + opposite of you =

_____ by _____

6. a journal + rhymes with "dove" + an article + opposite of calm + a young goat +

opposite of brother = _____ by _____

7. homonym for deer + opposite of Mrs. + a (female chicken + rhymes with "law") =

_____ by _____

8. homonym for beet + an article + tortoise + percussion musical instrument =

_____ by _____

9. opposite of down + an article + highway + opposite of quickly =

_____ by _____

10. an article + opposite of winter + homonym for "two" + opposite of live =

_____ by _____

NOW SEE IF YOU CAN MAKE UP A BOOK TITLE RIDDLE YOURSELF READ IT TO THE CLASS AND SEE IF THEY CAN FIGURE IT OUT!

HUMOROUS STORIES

SUGGESTIONS FOR THE TEACHER

Books with humorous stories are great favorites with children, such as *Curious George* by H. A. Rey, *Miss Nelson Is Missing* by Frank Allard, and *Arthur's Nose* by Marc Brown for younger readers. For older readers, there are the Ramona books by Beverly Cleary and *Tales of a Fourth Grade Nothing* by Judy Blume.

At one time when books about death, divorce, or the supernatural were being written and published almost to the exclusion of other types of fiction, it was difficult to find humorous books for the third, fourth, fifth, or sixth grader who begged for a "funny" book. Now, however, humorous books are once again being written, much to the joy of children and librarians!

The books chosen for Unit 4 are but ten of the many available. Most of them are not difficult for good readers and will be enjoyed by most students. Even gifted students will enjoy them since they, too, need to relax with a book that makes them laugh.

The unit can be introduced by showing Pied Piper's sound filmstrip *Humor* or by using specific titles such as *Ramona Quimby, Age 8* or *Ralph S. Mouse* by Random House. There are many titles from other companies also available.

After showing one or more of these filmstrips, discuss with the children what kinds of things make them laugh. Then discuss the different books that they have read and consider funny.

Display the books and give a brief book talk for each, using the summary given in this book or the jacket blurb if you do not want to give one of your own. If you wish to be more elaborate in your introduction of this unit's books, you might use a campaign button to introduce your book talk for *The Kids' Candidate*, a broom or a cookbook for *Anastasia on Her Own*, or a "who is this mystery person?" newspaper-like article about someone in the class for *Mysteriously Yours, Maggie Marmelstein*.

If you do not have enough titles for the number of children in your group, display other suitable titles that could be used with the general activity sheets at the end of the unit.

Since the selections in this unit are not difficult, this might be a good time to let the students choose the title of their first book by picking a title from a hat. In this way, all of the titles would be quickly read and reported on. If you prefer that students choose their own titles, let the students select the books based on the personalities of the students rather than on their reading abilities because humor is highly individual.

Once the students have begun reading and doing the activities, be sure to reserve some time during the sessions for the students to show their projects to the class. These projects will often inspire another student to read the book.

AUDIO VISUAL AIDS
AND RELATED BOOK TITLES

Here are a few of the many audio-visual items and book titles that can be used with this unit on humorous books.

Audio-Visual Items

Humor, sound filmstrip (Pied Piper)
Tales of a Fourth Grade Nothing, sound filmstrip (Pied Piper)
The Great Brain Reforms, sound filmstrip (Pied Piper)
Henry and the Clubhouse, sound filmstrip (Pied Piper)

Veronica Ganz, sound filmstrip (Pied Piper)
Ramona Quimby, Age 8, sound filmstrip (Random House)
The Adventures of Tom Sawyer, sound filmstrip (Random House)

Related Book Titles

Blume, Judy. *Tales of a Fourth Grade Nothing* and *Superfudge*.

Cleary, Beverly. All of the Ramona or Henry Huggins books.

Gilson, Jamie. *4B Goes Wild* or *Harvey, the Beer Can King*.

Hicks, Clifford. All of the Alvin Fernald books.

Hughes, Dean. *Nutty for President*.

Lowry, Lois. All of the Anastasia books.

Robinson, Barbara. *The Best Christmas Pagent Ever*.

Rockwell, Thomas. *How to Eat Fried Worms*.

Sachs, Marilyn. *Veronica Ganz*.

Twain, Mark. *The Adventures of Tom Sawyer*.

SUMMARIES OF UNIT 4 BOOKS

4-1   *Thirteen Ways to Sink a Sub* by Jamie Gilson (New York: Lothrop, Lee & Shepard, 1982. 140 pages). The fourth graders in 4B have been hoping for a substitute teacher all year, so they are delighted when their teacher finally gets sick and a substitute is called. They are ready to play a game called "Sink the Sub" in which each team tries to make the substitute cry. The team to "sink the sub" wins. The boys are sure they can "sink the sub," but the girls are equally as sure. When the class discovers that this is the substitute's first teaching job, they are even more sure she will be an easy mark and bound to be "sunk." This story of the ways the fourth graders try to make their smiling substitute cry is an entertaining one.

4-2   *Me and the Terrible Two* by Ellen Conford (Boston: Little, Brown and Company, 1074. 117 pages). Dorrie is very upset when her best and inseparable friend, Marlene, moves to Australia. She is even more upset to learn that twin boys of her own age have moved into the house left by Marlene and her family. To make things even worse, the twins seem to feel their purpose in life is to tease her constantly. Dorrie feels that the teasing is more serious than just plain teasing when the boys send her a bill from the veterinarian after Dorrie's dog scares the boy's pet guinea pig. Dorrie is outraged at the bill and even angrier when one of the boys knocks her down in the cafeteria and her lunch spills all over one of her friends. Even though the twin apologizes and says it was an accident, Dorrie is not convinced and feels that she and the twins will always be enemies. Dorrie is appointed chairperson of a school committee that has to think of some exciting thing to do for Children's Book Week. Aghast when one of the twins also is appointed to the committee, she nevertheless comes up with the good idea of printing a newspaper in which all the headlines and articles are based on books. Since Dorrie's father is the publisher of the town newspaper, he agrees to print it for the school. The newspaper is the hit of the Children's Book Week celebration. Dorrie is elated even though she feels sick and knows she is coming down with "something." The "something" turns out to be a virus, so she is confined to bed. None of her girlfriends visit her for fear of catching the virus, but the twins claim they are immune and visit her with a present—one of the babies of their pet guinea pig. Dorrie decides maybe they aren't so bad after all. Most students will enjoy reading this amusing story.

4-3   *The Great Brain* by John D. Fitzgerald (New York: Dial Press, 1967. 167 pages). Tom Fitzgerald, John's brother, is famous in his family for his "great brain". His "great brain" is usually being used to finagle money from his brothers, parents, or anyone else he happens to know! He might get kids to pay a penny each to see the Fitzgeralds' new indoor toilet, the first in town, or charge them a penny to lick the dasher when his mom makes home-made ice cream. He also uses his great brain to get John to do almost anything he asks—to almost get a hated teacher fired or to get a favorite Indian belt away from another brother. However, Tom also uses his brain to find two boys and their dog who are lost in a cave and to help a handicapped boy learn to do as much with his one leg as other boys can with two. The reformation of the "great brain" from a terrific "con" man to the inspiration of Andy, the handicapped boy, makes a readable, entertaining story that most students will want to read. (NOTE: If students like the Great Brain stories, you might suggest that they read about some other great fictional children manipulators such as Tom Sawyer, Alvin Fernald, and Soup. It might be fun for some of the students to prepare a poster of fictional "great brains."

4-4   *The Kids' Candidate* by Jonah Kalb (Boston: Houghton Mifflin, 1975. 140 pages). Barnaby Brome sees a poster promoting someone named McKinstry for the School Committee. Barnaby mischievously changes the sign to read "Vote Barnaby Brome for School Committee. Why not?" He doesn't know the consequences of his prank, because his friend Billy really believes "why not?" and goes to town hall to check on the qualifications to run for the school committee. When at the town hall he discovers that by a fluke the age requirements have been left out of the requirements for eligibility, Billy propels the unwilling Barnaby into running. All of the kids join together to help Barnaby run his campaign, but Barnaby learns something about the quality of Billy's friendship when the going gets tough for the youthful campaigners. This is a fast-moving story that most children will identify with and enjoy.

4-5   *The Cybil War* by Betsy Byars (New York: Viking Press, 1981. 126 pages). Simon Newton, whose father deserted his mother and him to "get back to the simple way of life," has been disappointed in many things. First of all, he is disappointed that his father has never come back to take him away to live with him. Then he is disappointed in not getting the part he wanted in the school play. NOW he discovers that his best friend, Tony Angotti, lied about him to Cybil Ackerman. Cybil, a red-headed girl with a zest for everything and a soft spot for Simon, has been the object of Simon's adoration ever since second grade when she was the only person other than Simon to vote for his essay on Arbor Day. Tony's lies have gotten Simon in trouble before, but his lies to Cybil and his efforts to get Cybil to like him instead of Simon are too much for Simon. Tony's friendship for Simon turns to hate. How Simon wins the "Cybil War" makes a fast-moving story that fourth through sixth grade students will enjoy.

4-6   *Anastasia on Her Own* by Lois Lowry (Boston: Houghton Mifflin, 1985, 131 pages). This is the fifth book about Anastasia Krupnik, and it is as readable and funny as any of the previous books. In this one, Anastasia is in the seventh grade. She thinks her mother's housekeeping job is easy and cannot understand why Mrs. Krupnik often forgets to take anything out of the freezer to defrost for dinner and never seems to have time to bake cookies or do things the other girls' mothers do. Anastasia and her father think that all Mrs. Krupnik needs is a schedule, so they make her one. Before Mrs. Krupnik gets to try the schedule for more than a short time, she is called to California as a consultant in her capacity as an illustrator. She leaves Anastasia in charge of the housekeeping. Anastasia feels confident, but soon learns that it is the unexpected in keeping house that makes a schedule difficult to follow. For Anastasia, the unexpected is her little brother, Sam, getting chicken pox, so she has to stay home from school to take care of him. Between giving Sam soda baths to help relieve his itching, telephone salespeople calling, and an inexhaustible supply of dirty laundry, each day's schedule is impossible to follow. Anastasia must write a new schedule, which is also impossible to keep. Anastasia is delighted when Steve Harvey calls to ask her to go to the movies on Friday night. This would be her first date and she can hardly wait to tell her father about it. The unexpected again happens when her father's old girlfriend turns up at his office that day and he feels compelled to ask her to the house for dinner on Friday night...and Anastasia would have to stay home to be chaperone. Anastasia is at first dismayed, but then she decides to ask Steve to dinner, too, and plans a romantic dinner...after making certain that her father understands it is for Anastasia and Steve and not for him and his old flame. The dinner is to be completed with passionate purple tablecloth (which she must make by dyeing the white one), purple flowers, and purple candles. Sam even gets into the romantic spirit by connecting his chicken pox spots with a purple felt-tip pen! The dinner is a disaster. Then the next day when Anastasia discovers that her father, too, is coming down with chicken pox, that she has dyed her father's shirts purple, and that her telephone purchases are a financial disaster, she gives up and puts in a hurried call to her mom to come home and rescue them. Most readers will enjoy this book.

4-7   *Alvin Fernald, TV Anchorman* by Clifford Hicks (New York: Holt, Rinehart and Winston, 1980. 140 pages). Alvin Fernald is interviewed on the Riverton TV station as the "Spotlight" feature of the local news station. He is interviewed because, as Alvin thinks to himself, "he was the best known kid in Marshall County." In the course of the newscast, Alvin makes the remark that he doesn't want to become a TV newscaster because that job would be too easy and not exciting. The real newscaster, a little irate both from that remark and from the fact that Alvin had tried to tell him what kind of questions he should ask, has an inspiration. He suggests on TV that Alvin should try being a television newsman and come back a week from that day to use five minutes of the newscast time to broadcast the local school news. Alvin, always confident, agrees. The television newscaster hopes that Alvin will fail, but instead, he, his pal Shoie, their friend Peter, and Alvin's little sister Daphne are a hit. The audience loves them and they become a twice-weekly regular feature of the Riverton television news. Pete is the producer, Alvin the anchorman (or anchorperson as Daphne insists), Shoie reads the sports news, and Daphne is the weather girl who forecasts the next day's weather by consulting her weather-sensitive big toe. Alvin becomes famous and is invited to have a spot on the national news. He agrees and because he has become interested in Pete's friend, Mr. Kubec, Alvin uncovers a mystery about the man and reveals it on the national broadcast. The mystery is an unsolved robbery of which Mr. Kubec was accused but of which he was innocent. Alvin proves the man's innocence in a dramatic live broadcast along with the relevation that Mr. Kubec is Pete's father. Feeling that television newscasting cannot be this exciting all the time, Alvin decides to give it up and find something else to do. This is a fast-moving story and the antics of Alvin, Shoie, and Daphne should make the young readers laugh.

4-8   *Mysteriously Yours, Maggie Marmelstein* by Marjorie Weinman Sharmat (New York: Harper & Roe, 1982. 151 pages). Maggie Marmelstein is now a sixth grader and, like the rest of the sixth-grade class, she is eager to try out to be the mystery writer for the school paper. Noah, the student editor, is to pick the winning entry but the name of the winner is to be an absolute secret. Only Noah and the winner will ever know who the mystery columnist is. Maggie wins and becomes the mystery writer. She is elated but disappointed that she cannot tell anyone that she is the mystery writer. She decides to feature a different student each week in her column. The first week, she writes a feature on her best friend, Ellen.

After the column is written, her next problem is how to get it to Noah without letting any of the snoopy sixth graders know. She and Noah solve the problem by exchanging their lunches during lunch time in the cafeteria. It is a successful trade, but some of the students are suspicious. The first column is a great success. Ellen is delighted to be so sought after and popular. The column's success goes to Maggie's head and she decides she can be a help to many of the students by featuring them in her column and thereby letting them and their classmates know what their problems are and how to solve them. Needless to say, the second column is too blunt and Dipsey, the featured student, is very unhappy. Maggie's problems multiply as both Thad and Henry, her friends, and Tamara Axelrod, her rival for Thad's affections, become suspicious and try to find out just who the mystery person is. Their efforts finally succeed and they discover that Maggie is the mystery writer. Maggie is disappointed but she thinks it is best since the power the column gave her is going to her head. This is the third book about Maggie Marmelstein and students who like this book may want to read the others, *Getting Something on Maggie Marmelstein* and *Maggie Marmelstein for President*.

4-9   *Buddies* by Barbara Park (New York: Alfred A. Knopf, 1985. 135 pages). Dinah feels she is unpopular, so when she sees an advertisement for Camp Miniwawa she decides to go. She's determined to pal around with the prettiest and most popular girls so that she, too, would be popular and admired. A problem develops in the person of Fern, who meets Dinah at the bus stop waiting to be taken to camp and who then latches on to Dinah and follows her everywhere she goes. Dinah cannot seem to break away from this girl, who is impossible in the eyes of all the girls who know her. Dinah decides that she wants to be best friends with Cass and Marilyn, who seem to be the most popular girls at camp. Marilyn is popular because her grandfather had started Camp Miniwawa and because whe is clever and funny. Cass is one of those popular girls who always look just right and who is the one everyone wants to be seen with. Marilyn and Cass are friendly to Dinah but keep giving her the ultimatum that she get rid of Fern or forget about being pals with them. Dinah tries, but she just can't tell Fern to go away, even though Fern keeps doing things that the girls consider disgustingly gross. At last, Dinah finally makes herself do something to Fern. She pushes Fern from the canoe the four of them are paddling. As Fern comes up from the water, Dinah sees the hurt look on her face. She tries to forget it and enjoy the rest of her camp days with Cass and Marilyn, but somehow the fun was gone. Twice she attempts to make up with Fern, but Fern wants nothing to do with her. Dinah knows that Fern sits alone everyday behind a rock, doing nothing but waiting for the time to pass. When Dinah arrives back home, her ideas of popularity are not the same as when she left and she is happy to see her best friend—not a popular girl but a good friend. This is a funny, but touching book that most readers will be able to relate to and enjoy.

4-10   *Soup on Wheels* by Robert Newton Peck (New York: Alfred A. Knopf, 1981. 101 pages). Robert loves Norma Jean Bissell, but he lives in fear of Janice Riker, who is the biggest and strongest kid in the class. Soup is Robert's best friend but Soup always seems to get Robert in trouble! One time he said that Robert hadn't been "It" yet in Janice's game of tag in which the one who is "It" is chased by everyone else. And another time he tricked Robert into ringing the fireman's bell just so he wouldn't have to work as hard. Still, Robert follows Soup in anything he suggests. When Soup suggests that he and Robert make a costume for the Vermont "Mardy Grah," Robert is a little doubtful until Soup asks him if he didn't want to beat Norma Jean and her new boyfriend. Of course, Robert does because he is jealous of Norma Jean and the new boy from the South who always looks so neat and has such beautiful manners! When Robert agrees, he doesn't realize that he will have to play the back end of the zebra or that he will have to be on roller skates—an especially terrifying feat since he has never before tried to roller skate! Soup says that roller skates are important because HOW you enter is more important than your costume. Robert is skeptical but he does want to show up Norma Jean and her new boyfriend who enter as Raggedy Ann and Raggedy Andy. The entrance of Soup and Robert is not quite what they had planned since neither of them know how to skate. Soup, as the front end of the zebra, skates so fast down a hill that he loses control and the two boys careen into the organizers of the "Mardy Grah." Miss Boland and Mr. Jubert. This is another amusing book about Soup and Robert. It is most often checked out by boys, but girls enjoy the funny antics as well.

PROJECTS FOR
THIRTEEN WAYS
TO SINK A SUB

1. Do you think Svetlana Ivanovitch knew the fourth graders were not being truthful about their names? _____ Why do you think so? _____

_____

2. What would you have done if you were the substitute in 4B and the children acted as they did in this story? _____

_____

3. At the end of the story, do you think most of the students liked the substitute and were sorry for the way they had acted? _____ What makes you think so? _____

_____

CHOOSE ONE OF THE FOLLOWING PROJECTS:

1. Pretend you are a student in 4B. Write a letter to Svetlana Ivanovitch, apologizing to her for all that happened on the day she was your substitute teacher.
2. Write a story about a different kind of substitute coming to Class 4B. Tell how the class tried to sink this different kind of substitute and what they did to do it. Tell what the substitute did and describe her appearance, voice, and attitude.
3. *Read Miss Nelson Is Missing* by Frank Allard. Write a story telling what happened when Miss Viola Swamp was the substitute in Class 4B.
4. Learn how to do some origami like Marshall was making in the book *Thirteen Ways To Sink A Sub*. After you have learned how to make an origami figure, pass out paper to the class and teach them how to do it.
5. Make a good set of rules for class to go by when a substitute is needed. Make rules you feel are fair, both to the class and to the substitute.

CAN YOU SINK THE SUB?

Follow the directions to see if you can sink the "sub."

1. Add the zip code of North Olmsted, Ohio, to the zip code of McMinnville, Oregon = _____

2. Subtract from the number you got in #1, the area code of Maryland = _____

3. Next subtract from your answer in #2 the year of President John Quincy Adams birth = _____

4. Divide this number by the number of senators each state is allowed in the Senate of the United States. = _____

5. Divide the number you got in question 4 by the number of surface zones of the earth. = _____

6. Subtract from this number the score of Nebraska in the 1983 Orange Bowl football game. = _____

7. Divide the number you got in the last question by the number of representatives there are in the House of Representatives in Washington, D.C. from the state of Arkansas. (As of 1984 = _____

8. Subtract from this number the number of counties in the state of California and your answer is_____

9. Divide the number you got in question eight by the number of eclipses of both the sun and the moon in 1984 and your answer is _____

10. Add to this number the score of Arizona in the 1983 Fiesta Bowl football game and your answer is _____.

11. Divide the number you got in question ten by the number of counties in West Virginia and your answer is _____.

12. If your answer in number 11 is the same as the number of original colonies in the United States, you sank the "sub"!

Did you sink the sub? _____ If not why don't you go back and try again!

PROJECTS FOR
ME AND THE TERRIBLE TWO

1. Ellen Conford has written many books for children. List below three titles which are in your library. Include the copyright date of each book.

A. _____ Copyright date: _____

B. _____ Copyright date: _____

C. _____ Copyright date: _____

2. Write a paragraph about Dorrie. Describe her appearance. Tell what her good qualities are and also her bad qualities. Tell if you would like her as a friend.

_____

_____

3. Why do you think Haskell and Conrad acted the way they did? _____

_____

_____

4. Look up Ellen Conford in *The Junior Book Of Authors* or another reference source and answer these questions about her. Use the back of this sheet to write.

A. When was she born? _____ B. Where was she born? _____

C. Why did she become a writer?

CHOOSE ONE OF THE FOLLOWING PROJECTS:

1. In the book, Dorrie and her committee wrote a newspaper using headlines and articles based on books. Make the front page of a newspaper using books or nursery rhymes as the basis of your headlines and stories. Make your page look as much like a newspaper as possible. Type your articles on a typewriter or computer, if possible. If not, then hand print your articles in newspaper form.
2. Pretend you are Dorrie and write a letter to Marlene in Australia. In the letter, tell Marlene all the things that have been happening since she moved. Use good letter form.
3. Pretend you are Marlene and write a letter to Dorrie. Tell Dorrie about the trip to Australia and life in Australia. (If you do not know much about Australia, look in an encyclopedia or another reference book.) Use proper letter form and make your letter several paragraphs long.
4. Make a page of want ads using nursery rhymes or books, such as the one in the book when Haskell suggests an ad for Little Bo Peep's lost sheep. Write at lease five ads.

HEADLINES FROM LITERATURE

In *Me and the Terrible Two*, Dorrie and her committee write a newspaper for Children's Book Week using headlines and articles based on books. Below are some headlines they might have used. See if you can figure out the famous titles. (HINT: The titles may be folk tales, fairy tales, books, or nursery rhymes.)

1. Boy and Girl Survive Tumble Down Hill

_____

2. Young Boy Swallows Pet Turtle

_____

3. Big Blow Destroys Two Homes—Brick Home Alone Remains Standing

_____

4. Woman with Strange Appetite Bites Off More Than She Can Chew

_____

5. Golden-Haired Girl Sought for Breaking and Entering

_____

6. Grandfather Searches for Four Missing Grandchildren

_____

7. Poor Boy Holds Winning Ticket in Chocolate Bar Contest

_____

8. Monkey Rides Off with Newsboy's Newspapers

_____

9. Boy Sought for Theft of Poultry, Money, and Musical Instrument

_____

10. Johnny Stout Rescues Kitty from Well

_____

Now take one of these headlines and, remembering the book, story, or nursery rhyme from which it is taken, write a newspaper article about the headline. Remember that news stories must tell what happened, to whom it happened, where it happened, and when it happened. You might have to make up some of the details but follow the story or nursery rhyme as closely as possible. (If you absolutely cannot figure out the titles for the headlines above, perhaps your teacher will give you a list of titles to choose from.) Use the back of this sheet to write your headline and article.

PROJECTS FOR
THE GREAT BRAIN

1. When the Great Brain rescued Frank and Allen and their dog, Lady, he rubbed liver on the soles of his and his Uncle Mark's shoes. Why?_____

_____

2. How did the Great Brain get even with the new teacher for paddling him when he would not be a tattletale? _____

_____

3. Do you think John really loves his brother, the Great Brain? _____ What evidence is there in the story for your answer? _____

_____

4. This story is set in a small town in Utah. Answer these questions about Utah.

  a. What is the population of Utah? _____

  b. What is the state motto? _____

  c. What is the state capital? _____

© 1988 by The Center for Applied Research in Education, Inc.

CHOOSE ONE OF THE FOLLOWING PROJECTS:

1. Tom Sawyer was another boy like the Great Brain who always had schemes and ideas and was rather a "con" man. Read *The Adventures Of Tom Sawyer* and tell the class how the Great Brain and Tom Sawyer were alike by telling some of the things each did.

2. This book is illustrated by Mercer Mayer who has illustrated many books, as well as writing many himself. Write a report on Mercer Mayer and then find five or six books which he has illustrated. Read your report to the class and show them the illustrations in the books which you have chosen.

3. Make a wordsearch using characters from this book. Be sure there are at least ten characters in your wordsearch. Make a Key for the wordsearch as well.

4. This story was set in 1896. Make a list of at least twenty things which were not yet invented in 1896. Check your list in a book of inventions, *Famous First Facts*, or another reference source to be sure of the time of their invention.

A MESSAGE FOR GREAT BRAINS

See if you can be a "Great Brain" and figure out the message below. Use the clues about some really "great brains" to help you.

1. If Thomas Jefferson was our fourth president, put a "J" in space 31. If he was our third president, put a "U" there.

2. If Thomas Jefferson was a writer, architect, and inventor, put a "D" in space 34. If he was a preacher and a teacher, write an "S" there.

3. The Louisiana Territory was purchased during Jefferson's term as president. If it was purchased from France, put an "F" in space 23. If it was purchased from Spain, put an "S" in space 23.

4. If Jefferson was born in Georgia, put an "F" in spaces 1 and 20. If he was born in Virginia, put an "A" in those spaces.

5. Benjamin Franklin was also a "great brain." If he was born in 1706, put an "T" in spaces 10, 22, and 26. If he was born in 1710, put an "E" in those spaces.

6. If Franklin was born in Lexington, put an "L" in space 7. If he was born in Boston, put a "B" there.

7. Benjamin Franklin was a statesman, scientist, inventor, writer, and publisher. If he published books for children, put a "D" in spaces 13, 27, and 32. If he published a newpaper and an almanac, put an "S" in those spaces.

8. If one of Benjamin Franklin's inventions was bifocal reading glasses, put a "G" in spaces 2 and 17. If he invented the mercury thermometer, put a "K" in those spaces.

9. Thomas Edison is considered by many people to be the greatest inventor who ever lived. If he was born in 1847, put an "R" in spaces 3, 8, and 18. If he was born in 1851, put an "H" in those spaces.

10. If the phonograph was Edison's favorite invention, put an "A" in spaces 5 and 9. If the telephone was Edison's favorite invention, put an "E" in those spaces.

11. If Edison was called the "Wizard of Inventions," put an "M" in spaces 11, 14, and 28. If he was called the "Wizard of Menlo Park," put an "N" in those spaces.

12. If Edison was born in Ohio, put an "O" in spaces 15 and 29. If he was born in New Jersey, put an "N" in those spaces.

13. The name "Einstein" has almost become a synonym for a "great brain." If his first name was Alfred, put an "F" in spaces 12 and 24. If his first name was Albert, put an "I" in those spaces.

14. If Einstein was born in the United States, put a "C" in spaces 4, 19, and 33. If he was born in Germany, put an "E" in those spaces.

15. If Einstein received the Nobel Prize for Physics in 1931, put an "S" in spaces 6, 16, 21, 25 and 30. If he received the Prize in 1921, put a "T" in those spaces.

THE MESSAGE IS _____

_____

If you solved the message, you are on your way to becoming a "great brain." If you didn't figure out the message, go back and check your answers.

PROJECTS FOR
THE KIDS' CANDIDATE

Barnaby Brome was the youngest candidate to ever run for the school committee. Use reference sources to find out who was the youngest person to do each of the following.

1. Who was the youngest person to ever become president of the U.S.A.?

   _____

2. Who was the youngest person to ever be *elected* president of the U.S.A.?

   _____

3. Who was the youngest published author? _____What was the title of the

   book? _____ At age _____

4. The youngest woman who ever became a tennis champion in a singles match

   was _____ who was age _____when she won.

5. Who was the youngest person to ever fly solo in an airplane? _____

   At what age?_____

© 1988 by The Center for Applied Research in Education, Inc.

CHOOSE ONE OF THE FOLLOWING PROJECTS:

1. Make a good campaign poster for Barnaby Brome. Make it at least 22″ X 18″. Make an eye-catching illustration and be sure your lettering is the best you can do. Tell in your poster why Barnaby should be elected to the School Committee.
2. Write at least three slogans for Barnaby's election campaign. Kathy Moo suggested the slogan Barnaby used... "Why Not?" but maybe you can think of three better ones.
3. Make a T.V. commercial for Barnaby. You may use a friend or friends to help you or you may do it yourself. Tell why Barnaby is the best candidate. Then see if you can use the school's video equipment to film your commercial and then show it to the class.

FOR GREAT SCHOOLS — VOTE FOR BARNABY BROME! HE HAS THE ANSWERS!

WHO SAID WHAT?

Part One

What are the first and last names of the people who said the following?
Who said:

1. "Billy, you're nuts. I don't even know what the school committee is! Why should I run?

_____

2. "We need a kid on the committee. Let's elect one of our own. I say, let's run our own candidate. The kid's candidate. Let's run Barnaby Brome!"

_____

3. "Dod't bake fud of by allergies." _____

4. "Blow your nose, young man. I'm going to stand right here. This is school property, and I'm running for the school committee and I'm not going to move one inch. I don't care

who drew the crowd." _____

5. "Mr. Cronkite...I'm _____, Barnaby Brome's press secretary.

Part Two

Chris Bort put together a Barnaby Brome platform. It had five articles for Barnaby's campaign in it. Write below what three of the articles were.

1. _____

2. _____

3. _____

Part Three

Now write five articles you might write for a campaign to run for the school committee for your school. (You may use the back of the paper if you need more room.)

_____

_____

_____

_____

_____

PROJECTS FOR
THE CYBIL WAR

1. Why do you think Tony told so many lies about Simon?

_____

_____

_____

2. Describe Cybil Ackerman. _____

_____

_____

3. Why do you think Simon wanted to be kidnapped by his father? _____

_____

_____

_____

CHOOSE ONE OF THE FOLLOWING PROJECTS:

1. Read another book about boys liking girls such as *Veronica Ganz* by Marilyn Sachs. Then compare it with *The Cybil War* by telling the class about the two books and how they are alike and how they are different.
2. Prepare a television commercial for this book. Use one of the most entertaining parts of the book as part of the commercial. The pet show incident or the movie date with Harriet, Tony, and Cybil might be good ones. If possible, borrow the school's video equipment and televise your commercial to show to your class.
3. Do you think Simon will ever be friends again with Tony? Write a story telling how Simon and Tony become friends again or write a story telling how Simon finds a new friend.
4. Use the card catalog in your school library to make a bibliography of books about friends and friendship. Include at least ten books and use the form for bibliographies recommended by your teacher or librarian.

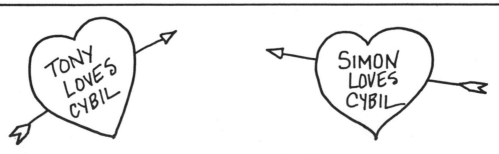

TRUE OR FALSE?

Tony was very adept at lying, but Simon finally began to recognize many of Tony's lies. How good are you at telling truth from fiction? Write true or false beside each statement. (You may use reference sources if you need to.) Be careful, some may be tricky!

	True or False?	Points
1. The tallest building in the world is in New York City.		
2. Whales are the largest fish in the world.		
3. The capital city of West Germany is Berlin.		
4. The winner of the men's 1000-meter speed skating in the 1980 Olympics was Eric Heiden.		
5. The capital of Oregon is Portland.		
6. Texas is the largest state in the United States.		
7. A gemsbok is an antelope.		
8. There are 5,280 feet in a mile.		
9. The Academy Award winner for best actress in 1982 was Meryl Streep.		
10. A calorie is a measure of weight.		
11. *Ramona the Pest* is by Betty Cleary.		
12. Constance Greene is the author of *Beat the Turtle Drum*.		
13. Canines and felines are members of the same animal family.		
14. Linen is a cloth made from a plant called flax.		
15. Merino is a breed of sheep.		
16. A bibliography is a book about a real person.		
17. An annotation is a summary of a book found on a card catalog listing.		
18. Animato is an Italian food consisting of fresh vegetables and appetizers.		
19. 796 is the Dewey Decimal number for sports.		
20. Indigo is a large city in India.		

Now check yourself. Give yourself 5 points for each answer you said was FALSE. Give yourself 10 points for each answer you said was TRUE. If your score is 145, you can tell fact from fiction. If you have a different score, go back and check your answers.

PROJECTS FOR
ANASTASIA ON HER OWN

1. Do you think Anastasia ran the household capably? _____ What could she have

   done to make the work go more smoothly? _____

   _____

   _____

   _____

2. How many books does your library have by Lois Lowry? _____ List the titles and
   copyright dates of three of them below.

   _____

   _____

   _____

3. Using *The Junior Book of Authors* or another reference source, write a paragraph about
   Lois Lowry on the back of this sheet.

CHOOSE ONE OF THE FOLLOWING PROJECTS:

1. Read another of the Anastasia books by Lois Lowry. Tell the class about the book and show
   the other books in the series.
2. Make a week's schedule for your own family, such as Anastasia did in this book. Put down
   what each family member does each day to help in the running of the household.
3. Anastasia's *ragout do veau aux champignons* was not a great success. Try to cook something
   by yourself using a recipe you have never used before. If it is something like cookies that could
   be brought to class, bring one for each class member to sample and then explain how it relates
   to this book. If it is a dinner dish, write a paragraph describing it and how you cooked it. Then
   have a family member write a paragraph about how successful (or unsuccessful) it was. Read
   the paragraph and explain how it relates to the book.
4. Anastasia is talked into buying an electric blanket and dancing lessons by telephone
   salesmen. Write a sales pitch for this book that a salesperson might use by telephone. Read
   your sales pitch to the class and explain what it has to do with the book.

HELP!

ANASTASIA'S WORDSEARCH

Answer the following questions about *Anastasia on Her Own*. Then find the answers in the wordsearch below. The words can be found horizontally, vertically, diagonally, forwards, and backwards.

1. What color did Anastasia think was passionate? _____

2. Besides being a wife and mother, what other job was held by Mrs. Krupnik? _____

3. Who asked Anastasia to go to the movies with him? _____

4. Who did Norman Kerkowitz like? (first and last names) _____

5. Where did Mrs. Krupnik have a consulting job? _____

6. What was the name of Anastasia's goldfish? _____

7. What was Anastasia's mother's first name? _____

8. What was Anastasia's father's first name? _____

9. What was the first thing Anastasia bought from a telephone salesman? _____

10. What was the name of the telephone salesman who sold her tap dancing lessons?

_____

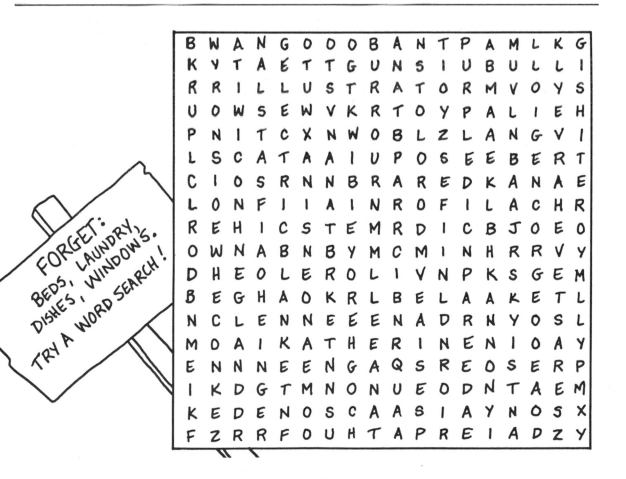

```
B W A N G O O O B A N T P A M L K G
K Y T A E T T G U N S I U B U L L I
R R I L L U S T R A T O R M V O Y S
U O W S E W V K R T O Y P A L I E H
P N I T C X N W O B L Z L A N G V I
L S C A T A A I U P O S E E B E R T
C I O S R N N B R A R E D K A N A E
L O N F I I A I N R O F I L A C H R
R E H I C S T E M R D I C B J O E O
O W N A B N B Y M C M I N H R R V Y
D H E O L E R O L I V N P K S G E M
B E G H A O K R L B E L A A K E T L
N C L E N N E E N A D R N Y O S L
M O A I K A T H E R I N E N I O A Y
E N N N E E N G A Q S R E O S E R P
I K D G T M N O N U E O D N T A E M
K E D E N O S C A A S I A Y N O S X
F Z R R F O U H T A P R E I A D Z Y
```

FORGET:
BEDS, LAUNDRY,
DISHES, WINDOWS.
TRY A WORD SEARCH!

PROJECTS FOR
ALVIN FERNALD, TV ANCHORMAN

1. How do you feel about Alvin? Do you think he was overconfident and conceited or do you feel he was someone you'd like for a friend? On the back of this sheet, describe Alvin and your feelings about him.

2. Daphne forecast the weather by consulting her big toe. Look in an encyclopedia or another reference source and see if you can find out other ways that people predict the weather (excluding scientific weather instruments). Write at least two different ways below. ONE EXAMPLE: Some people predict a hard winter by how many cones are on fir trees. _____

   _____

   _____

3. What did Alvin advise the president to do about the relations with the Middle East?

   _____

   _____

4. Why did Alvin decide to give up television newscasting? _____

   _____

CHOOSE ONE OF THE FOLLOWING PROJECTS:

1. Look up the profession of radio or TV newscaster in a reference book on occupations. Write a report on that profession, being sure to include educational requirements, qualifications, working conditions, and possible salaries. Read your report to the class.

2. Prepare a television newscast for your school. Include news items about the students and teachers, weather, sports, and any other items you think interesting and appropriate. If possible, use the school's video equipment and film the newscast to show the class. (Some schools have a weekly school newscast. If your school does not have one, you many want to start one if your teacher agrees.)

3. The book talks about Alvin's magnificent brain. Tom Fitzgerald, the main character in the Great Brain series is similar to Alvin in some ways. Read one of the Great Brain books and then compare Alvin and Tom. How are they alike and how are they different?

4. Write a new adventure for Alvin Fernald. Possible titles could be *Alvin Fernald, Spelunker*; *Alvin Fernald, Mountain Climber*; or *Alvin Fernald, Movie Star*. You might also want to make up your own title.

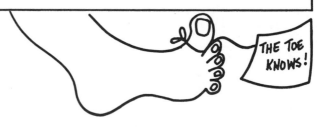

THE TOE KNOWS!

WATCH THOSE NUMBERS!

Alvin Fernald's friends claimed that he had a "magnificent brain"—and Alvin usually agreed with them Use your magnificent brain and your research knowledge to see if you can follow the directions below correctly. If you do, the last answer will be the copyright date of *Alvin Fernald, TV Anchorman.*

ALVIN FERNALD
BEST-KNOWN KID
IN MARSHALL COUNTY

1. In what year did John Steinbeck win the Nobel Prize for Literature? _____

2. Add the ZIP code of Dover, Delaware to answer in #1. _____ + _____

   = _____

3. Subtract the ZIP code of Amsterdam, New York from your answer in #2.

   _____ − _____ = _____

4. Subtract the area code of North Dakota from your answer in #3.

   _____ − _____ = _____

5. Divide your answer in #4 by the number of times that Katherine Paterson has won the

   Newbery Medal between the years of 1922 and 1985. _____ ÷ _____

   = _____

6. Subtract the year in which Betsy Byars won the Newbery Medal for her book *Summer of*

   the Swans from your answer in #5. _____ − _____ = _____

7. Subtract the last year of George Washington's presidency from your answer in

   #6. _____ − _____ = _____

8. Multiply your answer in #7 by the number of times the Summer Olympic Games have

   been held in London, England between the years 1896 and 1988. _____ ×

   _____ = _____

9. Add your answer in #8 the year of Mark Twain's birth. _____ + _____

   = _____

10. Subtract the year in which Ingrid Bergman won the Academy Award for Best Actress

    for her work in the movie *Anastasia* from your answer in #9. _____ − _____

    = _____

11. Add to your answer in #10 the number of deaths in the San Francisco, California

    earthquake of April 1906. _____ + _____ = _____

12. Subtract the number of people who died in a U.S. railroad wreck in Times Square, New

    York, on August 24, 1928 from your answer in #11. _____ − _____

    = _____

Was your last answer the same as the copyright date of the book *Alvin Fernald, TV Anchorman*? If not, check your answers and check with your teacher to be sure your edition of the book has the original copyright date.

PROJECTS FOR
MYSTERIOUSLY YOURS,
MAGGIE MARMELSTEIN

1. Maggie Marmelstein's first column about Ellen was a success, but her second column about Dipsey was not. What was the difference in the way Maggie wrote the two columns? _____

    _____

    _____

2. How did Thad and Henry finally find out that Maggie was the mystery writer?

    _____

    _____

3. Describe Tamara Axelrod and how you felt about her. _____

    _____

    _____

4. Marjorie Weinman Sharmat has written many other books for children. Look in the card catalog and write the titles of two of her other books that are not about Maggie Marmelstein. Write your answers on the back of this sheet.

CHOOSE ONE OF THE FOLLOWING PROJECTS:

1. Maggie Marmelstein enjoyed eating mystery muffins. Make some mystery muffins using the recipe at the end of *Mysteriously Yours*. Give each of your classmates a piece of a muffin and let them try to guess the mystery ingredients. (Chopped dried apricots or prunes, raisins, or butterscotch chips also could be used as mystery ingredients.) Then tell the class about *Mysteriously Yours, Maggie Marmelstein*.

2. Make a poster advertising this book. Use paint, felt-tip pens, or cut up pieces of construction paper to make your poster attractive and colorful. Make your poster at least 12" x 18" in size. Be sure to include the title, author, price, and an illustration. You also might include the publisher and a brief summary of the book.

3. Look up the author of *Mysteriously Yours, Maggie Marmelstein* in the *Junior Book of Authors* or another reference source. Write a report, be sure to show several of her books for children.

4. If you liked this book, write a letter to the author. Be specific about why you liked the book. Use the proper letter writing form suggested by your teacher or librarian. Let your teacher check the letter before you mail it to the author in care of the publisher.

"CREATIVELY YOURS, MAGGIE MARMELSTEIN"

As the mystery writer, Maggie Marmelstein featured a different student in each of her columns. Pretend you are a newspaper columnist and write a feature story about one of your friends. Draw a picture of your friend or put a snapshot in the space provided. If you need more space for your article, use the back of this sheet.

SPOTLIGHT ON _____

BY _____

PROJECTS FOR
BUDDIES

1. Describe Fern and tell if you would have liked her or

not. _____

_____

_____

_____

2. What could Dinah have done to help Fern? _____

_____

_____

3. Did you feel sorry for Fern? ____   On the back of this
   sheet, tell why you think she acted the way she did and what she could have done to
   change the way she acted.

CHOOSE ONE OF THE FOLLOWING PROJECTS:

1. The end of the book left Dinah unforgiven by Fern. Write a new chapter for the book telling
   how Fern and Dinah meet again, whether Fern has changed, and whether Fern forgives
   Dinah.
2. This book is not illustrated except for the book jacket. Make a large illustration for one
   incident in the book. Show it to the class and tell about the incident and about the book
   (Don't tell all about the book, however, so that the other children will want to read it, too.)
3. Get some friends and dramatize the skit that the four girls performed in the camp's talent
   show. Act it out as nearly as possible like the girls in the book. After the skit, explain the
   incident to the class.
4. Make a crossword puzzle or wordsearch titled "Going Camping." Use words in your puzzle
   or wordsearch that have to do with camping, such as swimming, horseback riding, bike
   riding, hiking, etc.

CAMPING WITH A BUDDY

Buddies by Barbara Parks is about the campers in a girls' camp. Camping is a favorite activity of boys and girls and their families everywhere. The people in the questions below are camping at different places, but they aren't telling where. You can find out where they are camping by using a map, your research skills, and the clues given.

1. Bob and Jim are camping with their Boy Scout troop. They are in a state that touches Nebraska, North Dakota, Montana, Wyoming, and Minnesota. They are in the state of _____.

2. Sally and Sue are camping in a state that touches Oregon, Idaho, Utah, Arizona, and California. They are in _____.

3. The Foster twins are camping with their parents in a state that touches South Carolina, North Carolina, Tennessee, Alabama, and Florida. They are in _____.

4. The McKnights decided to camp at a latitude of 40N and a longitude of 105W. They are camping in the state of _____.

5. The Brownings are camping at a latitude of 45N and 90W. They are camping in the state of _____.

6. Erin, Dustin, Jeff, Jeremy, and Nikki are at a camp with the latitude of 35N and 110W. They are in the state of _____.

7. Bob, Dan, Lori, and Eden are camping with their families in a state where you can visit the Carlsbad Caverns. They are in _____.

8. The Molloys are camping in the state where Crater Lake is located. They are in the state of _____.

9. Connie, Kelly, Chris, and Cindy are vacationing in a place where they can see Mount Whitney. They are in the state of _____.

10. Jerry, Mike, Paula, and Marilyn are camping in a state where they also can see the beautiful Mount Rainier. They are in the state of _____.

11. Mike, Alan, Steven, and Jim are camping with their family in a state where they also can visit the Field Museum. They are in _____.

12. The Carliles are camping in a state where they also can visit Mammoth Cave. They are in _____.

PROJECTS FOR
SOUP ON WHEELS

COME TO
VERMONT'S
1ST
"MARDY GRAH"!

1. Would you like to have Soup as your best friend? Describe him and tell why you would or would not like him as a friend. Use the back of this sheet for your answer.

2. Describe Janice Riker. _____

_____

_____

3. Soup and Robert lived in a small town in Vermont. Answer the following questions about that state:

a. What is Vermont's state motto? _____

b. What is Vermont's state flower? _____

c. What is Vermont's state bird? _____

© 1988 by The Center for Applied Research in Education, Inc.

CHOOSE ONE OF THE FOLLOWING PROJECTS:

1. Make a poster advertising Vermont's "Mardy Grah." Make the colors bright and visible by using paint, felt-tip pens, or colored construction paper. Put all the necessary information on the poster, such as time and date, where, and what activities are planned. (If any necessary information is unavailable from the book, you may make it up.)

2. Pretend you are a television or radio newscaster describing the contestants in the costume contest. Describe the various contestants as an announcer or newscaster would and then report the strange and exciting entrance of Soup and Robert as a roller-skating zebra. You might want to get two friends to play the parts of Soup and Robert and interview them. Tape your report and play it for the class or do it "live." Then explain how it relates to the book.

3. The Vermont "Mardy Grah" was an imitation of the Mardi Gras held annually in New Orleans. Research the Mardi Gras and give a report to the class. If possible, use pictures with your report. Then tell what the Mardi Gras has to do with *Soup on Wheels*.

4. Write a new adventure for Soup, Robert, Janice, and Norma Jean Bissell. Make the adventure at least 300 words long.

FIND THE MISTAKES

Janice Riker thought a "peninsula" was "Pennsylvania" and that you played "gulf" instead of "golf." Soup and Robert thought these mistakes were pretty funny, but do you think that they could spot all of the mistakes in the story below? Have your dictionary handy and see how many you can find.

The Party

Soup and Robert dicided to give a party. It would be a realy grate one. Their would be prizes for the best custume and the food would be terific!

They planed to have barbaqued chicken, potatoe salad, crossants and, for desert—an ice cream sunday!

The party was to be on Wensday and the boys were reddy an hour early. They waited and waited but noboddy came.

"Where is everyone?" Soup asked.

"There not coming, I think," said Soup with aggravation.

They should have recieved there invitations a long time ago," Soup said. "You mailed them last weak, didn't you?"

"Why know! I thought you mailed them," Robert gasped in surprise. "No wonder they're no guests coming!"

"Oh, well," sighed Soup, "there's a barel of food, so let's eat!"

There are 23 spelling mistakes in the story above. Underline each misspelled word and then write the correct spelling of each word below.

_____   _____

_____   _____

_____   _____

_____   _____

_____   _____

_____   _____

_____   _____

_____   _____

PROJECTS FOR YOUR CHOICE OF A HUMOROUS STORY

1. What is the title of the humorous book you chose?

_____

_____

2. Who is the author? _____

3. Who are two of the main characters? Tell at least two things about each of these

characters? _____

_____

_____

_____

4. On the back of this sheet, describe one humorous incident from the book.

CHOOSE ONE OF THE FOLLOWING PROJECTS:

1. Make a crossword puzzle or a wordsearch using the titles from at least ten humorous books.
2. Make up ten riddles for book titles. Read the riddles to the class and see if your classmates can figure out the answers (book titles).
3. Prepare a bibliography. Use the form for bibliographies recommended by your librarian or teacher.
4. Prepare a TV interview show and "interview" the author of the humorous story you read. Choose a friend to help you: one of you be the interviewer and the other be the "author." Rehearse both questions and answers and then present your interview to the class "live" or videotape it and show the tape to the class.

FIGURE OUT THE HUMOROUS TITLES

Here are some phrases that add up to the titles of some famous books. See if you can figure them out. Then look in the card catalog and find out who wrote the books.

1. an unlucky number + homonym for "weighs" + 2 + to "submerge" + A + a prefix meaning "under" =

_____

2. really great + kind of candy =

_____

3. consommé + 4 + Washington, Lincoln, Roosevelt, or Reagan =

_____

4. antonym for "you" + homonym for "no" + U + AL =*

_____

5. a four-base hit + the cost of something =

_____

6. THE + antonym for "first" + a wise teacher from India =

_____

7. THE + stupendous + mind =

_____

8. too thin + clavicle and tibia =

_____

9. antonym for "you" + AND + THE + synonym for "awful" + homonym for "too" =

_____

10. antonym for "goodbye" + antonym for "your" + what you are called + IS + mixed up + what comes before the chickens =

_____

11. antonym for "something's" + homonym for "fare" + antonym for "out" + comes after "fourth" + another name for the level you're at in school =

_____

12. "stories + rhymes with "dove" + A + what comes after "third" + another name for the level you're at in school + antonym for "something" =

_____

HISTORICAL FICTION

SUGGESTIONS FOR THE TEACHER

The books in Unit 5 are probably more difficult to read than those in many of the other units. However, the books are action filled and are usually enjoyed by students.

This unit can be introduced in many ways. If you are a bit of an actor or actress, you might want to dress in a period costume and let the class guess both the time period of the costume and also why you are wearing the costume.

A more conventional approach would be to have historical fiction books displayed and then show a sound filmstrip, such as Pied Piper's *Historical Fiction*. Examples of this type of fiction also can be shown in *The Courage of Sarah Noble, Caddie Woodlawn*, or *Johnny Tremain* (all from Random House).

After introducing the type of fiction the students will be reading, discuss the difference between history and historical fiction. Then give book talks about each of the books in the unit, using the summaries given or the jacket blurbs. Include any other historical fiction books you would like to use with this unit. These additional books could be used with the two activity sheets at the end of the unit.

In this group of books, *My Brother Sam Is Dead*; *Wait for Me, Watch for Me, Eula Bee*; and *Three Knocks on the Wall* are probably the most difficult. *The Terrible Wave* is perhaps the most readable and *Snow Treasure* is probably the easiest.

As a culmination to Unit 5, you can show an historical fiction movie. Try to show a film based on a book that was not read to further your students' reading of historical fiction.

AUDIO-VISUAL AIDS
AND RELATED BOOK TITLES

Here are a few of the many audio-visual items and book titles that can be used with this unit on historical fiction.

Audio-Visual Items

My Brother Sam Is Dead, sound filmstrip or listening cassette (Random House)

The Matchlock Gun, sound filmstrip or listening cassette (Random House)

Johnny Tremain, listening cassette (Random House)

Across Five Aprils, sound filmstrip (Random House)

Historical Fiction, sound filmstrip (Pied Piper Productions)

Davy Crockett, film (Walt Disney)

Amos Fortune, Free Man, cassette or sound filmstrip (Random House)

On the Banks of Plum Creek, record or cassette (Random House)

By the Shores of Silver Lake, record or cassette (Random House)

The Perilous Road, cassette or sound filmstrip (Random House)

The Upstairs Room, sound filmstrip, record, or cassette (Random House)

Related Book Titles

Blos, Joan. *A Gathering of Days.*

Brink, Carrie. *Caddie Woodlawn.*

Dalgliesh, Alice. *The Courage of Sarah Noble.*

De Jong, Meindert. *The House of Sixty Fathers.*
Edmonds, Walter. *The Matchlock Gun.*
Forbes, Esther. *Johnny Tremain.*
Hunt, Irene. *Across Five Aprils.*
Keith, Harold. *Rifles for Watie.*
Levitin, Sonya. *Roanoke.*
Reis, Joanna. *The Upstairs Room.*
Steele, William O. *The Perilous Road.*

SUMMARIES OF UNIT 5 BOOKS

5-1 *The Sign of the Beaver* by Elizabeth George Speare (Boston: Houghton Mifflin, 1983. 135 pages). Matt is more than a little afraid as he watches his father head off through the Maine forest to bring back Matt's mother, sister, and the new baby. He knows someone needs to stay to watch over the new cabin he and his father had just built, but it is 1768 and he knows there is no one near to help him except the Indians who seem to be near but could only be sensed and not seen. Matt tries to be brave and to keep busy, but when a passing stranger spends the night with him and then steals his gun, Matt becomes worried for his survival! One day, Matt, unused to the wild life, tries to get some honey from a tree. The bees chase him to the river and sting him so badly that he is only dimly aware of his rescue by the Indians, who bring him back to his cabin and give him healing medicines. Later, one of the Indians returns with his grandson, Attean. Matt wants to give the Indian something to show his gratitude, so Matt gives the Indian his only book, *Robinson Crusoe.* The old Indian admits that he cannot read, but asks Matt to teach Attean. So Attean, seemingly unwilling and hostile, begins coming to the cabin to learn to read. In the months that follow, Matt learns even more from Attean about how to live in the forest than Attean learns from him about reading. He and Attean slowly become friends as Matt waits for the long overdue return of his father and family. This is another well-written and interesting story by the two-time Newbery award winner, Elizabeth George Speare.

5-2 *The Terrible Wave* by Mardon Dahlstedt (New York: Coward McGann, 1972. 125 pages). This is an engrossing story of fictional characters in an actual setting—the Johnstown, Pennsylvania flood of May 31, 1889. Megan Maxwell, the daughter of a rich and influential owner of a department store, is the main character. She is swept away by the wall of water that hits the Maxwell home when the dam built above Johnstown breaks. Megan finds herself floating on a mattress separated from her family and not knowing if they are dead or alive. She is rescued by Brian O'Meara, a young man who jumps from the window of a floating house to save her, and by Septimus Shaw, an old man in a floating wagon that manages to stay afloat until they get to higher ground. This story of the flood and of Megan's search for her family is descriptive and fast moving and should be enjoyed by most children in upper elementary grades.

5-3 *Wait for Me, Watch for Me, Eula Bee* by Patricia Beatty (New York: William Morrow & Company, 1978. 221 pages). Thirteen-year-old Lewallen Collier is part of a large family in west Texas in 1861. His father and older brother leave the family to join the Confederate Army. They leave behind Lewallen; the youngest brother, Daniel; the mother; Uncle Josh; and the three-year-old sister, Eula Bee. Lewallen's father's last words to him are that he, Lewallen, is to watch over Eula Bee. One terrible day, Comanches swoop into the farmyard killing his mother, uncle, and Daniel, and capturing Eula Bee and Lewallen. On the march back to the Indian camp, Lewallen discovers that the children of their despised Mexican neighbors, the Cabrals—Tomas and Angelita—also have been captured. Tomas warns Lewallen to "show bravery," so Lewallen begins to sing and whistle Eula Bee's favorite song, "Lorena," as loud as he can to comfort her and let her know he is near. At the camp, Lewallen becomes the slave of the hunter Many Horses. Eula Bee and Angelita are to be the children of Yellow Wolf, and Tomas is the slave of Small Buffalo. Lewallen is glad he was not given to Small Buffalo, because he was the one who had killed his family members and flaunted their scalps around the camp. Lewallen finds out that Many Horses' wife, Grass Woman, was a white woman who had been taken captive long ago. She speaks English and is a help to him. During a buffalo hunt, Lewallen saves the life of Many Horses, so he becomes more trusted and is allowed to herd the ponies. He tells Tomas that this might give him a chance to escape, which he does. Lewallen manages to reach a fort, but there are not enough people to ride with him to find his sister. However, his former despised neighbor, Cabral, is at the fort, so he joins Lewallen to find Eula Bee and his two children. When they finally locate the Indian camp, after being away for many months, Cabral goes in alone to find the children because he knows the Indian ways and their language. While Cabral is in the camp, Lewallen sees the Cavalry coming. He tries to stop them to tell of Cabral and the other white captives, but cannot attract their attention. When Lewallen finally gets into the camp, he finds that the Cavalry has killed many men and some women and children, including Cabral and Tomas. From an Indian woman, Lewallen learns that Angelita had died of an illness during the winter and that Eula Bee is gone. Lewallen finally finds Eula Bee with the help of members of Cabral's family in San Antonio. By this time, Eula Bee has forgotten her former life and has become like an Indian child. She finally remembers her brother after some time when he sings her favorite song, "Lorena." The author adds some information at the end of the book authenticating the material she used about the people of the time. The story is fast paced and, while very realistic about the atrocities committed by both the white people and the Indians, most children will find it very readable.

5-4 *Journey to Topaz* by Yoshiko Uchida (New York: Scribner's, 1971. 149 pages). Yuki Sakane, a native-born American of Japanese descent, is a happy child in 1941 living with her parents in San Francisco. Her happy life is changed, however, by the December 7, 1941 bombing of Pearl Harbor. Shortly after the news of the bombing, her father is arrested by the F.B.I. and taken away, not because he has done anything but because he is Japanese. Soon the family learns that they, along with thousands of other Japanese on the West Coast, would be sent to camps away from the coast. Yuki, her mother, and her college-age brother, Ken, have to give up their home and take only what they can carry to a camp in Topaz, Utah. The camp is not yet ready for occupancy, so they are given only a single room with three cots on which to sleep. The walls of the room, which is part of a barracks-like building, do not even have sheet rock put on them yet. Topaz is in a desert and is so hot and dusty that it is difficult to breathe. Yuki makes friends with Emi, a girl her own age who lives with her grandparents. Emi develops tuberculosis and is isolated in a hospital ward where Yuki sneaks in often to see her. This is a story of a child caught up in the hysteria of war-time fear, written by an author who herself experienced this treatment of the Japanese-Americans as a child during the second World War. It is a simple but thought-provoking story.

5-5 *My Brother Sam Is Dead* by James Lincoln Collier and Christopher Collier (New York: Four Winds, 1974. 216 pages). In April of 1776, Tim's brother Sam appears at the family's inn dressed in a uniform. He says he is going to join the rebels in the war against the king and England. His father is furious because his sympathies and most of the townspeople's are with the Tories who are loyal to the king. Sam is convinced that the rebels are right and is determined to help them. After a fight with his father, Sam steals his father's only gun and runs away to join the fight. Tim misses Sam and hates the disagreement in the family. His father, while leaning toward the Tory side, is principally just opposed to war and tries to tell

Tim of the horrors of it. Tim is confused about who is right. Sometimes he thinks his father is and other times he thinks Sam is, but he always wishes that Sam would come home. One winter, Tim and his father start out to sell some cattle to get provisions for running the inn. On the way back, they are accosted by "cowboys," men who pretend to rob for the rebel cause but who are really thieves who rob for themselves. Tim's father is taken away, but Tim manages to outwit them and get home. He is now the only "man" in the household and seems to grow up overnight. He helps his mother run the inn and takes over the responsibilities formerly held by his father and Sam. One day Tim learns that Sam's army troop is quartered nearby. He manages to see Sam and both he and his mother try to persuade Sam to come home. Sam refuses, saying that he has vowed to fight until liberty is won. One night, Sam slips away to see Tim. While they are together, they hear their few remaining cattle make a commotion. They know someone is stealing them. Sam runs after the robbers, but a little later Tim is horrified to see that Sam is under arrest for the theft. Sam's commander is strict and is determined that Sam be executed as an example to any would-be thieves and to show the townspeople that the men are disciplined. Despite Tim's and his mother's pleas and explanations that Sam was trying to recover the cattle and not steal them, Sam is executed while Tim watches. This is a poignant story of the irrationality and brutality of war. Mature readers will be able to read it.

5-6 *An Orphan for Nebraska* by Charlene Joy Talbot (New York: Atheneum, 1979. 203 pages). Eleven-year old Kevin O'Rourke arrives in New York in 1872. He is alone because his father had died before the voyage and his mother has died on the long ocean trip from Ireland to New York. Kevin's Uncle Michael in New York had sent tickets for both him and his mother, which is why they had begun the voyage. Kevin expects his uncle to meet him when the ship docks, but no one is there to greet him. When Kevin arrives at his uncle's rooming house, the landlady tells him that his uncle is in jail. Kevin has a few coins, but knows he will have to make his own living. After visiting his uncle in jail and finding out that he will be in jail for two more years, Kevin begins earning pennies as a newspaper boy. One cold night with no place to sleep, Kevin finds out about the Newsboys' Lodging House. Besides giving the many homeless newsboys food and a place to stay, the people in the House work with the Children's Aid Society to send orphaned homeless children to the West where such children are wanted and needed. Kevin hears about the West and is excited to go. He goes with a group of other children to Nebraska where the people of the small town of Cottonwood City choose the children to be their own. Kevin is not chosen because the hearty farmers feel he is too little for the work and too fair-skinned for the hot sun. Dejected, Kevin is afraid he will have to be on his own again. At the last moment, the town's newspaper editor comes. His name is Yuke and he does not intend to adopt an orphan but only to write a news story about the adoptions. His friends talk him into adopting Kevin since he is one of the very few children who can read and write and, thus, be a help to Yuke as a printer's helper in the newspaper office. Yuke and Kevin become fond of each other and Kevin finds the life in Nebraska much to his liking. While this book is fiction, it is based on fact and should hold the students' interest.

5-7 *Snow Treasure* by Marie McSwigan (New York: Dutton, 1942. 156 pages. Also available in paperback from Scholastic). When the German Army comes to Norway in 1940, the people are determined that Norwegian gold in the form of bullion will not fall into Nazi hands. Peter Lundstrom, his sister, and their friends are recruited to carry the bullion on their sleds from where it is hidden to another hiding place close to a fishing boat. They are to bury the gold bullion under the snow and then build a snowman over each hiding place where the gold is buried. Later, Peter's Uncle Victor will load the gold onto a fishing boat hidden nearby. When all the gold has been transferred to the boat, the boat will sail to the United States and be kept safe for Norway until after the war. Since the children can carry only a few bars of the bullion on their sleds and each team of children can go only every other day because they need to rest, the transfer of the gold takes several weeks and is carried out under the very eyes of German soldiers who are billeted near the beach. Peter is frightened on one of the last trips when a German soldier appears as the boy is building the snowman. Before Peter could say anything, Uncle Victor appears, overcomes the soldier, and takes him to the fishing boat. Once there, the soldier claims to be Jan Lasek, a Polish citizen who wants to go to the United States with them. He had been planning to go to the United States when the war broke out, but his passport had been stolen by the Germans so that it could be used for a spy, and he had been forced to join the German Army as a translator. Uncle Victor and the others do not know whether to believe him, but they dare not let him go. Soon after, as Peter and his sister Lovisa are building a snowman to hide the bullion, a group of German soldiers arrive. The commandant becomes infuriated when neither child answers when asked if they have seen the missing soldier, Jan Lasek, so he begins kicking and destroying Lovisa's snowman. Peter, sure that the commandant will kick the lightly buried bullion, hits him on the ear with a snowball to distract him. The ploy works, but Peter is carried to the German camp and shut up in a barracks. That night, Jan Lasek puts on his German uniform, sneaks into the barracks, rescues Peter, and takes him back to the fishing boat which is ready to sail for the United States with the gold. Having to leave Norway because of his danger from the Germans, Peter is excited and happy to know that he and the other children have saved Norway's gold. Although no proof of this story has ever been found, it was widely believed to be true for many years after World War II. It is an adventure that can easily be read by any able reader in the middle grades.

5-8   *Fire in the Wind* by Elizabeth Baker (Boston: Houghton Mifflin, 1961. 244 pages). Jeff Bellinger lives on the outskirts of Chicago with his parents. It is October of 1871, and Jeff's main interests in life are his horseshoe collection and earning money to have a horse of his own. He has only one good friend, Arthur Arnold, the son of a rich man who owns a race horse and collects many things—among them a collection of Abraham Lincoln papers. Arthur is timid and neither boastful nor proud of his family's many possessions. At school, Jeff meets Newman, a big 14-year old who loves school but is often fighting because the other boys tease him about being so old and only in the fifth grade. Newman saves Arthur from the schoolboys who are stealing his lunch every day, so Jeff and Arthur take Newman to Arthur's house to see if his father will give Newman a job as a stableboy. Mr. Arnold gives him the job, but shortly after, Mr. Arnold's expensive race horse and his valuable collection of Lincoln papers are stolen and Newman has disappeared. Newman is, of course, suspected of being the thief, but Jeff is positive he is not. He gets into many adventures trying to prove Newman's innocence. Newman is finally proven innocent with the help of Jeff's dad, a Chicago police detective, and the race horse and valuable papers are recovered. Then on October 8, the great Chicago Fire erupts. Arnold's house and all the surrounding homes are destroyed by the fire. Jeff's house survives because of Jeff's and his father's long hours and much effort of fighting the fire with stored-up water and some garden tools. The book ends with the stirrings of a new birth for the city of Chicago. *Fire in the Wind* is action filled and should hold the interest of the reader. (NOTE: Activity 5-8B does not have a direct reference to this book, so the puzzle could be used during National Fire Prevention Week or at another suitable time, even if the book has not been read or is not available.)

5-9   *Three Knocks on the Wall* by Evelyn Sibley Lampman (New York: Atheneum, 1980. 182 pages). Marty is in the seventh grade in a small town in Oregon during the first World War. She is a rather free-thinker for a girl of that time and scandalizes the town by once walking downtown with a young Indian girl and then, later, by being a friend to Edna Pope. Edna is the best dressmaker in the area and, while she is sought after for her sewing skills, she is ostracized in other ways because her mother had been unmarried and Edna had never known her father. Next to Marty's house is a big house completely surrounded by a high wall. A formidable old lady, Mrs. Hutchinson, and her timid thirty-ish year-old daughter, Rebecca, live there. No one is ever welcome in the Hutchinsons' house or yard, so no one has ever gone there, least of all Marty. One day while Marty is in her yard, she hears some knocks on the high wall between her yard and the Hutchinsons'. She knows Mrs. Hutchinson and Rebecca are at church, but she thought that perhaps Rebecca had sneaked out and come home. Marty knocks back. In subsequent Sundays, Marty devises a signal of two knocks for "no" and three knocks for "yes." With this code, she finds out that the person knocking on the wall is not Rebecca but her ten-year-old daughter, Sinette, which means "small sin." Sinette and Marty become secret friends and, although they never see one another, they talk often. Marty changes Sinette's name to Antoinette and tries to tell her about all the things that happen to her at school and at home since Antoinette has never been out of her own yard. Marty soon realizes that Mrs. Hutchinson has kept Antoinette hidden because she is ashamed of her due to Rebecca's being an unwed mother. When the influenza strikes the small town, Marty and her mother get it, but recover. One night, Antoinette, shivering from rain and wearing no coat, comes to their door. Marty, who has never seen her before, knows it is her secret friend. Antoinette says that both her mother and grandmother are very sick. Marty's mother and Edna Pope, who was visiting, dry off Antoinette and put her to bed. Then Marty's mother goes to the Hutchinson house. When she returns, she says that old Mrs. Hutchinson is dead and Rebecca is very sick. Antoinette stays with Edna Pope while her mother recovers. Edna becomes so attached to Antoinette that when she is leaving for St. Louis to set up a bigger dressmaking business, she takes Rebecca as a partner, so the two of them and Antoinette go to St. Louis to live. This is an interesting story of the lives of people during World War I. It shows the many details of life and the morals of that time.

5-10 *When Hitler Stole Pink Rabbit* by Judith Kerr (New York: Coward McCann, 1971. 191 pages). Anna lives with her parents and brother, Max, in Germany in 1933. She knows she is Jewish, but since the family is not religious and does not observe Jewish customs, she does not feel that she is different from her friends and neighbors. One night, her father disappears and Anna is told that he is on a trip. She also is told that she must not tell anyone that he is gone, but only to say that he is in bed with the flu. Anna is worried because she knows he should not be travelling since he really had been ill. She knows it is strange that she cannot tell anyone that he is gone. One day, the family hurriedly packs and leaves, taking almost nothing with them. Anna knows that it is because they are afraid that the Nazi party will win the coming election and then possibly they will take away their passports and persecute them in other ways. In some way, Anna knows that it is not only because they are Jewish but also because Papa, a famous author, had written things derogatory about the Nazi party. Anna is anguished over leaving some of her beloved toys, such as her pink rabbit, but she is a little excited about the trip. They go on a train to meet her Papa. At the German border, they are afraid that their passports will not be accepted, but they pass without incident. They are finally met by Papa at Zurich in Switzerland. In Zurich, they live in a far different situation than they had at home. Their Papa cannot find much writing work, since there is a depression in Switzerland. Money is always scarce and they can tell that their mother is worried about it. The family is frightened because they hear that the Nazis have put a "price" on Papa's head. One day, the family moves to Paris, France, hoping that Papa can get more work. The children have to start in new schools where only French is spoken and they are completely unfamiliar with the language. Both Anna and her brother learn the language and try to adjust to their new home. The book tells of the family's struggles to find a place for themselves and ends with the family leaving for England where Papa has sold a screen play. The book ends before the start of World War

II but does tell of the prejudice and persecution of the Jews in Germany even before the start of the war. It is a book written from the daughter's point of view, so it may be more appealing to the girls in your group.

PROJECTS FOR
THE SIGN OF THE BEAVER

1. Matt and his family left Massachusetts for Maine. Massachusetts was settled before Maine. When did Massachusetts become a state? _____

   When did Maine become a state? _____

2. What tribes of Indians live in Maine? _____

   _____

   Were any of these tribes mentioned in this book? _____ Which tribe or tribes was

   mentioned? _____

3. Do you think Matt could have survived if it had not been for Attean? _____
   On the back of this sheet, write why or why not.

CHOOSE ONE OF THE FOLLOWING PROJECTS:
1. Build a model of a log cabin like the one built by Matt and his father. Try to make it as close as possible to theirs.
2. Make a diorama of the forest and the log cabin built by Matt and his father. Include Matt and his father or Matt and Attean in the diorama.
3. *The Sign of the Beaver* is not illustrated. Make a painting or a drawing to illustrate some incident in the story. The Indian dance at Attean's village is a good selection or choose anything else from the story that you feel could be illustrated. Show it to the class and tell the class something about the story.
4. Check out a book on Indian crafts and make one or two of the things that Attean taught Matt to make or use. Show the class what you have made and explain how the items relate to the story.
5. The Sign of the Beaver does not tell exactly where Attean and his tribe go. Write a story of Attean and what happens to him after he and his family leave their old home near Matt.

LOST IN THE WILDERNESS

In *The Sign of the Beaver*, Attean knew how to live from the land itself. He needed no tools nor equipment except those he made himself. If you were ever lost in the wilderness, could you survive? Finish this story by imagining what you would do if you were left in the wilderness for a length of time. If you need more space to write your story, use the back of this sheet.

What am I going to do? Here I am sitting in the shade of our wrecked car in a lonesome, seldom-visited canyon. My father and I are lucky that we weren't badly injured when our car lost its brakes and we crashed into a boulder. But because I had twisted my ankle, my father has left me to go get help.

It has been five hours already. "What if he is lost and he never gets back to me?" I thought.

I have to at least do something to find some water, but I don't want to go far away from the

car or my father will never be able to find me. I know I'll _____

_____

_____

_____

_____

_____

_____

_____

_____

_____

_____

PROJECTS FOR
THE TERRIBLE WAVE

1. How many lives were lost in the Johnstown flood? (Use an almanac.) _____

2. What was the worst flood that ever occurred? _____

3. When did this flood occur? _____

4. How many lives were lost in this flood? _____

5. What is the Zip Code for Johnstown, Pennsylvania? _____

6. What is the present population of Johnstown, Pennsylvania? _____

CHOOSE ONE OF THE FOLLOWING PROJECTS:

1. Pretend you are caught in a flood and write what happens. Tell the story as though it had really happened to you and you are telling it a year after the experience. Make your story as realistic and exciting as you can. Use actual buildings and/or places in your town as part of the setting.

2. Paint a picture of the Johnstown flood as described in *The Terrible Wave*. Make your picture at least 12" x 18" and be ready to show it to the class.

3. In the story, the little boy Stefan is so frightened that he cannot speak. The author does not tell us if he ever speaks again. Write a story about Stefan telling if he ever talks again. If so, when does he begin talking again and why. If he begins to talk again, does he remember his real family and anything else about his life before the flood? Be ready to read your story to the class.

4. Research dams and flood control and prepare a report on the dams of today. Tell if they are safer than the dam that broke and flooded Johnstown. If they are safer, tell how they are built now.

5. Write a letter to the Johnstown Chamber of Commerce asking for information about the city and the dangers (if any) of a flood occurring there again.

HELP MEGAN ESCAPE THE FLOOD

Follow the directions to help Megan arrive at the hillside and safety!

1. If Megan's family was rich, go 5 spaces south. If Megan's family was poor, go 3 spaces south.

2. If the date of the flood was May 31, 1887, go 4 spaces west. If the date was May 31, 1889, go 4 spaces east.

3. If Megan saw the giant wave coming, go 3 spaces south. If she did not see the wave coming, go 6 spaces south.

4. If there were four people who were carried to safety in Septimus Shaw's wagon, go 5 spaces east. If there were seven people in the wagon when it reached the hill, go 5 spaces west.

5. If the wagon floated for a day before it reached the hillside, go 7 spaces south. If it took less than two hours, go 4 spaces south.

6. If Stefan was found floating on wood in the water, go 5 spaces east. If he was found on a boulder, go 7 spaces west.

7. If Brian was graduated from high school, go 3 spaces south. If he was still in high school, go 7 spaces south.

8. If the people gathered in the Adams Street School, go 12 spaces east. If they gathered in the old Lutheran church, go 8 spaces east.

9. If Megan found her father before Daisy found her company, go 1 space north. If Daisy found her company first, go 4 spaces north.

10. If all of Megan's family lives through the flood, go 3 spaces east. If two of Megan's family died in the flood, go 9 spaces east.

11. If Megan found Hulda before she found Senator, go 4 spaces south. If Megan found Senator before finding Hulda, go 2 spaces south.

12. If Stefan learned to talk, go 2 spaces south. If he did not talk in this book, go 2 spaces east.

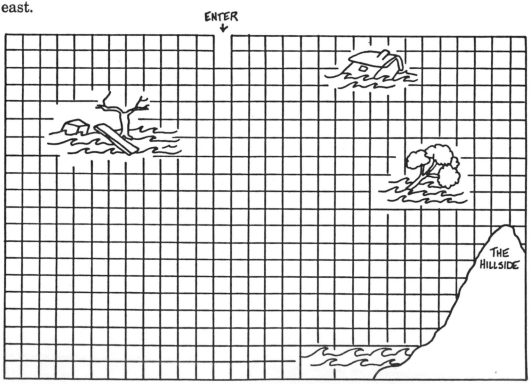

PROJECTS FOR
WAIT FOR ME, WATCH FOR ME, EULA BEE

1. Name at least three people who helped Lewallen find Eula Bee. _____
_____

2. Both the Indians and the white people did terrible things to each other. Why do you
think they acted this way? _____
_____
_____

3. Why did the Comanches take children as captives? _____
_____
_____

4. What do you think happened to Lewallen and Eula Bee after they were safe at the fort?
Did their father and brother return from the war or did they have to find a way to take
care of themselves? Write your answer on the back of this sheet.

CHOOSE ONE OF THE FOLLOWING PROJECTS:
1. Research the Comanche Indians and write a report on them. Use a map or draw one to
show the class where the Comanches lived. Tell about their life, their recreation, their
customs, their arts, etc.
2. Small Buffalo was a Kiowa. Research the Kiowa Indians and write a report on them for the
class, showing on a map where they lived, their life, customs, arts, etc.
3. This book is not illustrated. Make an illustration of the children in the Indian camp. Make
it large and colorful using felt-tip pens, paints, or construction paper. Show the illustration to the class and tell your classmates about the Indian children's lives and a little about
the book.
4. Research some of the tools or crafts of the Comanches or Kiowas. Make a model of one of
these tools or crafts. Show your model to the class and explain how it relates to the book.

EULA BEE'S WORDSEARCH

Complete these statements about *Wait for Me, Watch for Me, Eula Bee* and then find your answers in the wordsearch below. Your answers can be found horizontally, vertically, diagonally, forwards, and backwards.

1. Lewallen was captured and became a slave of _____.

2. _____ was the wife of the Indian who owned Lewallen.

3. Martin _____ was the boy who helped Lewallen find Eula Bee.

4. _____ was the Kiowa who wanted a red sash.

5. The one who cut off the Kiowa's long black braid was _____.

6. _____ bit Lewallen's hand and kicked him when he tried to save her.

7. _____ warned Lewallen to "show bravery."

8. _____ took Lewallen with him when he tried to find Tomas, Angelita, and Eula Bee.

9. _____ died of an illness after she was captured by the Indians.

10. Most of the Indians who captured the children were _____.

11. Small Buffalo was a _____.

12. The name of the song that Eula Bee liked Lewallen to sing was _____.

A	M	B	G	C	E	A	R	M	S	A	R	N	S	R
C	A	B	R	A	L	B	Q	U	I	N	T	E	R	O
S	N	M	A	D	E	F	L	J	T	U	S	V	R	Q
Z	Y	O	S	L	W	G	T	K	S	I	I	L	P	U
I	H	P	S	M	A	L	L	B	U	F	F	A	L	O
P	O	N	W	T	L	H	T	A	H	V	C	B	O	N
T	R	R	O	U	L	I	S	E	G	S	B	E	V	K
Y	S	O	M	G	E	J	H	F	A	W	A	E	I	M
M	E	N	A	T	N	C	E	M	E	E	D	O	W	L
S	S	O	N	F	N	K	O	T	X	C	W	A	D	C
O	J	T	H	A	E	T	Z	Y	A	A	V	B	T	E
L	K	I	M	A	T	I	L	E	G	N	A	A	D	E
L	L	O	R	E	N	A	Q	U	S	T	V	W	O	Z
U	C	M	L	N	O	O	P	R	A	U	C	B	A	E

PROJECTS FOR
JOURNEY TO TOPAZ

1. The Japanese-Americans were isolated and sent to camps in the United States during World War II. The German-Americans and the Italian-Americans were not sent to camps even though we also were at war with Germany and Italy. Why do you think this happened? Write your answer on the back of this sheet.

2. Even though the Japanese-Americans were treated badly, Yuki and her family had some non-Japanese friends in their city who were outraged about their treatment.

   Name two of these friends. _____

   _____

3. Some of the Japanese-Americans at the camp were called *Issei* and others were called *Nisei*. What is the difference between *Issei* and *Nissei*? _____

   _____

   _____

4. Yuki's friend Emi was kept isolated in a hospital ward because she had tuberculosis. Do people with tuberculosis have to be kept isolated in a hospital today? ____ Why? ____

CHOOSE ONE OF THE FOLLOWING PROJECTS:

1. Research the Japanese in America and write a report describing their many contributions to the United States. Present your report to the class and explain what it has to do with *Journey to Topaz.*

2. If you know any Japanese-American who experienced what Yuki and her family did during World War II, invite him/her to speak to the class about the experience. Prepare some questions to ask the speaker and invite the class to ask questions after the speaker's talk. After the guest speaker has spoken to your class, write a thank-you letter to him/her.

3. Make your own wordsearch using characters and places from the book. Have at least ten words in your wordsearch. Prepare both the activity sheet and an answer key.

4. Write a story about what happens to Yuki and her family after they move to Salt Lake City. Make your story at least 300 words long. Read your story to the class.

TOPAZ, UTAH

WHAT DOES IT SAY?

Follow the directions to figure out the message. All answers can be found in the *World Book* or another similar encyclopedia.

‾1‾ ‾2‾ ‾3‾ ‾4‾ ‾5‾ ‾6‾ ‾7‾ ‾8‾ ‾9‾ ‾10‾ ‾11‾ ‾12‾ ‾13‾ ‾14‾ ‾15‾ ‾16‾ ‾17‾ ‾18‾ ‾19‾ ‾20‾ ‾21‾ ‾22‾ ‾23‾ ‾24‾ ‾25‾ ‾26‾ ‾27‾

‾28‾ ‾29‾ ‾30‾ ‾31‾ ‾32‾

1. Put an "O" in spaces 3 and 7 if Japan has approximately 146,000 square miles. Put an "I" in those spaces if it has approximately 210,000 square miles.

2. Put an "E" in spaces 9, 13, 18, 21, 27, and 31 if Japan's flag is blue and white. Put an "A" in those spaces if the flag is red and white.

3. If Japan's oldest religion is Buddhism, put an "S" in spaces 12, 24, and 29. If the oldest religion is Shinto, put an "R" in those spaces.

4. If Japan's northernmost island is Hokkaido, put a "P" in spaces 1 and 4. If it is Honshu, put a "B" in those spaces.

5. Put an "L" in spaces 5, 10, and 11 if Japan's southernmost main island is Kyushu. If it is not Kyushu, put a "P" in those spaces.

6. If rainfall in Japan is scarce, put an "H" in spaces 17 and 22. If rainfall is abundant, put an "M" there.

7. If Japanese law requires that children go to school for nine years, put a "G" in space 28. If Japanese children must go to school for 12 years, put a "K" in that space.

8. If Japan's capital city is Tokyo, put a "T" in space 32. If Tokyo is not the capital city, put a "Y" in that space.

9. If Shikoku is Japan's smallest island, put an "S" in space 16. If it is not the smallest island, put a "B" in that space.

10. If Japan's national anthem is "Kimigayo," put a "K" in space 19. If it is not the national anthem, put an "L" in that space.

11. If Japanese people still wear the traditional kimono most of the time, put an "O" in space 25. If most Japanese wear western-style clothes, put an "I" in that space.

12. If Fuji is Japan's highest mountain, put an "F" in space 8. If it is not the highest mountain, put an "R" in that space.

13. If Japan's basic unit of money is the sen, put a "D" in spaces 14 and 26. If the basic unit of money is the yen, put a "C" in those spaces.

14. If Japan's ruler is called an emperor, put an "E" in spaces 2, 6, 15, 20, 23 and 30. If the ruler is not called an emperor, put an "A" in those spaces.

THE MESSAGE IS: _____

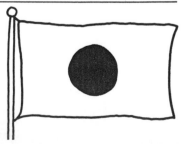

USE REFERENCE
SOURCES TO LEARN
ABOUT JAPAN!

PROJECTS FOR
MY BROTHER SAM IS DEAD

1. Describe Tim's feelings toward his brother Sam. _____

_____

_____

2. Who were the cowboys? _____

_____

3. Why wouldn't the general grant a stay of execution for Sam even after Tim and his

mother explained the circumstances of why Sam was with the cattle? _____

_____

_____

4. At the end of the book, the author writes "I keep thinking that there might have been another way, besides war, to achieve the same end." In what other way might we have achieved our independence? Write your answer on the back of this sheet.

CHOOSE ONE OF THE FOLLOWING PROJECTS:

1. Read a biography of one of the Revolutionary heroes, such as Paul Revere, Patrick Henry, George Washington, etc. Write a report on how the biography differs from the book *My Brother Sam Is Dead* in its account of the war. Present your report to the class.
2. This book is not illustrated. Make a large colorful illustration of some event in the story. Some suggestions are when Sam in his uniform talks to Tim or when Tim confronts the cowboys in the snow. Show your illustration to the class and explain the incident.
3. Make a comparison of a British soldier's uniform and equipment, and a Rebel's uniform and equipment. Draw and color pictures of the uniforms or create finger puppets.
4. Make a chart comparing an inn of the 1700s with a motel of today. You may cut out pictures or draw the items that would have been found in an inn during Tim's time and put them on one half of the chart. Then do the same with items you could find in a motel of today and put them on the other half of the chart. Display your chart and explain it to the class.

WORDS OF THE AMERICAN REVOLUTION

There were many great people in the United States during the American Revolution. Below are some quotations by some of them. Use a book of quotations to find out who said each one and then find the author's name in the wordsearch below. (Remember to look for key words in each quotation.)

1. "A national debt, if it is not excessive, will be to us a national blessing."

   _____

2. "Observe good faith and justice toward all nations."

   _____

3. "I only regret that I have but one life to lose for my country."

   _____

4. "I am not a Virginian, but an American."

   _____

5. "Liberty cannot be preserved without a general knowledge among the people…"

   _____

6. "I cannot ask of heaven success, even for my country, in a cause where she should be in

   the wrong."

   _____

7. 'Suspicion is the companion of mean souls, and the bane of all good society."

   _____

8. "The God who gave us life, gave us liberty at the same time."

   _____

9. "Lost time is never found again."

   _____

```
J H O L W H W B T B D T E I S O E A P T H A
A O I L D W A N O A N H K D T B H P Y W T R
L A N O T G N I H S A W E G R O E G C O U N
E N A N I E I B R O N W I N E H I D L I O I
X A B E Y O L N K O H G W P L O T O D M S N
A N M I S D K P A T R I C K H E N R Y S T N
N A H R T W N B O L R E I C O L W O P M E A
D S E E R R A S H A E N S A M I S A R A A E
E T H S R O R Y M E B B A S E E S O D D L Y
R M M U N E F N T O N I N E D O O T Y A S B
H I E O A K N I H Y R I E W L M U D H N R O
A D R N O T I S D P I C A C I E C N A H Y I
M O G O E T M I O R W N S P L L A M U O C H
I N E M D O A S T I I L I V S H H O O J L L
L I O N O T J K E N T M Y R T A M E L I O E
T S D J O H N Q U I N C Y A D A M S I L A K
O U L I D E E A D I L I N M B Y L O M Y O T
N I E N I S B C A M L F I L R O T H H E R T
S M M A M N O S R E F F E J S A M O H T S A
```

PROJECTS FOR
AN ORPHAN FOR NEBRASKA

1. Why was Kevin able to read when most of the other orphans and newsboys could not?

   _____

2. Why was Uncle Michael in jail? _____

3. Why wasn't Kevin picked by the farmers and townspeople of Cottonwood City?

   _____

4. Yuke finally took Kevin to live with him. What was Yuke's real name and occupation?

   _____

CHOOSE ONE OF THE FOLLOWING PROJECTS:

1. Many of the houses in Nebraska and other plains states at the time of the story were made of sod because there were very few trees for lumber and no other material was available. Make a model of a sod house. Look up sod houses in encyclopedias or other reference sources if you are unsure of how they were built.
2. This book is not illustrated. Make a large colorful illustration of some incident in the book, such as the children walking from the school hand in hand during the blizzard. Show your illustration to the class and tell something about the incident illustrated.
3. Look in a cookbook that offers pioneer recipes. Choose one, make it with the help of a parent, and bring it to class to share. Tell the class about pioneer food and what it has to do with *An Orphan for Nebraska*.
4. Write a story of Kevin and Yuke's ride west as described in the last chapter of the book. Make your story at least 300 words long. Be sure to tell in your story if Yuke and Kevin decide to stay in the west or whether they decide to return to Cottonwood City.

ALL ABOUT NEBRASKA

Nebraska, like the other states of the great plains region, has violent weather including tornadoes and blizzards. Answer these questions about Nebraska. Then give yourself 3 points for each answer you marked "true" and 1 point for each answer your marked "false." Then add your points. If you answered each question correctly, your score will be the order number of Nebraska's entry as a state into the United States.

	True	*False*	*Points*
1. There was a major tornado in Nebraska on June 3, 1980.	___	___	___
2. The most deaths in a major tornado in the United States were 350 deaths on April 3-4, 1974.	___	___	___
3. There was a severe blizzard in the United States on March 11-14, 1888.	___	___	___
4. Nebraska is 15th among the United States in square miles of land.	___	___	___
5. Nebraska became a state on March 15, 1879.	___	___	___
6. Nebraska's highest recorded temperature was 118°F on July 24, 1936.	___	___	___
7. Nebraska's lowest recorded temperature was −47°F on February 12, 1899.	___	___	___
8. Nebraska's state motto is "Equality before the law."	___	___	___
9. Nebraska's state tree is the red maple.	___	___	___
10. Nebraska's state flower is the goldenrod.	___	___	___
11. Nebraska's capital city is Omaha.	___	___	___
12. Nebraska has three U.S. representatives to the House of Representatives.	___	___	___
13. Nebraska is the only state in the United States with a unicameral (one house) legislature.	___	___	___
14. Lincoln is the largest city in Nebraska.	___	___	___
15. The name "Nebraska" comes from an Indian word meaning "flat land."	___	___	___
16. Nebraska is a state that has many large cities.	___	___	___
17. President Gerald Ford was born in Omaha, Nebraska.	___	___	___

TOTAL _____

Did your answers total 37 points? Nebraska was the 37th state to enter the Union. If your answers did not total 37, go back and check your answers. If you cannot find your mistakes, ask your teacher or librarian for help.

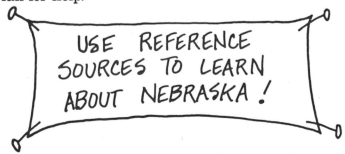

USE REFERENCE SOURCES TO LEARN ABOUT NEBRASKA!

PROJECTS FOR
SNOW TREASURE

1. Why were the children instead of adults recruited to carry the gold to the fishing

    boats? _____

    _____

2. Why did Uncle Victor at first say that Jan Lasek could not go to America with him, only

    to change his mind later? _____

    _____

3. Why was Peter, but not the other children who helped with the "snow treasure," taken

    to the United States? _____

    _____

4. How did the people of the village keep the German commandant from reopening the
    schools, which would have prevented them from transporting the gold? Write your
    answer on the back of this sheet.

CHOOSE ONE OF THE FOLLOWING PROJECTS:

1. Make a diorama of the children hiding the gold. Some children in your diorama could be
   coming down the mountain on their sleds while others are building the snowmen. You
   could include pine trees, Uncle Victor, and anything else you feel would add interest to
   your diorama. Make a label for your diorama that includes the title and author of the book.
   Show your diorama to the class and talk about it. Then display it in the classroom or the
   library with your teacher's or librarian's approval.
2. What do you think happened to Peter? He would have had to stay in the United States
   until the war was over, so he would have been away from his family for a long time. Write a
   story about Peter and what happened to him before he could be reunited with his family.
3. Research Norway and write about the country and its people. Read your report to the class
   and tell what it has to do with *Snow Treasure*. If possible, also show pictures, slides, or travel
   posters of Norway with your report.
4. Research Norway's part in World War II. The word "quisling" was coined during World War II.
   What does it mean and what was its relation to Norway? Write a report and then read it to the
   class.

A SNOWY WORDSEARCH

The gold of Norway was saved because of the children's skill in the snow. Use your research skills to answer the following questions about wintertime activities and snow. Then find your answers in the wordsearch. The words can be found vertically, horizontally, diagonally, forwards, and backwards.

1. Who said: "Snow had begun in the gloaming,/And busily all the night,/Had been heaping field and highway/With a silence deep and white"? _____

   _____

2. Who said: "Snow had fallen, snow on snow,/Snow on snow,/In the bleak midwinter/Long ago"? _____

3. Where did 76 inches of snow fall in a 24-hour period? It was the world's largest snowfall in such a time period (as of 1985). _____

4. Norwegians are experts at winter sports. How many times did they win the Winter Olympics through 1984? _____

5. The Winter Olympics were held in Norway in 1952. In which Norwegian city were they held? _____

6. The children in *Snow Treasure* were good at sledding. Bobsledding is a Winter Olympics sport. Which country won the 4-man bobsledding event in 1964? _____

7. A luge is a type of sled and it, too, is a Winter Olympics sport. Which country won the men's doubles in the luge in 1964? _____

8. Who won the men's cross-country skiing (15 kilometers) in the 1984 Winter Olympics?

   _____

9. Downhill skiing is an event of the Alpine Skiing in the Winter Olympics. Who won the women's downhill skiing in the 1968 Winter Olympics? _____

   _____

10. Who won the men's giant slalom skiing in the 1952 Winter Olympics? _____

    _____

11. Who won the women's singles in figure skating in the 1936 Winter Olympics?

    _____

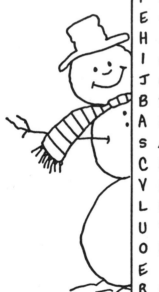

```
A O B B M L A P A W T S C H R N E A S D
R D E A P A R G N O C I N E E G G I O F
D A C R P R R J B R H R G M R U C L R S
F R E D B B Y N I N R O E O O N E A D T
E O G S A O M N W F I V E E H D G M O E
H L L E W O L L L E S S U R S E M A J I
I O A N L A I K N V T L L O A S R L L N
J C N L D A L B A M I O C M U V Q J L E
B E L A M I C K N E N Y N I S A N N O R
A K N I D R E O L G A P A L L N P O X I K
S A T E R E T H R S R V N O T R E G Y K
C L N B E S D E N H O O I L O B E R A S
V R E A S I W E I E S S L E E L L T Y E
L E D N N M W L S P S N L E D D H A S N
U V E R O A N E T P E O T O S E L R K R
O L E U R O W N E I T N G M I O E A P T
E I N E H A J N O S T L E A D Z R A U N
R S I B R A S E H A I R T S U A T H Z G
```

PROJECTS FOR
FIRE IN THE WIND

1. Describe Jeff and tell if you would like him for a friend. _____

_____

_____

2. Cornelius "Swapfor" McGrory was just a boy but he didn't go to school. He was always trading things with anyone he could find. Could a boy do

such things today? Why or why not? _____

_____

3. Mr. Arnold was determined to save his beautiful home from the fire.

Why did he have to give up? _____

4. Why were Jeff and his father able to save their house when Mr. Arnold and thousands of others were unable to save their homes? Write your answer on the back of this sheet.

CHOOSE ONE OF THE FOLLOWING PROJECTS:

1. Research the great Chicago Fire of 1871. Do people really believe it was started by Mrs. O'Leary's cow knocking over a lantern or is that just a legend? Make your report at least 300 words long and include how many days the fire burned, the loss in lives and in money, the efforts made to put out the fire, and whether you think such a fire could occur today.

2. Compare the fire equipment of today with the fire equipment of 1871. Show the comparison in a presentation to the class using charts, pictures, and illustrations. Include in your report your opinion on whether today's equipment would make such a fire as the great Chicago Fire an impossibility.

3. Make a large poster advertising *Fire in the Wind*. Remember, an advertisement needs to create interest and needs to tell what is for sale, why people should want to buy it, where it can be purchased, and how much it costs. Use bright colors and make your poster at least 12″ x 18″.

4. There was no radio or television in 1871, but pretend there was and make a "you are there" type of radio or television broadcast of the Chicago Fire. Pretend you are a reporter actually witnessing the fire. Your report should include facts, opinions of how the fire started, and interviews with people (two or three of your friends) who are either fleeing the fire or trying to put it out. You might want to listen to or watch several actual news broadcasts to see how they are done.

A FIREY PUZZLE

The Chicago Fire in *Fire in the Wind* and countless fires like it cause the loss of life or injury to many people every year. Millions of dollars also are lost because of fire. Solve the puzzle below by using your research skills. Answer each statement and then cross off your answer in the letter grid below. The remaining letters will spell a message. (Blackened squares in the grid are periods in the message.)

1. National Fire Prevention Week is in the month of _____.

2. People have used fire for over a million years. The earliest evidence of the use of fire

   was found in the country of _____ on the continent of _____.

3. Another name for a fireball is a _____.

4. An insect that glows in the dark could be a _____.

5. Pyrotechnics is another name for _____.

6. Things that will not burn easily are called _____.

7. A _____ firefighter does not get paid.

8. A piece of portable equipment used in public buildings and other places to put out fires

   is called a fire _____.

9. A famous ursine symbol of being safe with fire is _____.

10. In order to burn, a fire must have _____.

© 1988 by The Center for Applied Research in Education, Inc.

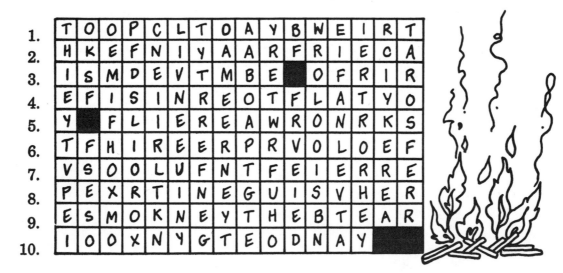

1.	T	O	O	P	C	L	T	O	A	Y	B	W	E	I	R	T
2.	H	K	E	F	N	I	Y	A	A	R	F	R	I	E	C	A
3.	I	S	M	D	E	V	T	M	B	E	■	O	F	R	I	R
4.	E	F	I	S	I	N	R	E	O	T	F	L	A	T	Y	O
5.	Y	■	F	L	I	E	R	E	A	W	R	O	N	R	K	S
6.	T	F	H	I	R	E	E	R	P	R	V	O	L	O	E	F
7.	V	S	O	O	L	U	F	N	T	F	E	I	E	R	R	E
8.	P	E	X	R	T	I	N	E	G	U	I	S	V	H	E	R
9.	E	S	M	O	K	N	E	Y	T	H	E	B	T	E	A	R
10.	I	O	O	X	N	Y	G	T	E	O	D	N	A	Y	■	

THE MESSAGE IS: _____

_____

PROJECTS FOR
THREE KNOCKS ON THE WALL

1. Did you like the character of Marty? Why or why not? _____

_____

_____

2. What did most of the girls give Eldon for a birthday present? _____

   What would be an acceptable gift for a girl to give a boy at a birthday party today?

_____

3. Why did Mrs. Hutchinson put up the high wall around her house? _____

_____

4. What could Rebecca have done to make Antoinette's life a happier one? Write your
   answer on the back of this sheet.

CHOOSE ONE OF THE FOLLOWING PROJECTS:

1. The prices of 1918 were much different than the prices of today. Below are some prices of
   items in 1918 as reflected in *Three Knocks on the Wall*. Go to the stores and write down
   today's prices of these items. Figure out the percentage of increase if you can. Report on these
   prices to the class.

   eggs—49¢ a dozen
   long licorice whip—1¢
   large well-kept two-story house—$1,000

   percale material—18¢ a yard
   spool of thread—15¢
   checked gingham material—22¢ a yard
   pair of men's socks—25¢

2. The influenza epidemic during World War I was terrible and worldwide. Research this
   epidemic and make a report on it to the class. Tell if it is likely that another epidemic like this
   is probable today.

3. Write a report to read to the class on how Marty's life in 1918 is different from your life today.
   Include at least ten ways in which your life is different from Marty's.

4. Research the clothing styles of 1918. Make clothes of the style of that period (you can use paper
   cutouts) and dress a paper doll in them. Show the doll to the class and explain it in relation to
   Three Knocks on the Wall. If you are good at sewing, you might want to sew some clothes.

© 1988 by The Center for Applied Research in Education, Inc.

HELP ANTOINETTE

Find Antoinette behind her high wall and rescue her by using your research skills and by following the directions carefully.

1. In *Three Knocks on the Wall*, Marty often says, "The world must be made safe for democracy." If General George Pershing originally said this quotation, go 6 spaces south. If Woodrow Wilson originally said it, go 3 spaces south.

2. If the United States had over 116,000 dead in World War I, go 6 spaces east. If the United States had over 320,000 dead, go 10 spaces east.

3. If the United States entered World War I in 1915, go 2 spaces south. If the United States entered the war in 1917, go 5 spaces south.

4. If the war ended on November 11, 1919, go 5 spaces east. If it ended on November 11, 1918, go 7 spaces west.

5. If Woodrow Wilson was president when the United States entered World War I, go 7 spaces south. If Calvin Coolidge was president at that time, go 3 spaces south.

6. *Three Knocks on the Wall* is set in Oregon. If there are approximately 96,980 square miles in Oregon, go 9 spaces east. If there are 110,650 square miles of land, go 4 spaces east.

7. If Oregon's nickname is "the Opportunity State," go 6 spaces north. If its nickname is "the Beaver State," go 4 spaces north.

8. If Oregon's state bird is the western tanager, go 10 spaces east. If its state bird is the western meadowlark, go 5 spaces east.

9. If Oregon became a state on February 14, 1859, go 6 spaces south. If it became a state on February 14, 1867, go 2 spaces south.

10. If Oregon's state tree is the jack pine, go 6 spaces east. If it is the Douglas fir, go 4 spaces east.

If you followed the directions and were accurate in your research, you should be at the ladder to rescue Antoinette. If not, check your answers and try again!

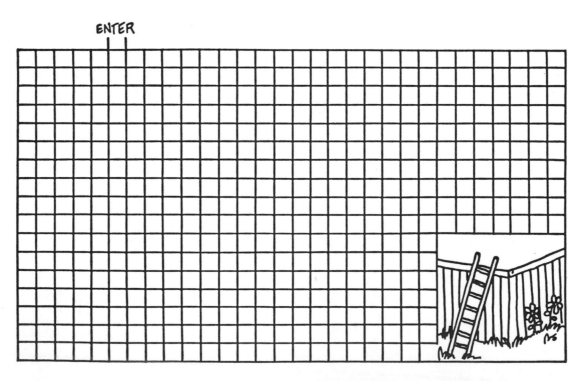

© 1988 by The Center for Applied Research in Education, Inc.

PROJECTS FOR
WHEN HITLER STOLE PINK RABBIT

1. Why must Anna and her family leave their home in Germany? _____

   _____

   _____

2. How did Onkel Julius change his attitude to what was happening in Germany during

   this time? _____

   _____

   _____

   _____

3. Do you think a persecution of a group of people, such as that which the Jewish people experienced in Nazi Germany, could occur in the United States? Why or why not? Write your answer on the back of this sheet.

CHOOSE ONE OF THE FOLLOWING PROJECTS:

1. At the end of the book, Anna and her family were in England. World War II had not yet begun, but its beginning was near. Write a story of Anna and her family and their experiences in England during the war.
2. Read *The Upstairs Room* by Joanna Reis, *The Diary of Anne Frank*, or *The Winged Watchman* by Hilda Van Stockum, all of which tell of things that happened to the Jewish people in Germany during the Nazi reign. Report to the class on the book you read.
3. Pretend that you are forced to leave your home and friends, as Anna was. Write a seven-day diary of what happens each day. Be sure to tell why you must leave, where you are going, and what you will take with you (remembering that you may take only what you can carry).
4. Make a large poster advertising this book. It should be at least 12″ x 18″ and be colorful and attractive. Information on the poster should include the title, author, why anyone should want to read or buy the book, and where the book may be found or purchased.

AN HISTORICAL FICTION PUZZLE

When Hitler Stole Pink Rabbit is an historical fiction book. Here is a crossword puzzle featuring some other titles and authors of historical fiction.

ACROSS

1. Last name of author of *The Sign of the Beaver*
4. Last name of the author of *The Perilous Road*
8. Last name of author of *A Gathering of Days*
10. An aid to rowing a boat
12. Last name of author of *Caddie Woodlawn*
15. Last name of author of *Moccasin Trail*
17. Homonym for "two"
18. Homonym for "sea"
19. Another homonym for "two"
20. Dug out ore
22. You and I together are _____
23. To enlarge
25. I am, but he _____
27. An exclamation
28. Present tense of "did"
29. Takes care of
31. Past tense of "lead"
34. An article (part of speech)
35. A globular object
36. Discharges fluid
38. Antonym for "light"
41. Antonym for "dry"
42. A child's toy representing a baby
45. A female sheep
46. Last name of authors of *My Brother Sam Is Dead*
48. A sweet potato
49. To make a mistake
50. Ran away from
51. Consumed a meal
52. Shine
53. Antonym for "he"
57. Last name of author of *Justin Morgan Had a Horse*
58. Outgoing (as in tides)
59. Last name of author of *Snow Treasure*

DOWN

1. To expectorate
2. Part of your arm or a kind of macaroni
3. Last name of author of *The Upstairs Room*
5. Last name of author of *The Matchlock Gun*
6. Something to burn in your fireplace
7. You hear with this
9. Last name of author of *The Horse Catcher*
11. A male sheep
13. Antonym for "old"
14. Last name of author of *Rifles for Watie*
16. Last name of author of *Little House on the Prairie*
19. Number of categories in the Dewey Decimal System
21. A negative answer
24. Antonym for "shallow"
26. This is used for transportation in the snow
28. Last name of author of *The Courage of Sarah Noble*
30. To write or say the letters of a word
32. A period of time
33. Last name of author of *A Fire in the Wind*
37. Antonym for "sour"
39. A necessity if your house is locked
40. Last name of author of *Three Knocks on the Wall*
42. A female deer
43. Antonym for "young"
44. To raise up
46. To move upwards
47. Something good for cleaning
54. Antonym for "she"
55. The letter following "M"
56. He is, but I _____

PROJECTS FOR YOUR CHOICE OF AN HISTORICAL FICTION BOOK

1. What is the title of your book? _____

_____

2. Who is the author? _____

3. During what years or period of history does your book's action take place?

_____

4. Are the characters people who actually lived or are they completely fictional? Describe

two of them. _____

_____

_____

5. Briefly tell the plot of your book. Use the back of this sheet for your answer.

CHOOSE ONE OF THE FOLLOWING PROJECTS:

1. Research the time of the story you read. Write a report on the lives of the people of that time, what was taking place in history, and the inventions that were available at that time. Give your report to the class and tell how it relates to the book.

2. Find out the names of at least ten actual historical figures who were alive at the time of your book's action. Create a wordsearch puzzle using these people's names. Be sure you also make an answer key for your wordsearch.

3. Make a large poster advertising your book. Make the poster colorful. Be sure to tell the title, author, something about the book, the price, and where it can be found. Perhaps your teacher or librarian will display the poster.

4. Make a bibliography of the historical fiction available in your school library. Be sure to include at least 15 titles and use the bibliographic form recommended by your teacher or librarian.

AN "HISTORICAL" MESSAGE

Look in the card catalog and find the authors of the historical fiction books below. Write their names on the lines and then cross off the name or names on the matching line of the grid. When you have finished, the remaining letters will spell a message.

1. The first and last names of the author of *A Gathering of Days*

   _____

2. The first and last names of the author of *The Upstairs Room*

   _____

3. The first and last names of the author of *Caddie Woodlawn*

   _____

4. The last name of the author of *My Brother Sam Is Dead* _____

5. The last name of the author of *The Matchlock Gun* _____

6. The last name of the author of *The Courage of Sarah Noble* _____

7. The first and last names of the author of *Johnny Tremain*

   _____

8. The first and last names of the author of *Rifles for Watie*

   _____

9. The first and last names of the author of *Across Five Aprils*

   _____

10. The first and last names of the author of *Moccasin Trail*

    _____

11. The first and last names of the author of *The Horse Catcher*

    _____

12. The first and last names of the author of *The Dark Frigate*

    _____

© 1988 by The Center for Applied Research in Education, Inc.

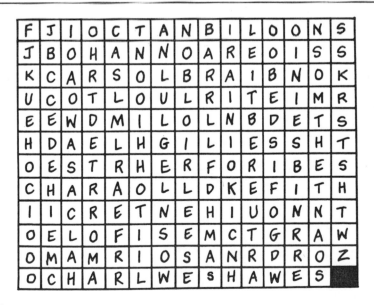

F	J	I	O	C	T	A	N	B	I	L	O	O	N	S
J	B	O	H	A	N	N	O	A	R	E	O	I	S	S
K	C	A	R	S	O	L	B	R	A	I	B	N	O	K
U	C	O	T	L	O	U	L	R	I	T	E	I	M	R
E	E	W	D	M	I	L	O	L	N	B	D	E	T	S
H	D	A	E	L	H	G	I	L	I	E	S	S	H	T
O	E	S	T	R	H	E	R	F	O	R	I	B	E	S
C	H	A	R	A	O	L	L	D	K	E	F	I	T	H
I	I	C	R	E	T	N	E	H	I	U	O	N	N	T
O	E	L	O	F	I	S	E	M	C	T	G	R	A	W
O	M	A	M	R	I	O	S	A	N	R	D	R	O	Z
O	C	H	A	R	L	W	E	S	H	A	W	E	S	

THE MESSAGE IS: _____

_____

ANIMALS IN FICTION

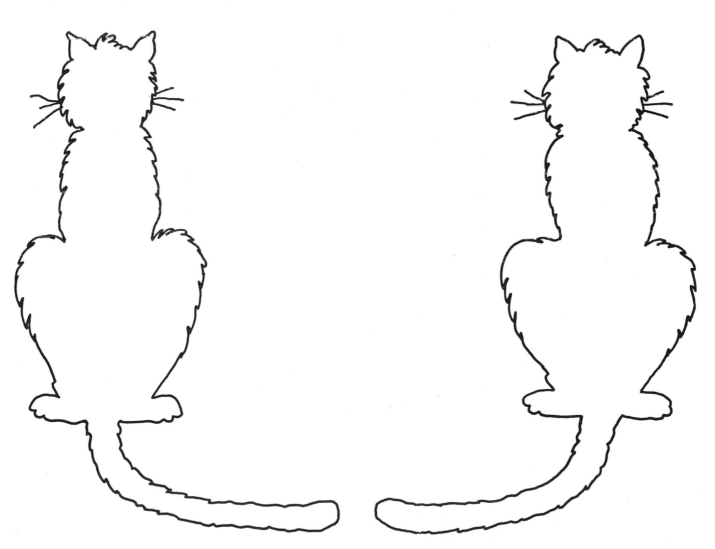

SUGGESTIONS FOR THE TEACHER

Books about animals have always been popular with children. Many of the favorite books about animals are ones that have endured for many years. Some, like *Lassie Come Home,* have been filmed for movies and for television so many times that children, believing that they know all about the book, have missed the pleasure of reading them. Another reason to include older titles is that books about animals do not become dated as quickly as other types of books and can be enjoyed for many generations.

Introduce Unit 6 by showing a sound filmstrip, such as *Animals* from Pied Piper, or by renting a movie such as *The Incredible Journey* or *Big Red* from Walt Disney. Then discuss with the children the elements that are usually present in animal fiction. These include danger, bravery on the part of the animal, and sadness.

After the discussion of animal books, give a brief book talk about each book in the unit using your own ideas about the book, the summaries in the unit, or blurbs from the book jacket. Allow the children to select their own books to read unless there are wide reading abilities. If this is the case, you may want to keep in mind that *Where the Red Fern Grows* and *Lassie Come Home* are among the more difficult to read and *A Morgan for Melinda* and *Misty of Chincoteague* are easier to read.

When the books have been read and the activities/projects are completed, save time during each class for the students to exhibit and discuss their projects.

To further enhance the students' interest in reading about animals, here are some additional suggestions to consider:

1. CREATIVE WRITING: Let the students bring a picture of their pets to class and have them write about the pets. The stories can then be arranged into a class book.
2. PET DAY: After obtaining permission from the school administrator and the parents, arrange a "Pet Day" when the students can bring their pets to class. The students can introduce their pets and talk about them.
3. GUEST SPEAKERS: Invite a veterinarian to visit the class and speak to the students on the care of pets. A dog control officer could speak to the students about abandoned animals and the local Humane Society. A game warden could speak about the wild animals in your area.
4. FIELD TRIPS: If possible, you and your students could visit a horse farm, a kennel, or a pet store.
5. CULMINATING MOVIE: In addition to introducing the unit, a movie could also culminate the unit. You might show *Lassie Come Home* or *The Black Stallion.* Many such movies can be rented from movie rental companies.

AUDIO-VISUAL AIDS
AND RELATED BOOK TITLES

Here are a few of the many audio-visual items and book titles that can be used with this unit on animals in fiction.

Audio-Visual Items

Old Yeller, sound filmstrip (Random House)
The Cat Who Went to Heaven, sound filmstrip (Random House)
Rascal, listening record or cassette (Random House)

Gay Neck, sound filmstrip (Random House)

Animals, sound filmstrip (Pied Piper)

The following are motion pictures from Walt Disney that can be rented:

Big Red
Old Yeller
Rascal
The Cat from Outer Space
Never Cry Wolf
The Ugly Dachshund
That Darn Cat
Sammy, the Way Out Seal

Related Book Titles

Armstrong, William H. *Sounder.*
Ball, Zachary. *Bristle Face.*
Gipson, Fred. *Savage Sam.*
Henry, Marguerite. *King of the Wind.*
Kjelgaard, Jim. *Snow Dog.*
London, Jack. *White Fang* or *Call of the Wild.*
Morey, Walt. *Gentle Ben* or *Gloomy Gus.*
Salten, Felix. *Bambi.*
Terhune, Albert Payson. *Lad, a Dog.*

SUMMARIES OF UNIT 6 BOOKS

6-1   *Sasha, My Friend* by Barbara Corcoran (New York: Atheneum, 1969. 203 pages). Hallie
Winthrop, whose mother has died in an automobile accident, is sorry for herself as she flies
to Montana with her father. They must go to his isolated ranch because his doctor says it
will help her father regain his health. Hallie wants to help her father, so she tries to make
the best of having to leave her friends in California. At first, Hallie finds life as lonesome as
she expected on the ranch. When she ventures out of the trailer, she does make friends with
an old Indian living nearby and with the Penneys and their daughter, Birdie, who is about
Hallie's age but confined to a wheelchair. Hallie likes all of the Penney family except for
Birdie's brother, John, who seems to be cruel and vindictive. While walking one day with
Black Thunder, her old Indian friend, they find a dead female wolf that has been killed by a
trap. When they investigate, they find a live pure white wolf pup in the female wolf's den.
Hallie begs to keep the pup against the advice of both Black Thunder and her father. She
raises the wolf pup, named Sasha, as a pet even though she knows it must be returned to the
wild when it is grown. *Sasha, My Friend* tells how Hallie learns to do many things for
herself as she grows up in Montana. There is sadness in the story when Sasha is killed by a
trap set by John Penney, but there also is adventure and joy as Hallie realizes she has
learned to appreciate her new life in Montana.

6-2   *Runaway Stallion* by Walt Morey (New York: E. P. Dutton, 1973, 217 pages). Althoug Jeff and
his family moved to the ranch from the city a year ago, he still misses the city and longs to
return. Perhaps if he had a horse of his own, he wouldn't mind living on the ranch and the
other kids wouldn't call him "Clodhopper." Jeff has had his eye on a black colt with a star on

its forehead that belongs to the Deckers. The Deckers and their son, Billy, have not been friendly to Jeff and his family, so Jeff doesn't think there is much chance of ever owning the black colt. One night, Jeff is awakened by a violent thunderstorm. Looking out of his window, he catches a glimpse of a magnificent, powerful stallion whose mane and tail stream in the wind as it gallops away. From that moment on, Jeff is determined to find the horse and make it his own. Jeff eventually finds the beautiful red stallion and rescues it from certain death. He names the stallion "Goblin" and tries to persuade his family to let him keep it. Everyone could see that the horse is well trained, so it must belong to someone. Jeff is told he can keep the horse only if no answer comes to an advertisement about the stallion in the newspaper. This is an exciting story about a boy who saves a famous lost racehorse named "Fly-By" and who grows up in the process of caring for the horse and then having to give it up. Most students will enjoy the book for the adventure as well as for the horse story.

6-3 *Rascal* by Sterling North (New York: E. P. Dutton, 1963, 189 pages). Although part autobiographical, *Rascal* is classified as fiction. It is the story of a boy and his pet raccoon named Rascal who live in Wisconsin in 1917 and 1918. Rascal is "adopted" as an infant by Sterling, who already has a large dog, a crow, various cats, and other wild pets that come and go. Sterling's mother is dead and his father, a lawyer, lets Sterling do almost anything he pleases. Rascal becomes like a family member and comes and goes as he pleases since he can easily unlatch the door. Rascal often gets into trouble because of his gourmet appetite and his curiosity. The neighbors at last insist that Sterling keep Rascal on a leash except when he is in a cage. Sterling knows he must, but is sad and distraught at the thought of caging his beloved friend. His father, to console his son, takes both Sterling and Rascal for a two-week camping trip in the woods. It is an idyllic time and ends when school begins. Sterling must go back to school, where even Rascal spends a day! At last Sterling realizes nature's pull is changing Rascal and he knows that he must let the raccoon go. This is a much-honored book about an engaging raccoon and the boy who loves him.

6-4 *Where the Red Fern Grows* by Wilson Rawls (New York: Doubleday and Company, 1961. 212 pages). Ten-year-old Billy lives in the Ozarks and longs to have a pair of hunting hounds. He begs his parents to buy them for him even though he realizes that they cannot possibly afford to buy the dogs. At last he decides to earn the money for the dogs himself. For two years he picks blackberries in his bare feet and sells them. He does whatever he can to earn the money for the dogs. He tells no one of his plans, even though for two years he has been saving an advertisement listing the dogs at $25 each, a tremendous amount of money for those days. When Billy finally saves the $50 for the two dogs, he takes the money and the advertisement to his grandfather, who is greatly moved by the boy's determination. Although he is afraid that the hound puppies will no longer be available at the price in the old ad, the grandfather sends for them anyway. Billy is ecstatic when he learns that the puppies are not only still available, but the price has gone down and he will receive $10 change! Billy's life with his dogs, Old Daniel and Little Ann, is recounted with love and understanding of a boy's love for dogs and their love for him. The book has both pathos and tears, but also victory and joy.

6-5 *A Morgan for Melinda* by Doris Gates (New York: Viking Press, 1980. 189 pages). Unlike most girls her age, Melinda has no desire to own a horse nor to learn to ride one. Her father, however, has his heart set on a horse for Melinda and on teaching her to ride. Melinda does not want to admit to her father that she is afraid of horses. She wants to be the kind of daughter she thinks her father wants because she wants to make up to him for the loss of his son, her brother Martin, who had died of leukemia. Melinda tries to delay learning to ride and owning a horse, but when her father is offered a beautiful Morgan stallion at an unbelievable price, she cannot disappoint him. With his help and the help of a loving old lady named Missy, Melinda learns to love her horse, to ride him, and even to *enjoy* riding. Missy, an author, also encourages Melinda in her writing. Melinda grows emotionally as she learns to care for, ride, and love her beautiful horse. This book is one that most fifth- and sixth-grade girls will enjoy.

6-6 *Old Yeller* by Fred Gipson (New York: Harper & Row, 1956. 158 pages). Travis is 14 years old when his Pa has to take cattle to Kansas and leave him in charge of the farm, his mother, and his five-year-old brother Arliss. Travis is confident that he can handle things and is proud to be treated like a man. One night, he discovers that a side of meat has been stolen by a big yellow dog. Travis is so angry that he wants to chase the dog away, but Arliss wants to keep the dog. Arliss gets so angry at Travis that Travis lets the dog stay. It is a good decision because the dog, named Old Yeller both because of his color and because of his funny yell-like bark, proves to be valuable help and a lovable companion. Old Yeller is a great help in keeping the raccoons out of the vegetable patch and in rounding up the pigs so that Travis can put the family mark on them. Twice, Travis is saved by Old Yeller's bravery and his mother's life, too, is spared because Old Yeller manages to hold off a rabid wolf. Before Pa gets home, Travis has learned to love the big yellow dog, who is unafraid in defending Travis and the family. Like so many animal stories, this one brings a lump to your throat, but it is action filled, exciting, and well written.

6-7 *Lassie Come Home* by Eric Knight (New York: Holt, Rinehart and Winston, 1940. 229 pages). Although this book has been made into movies and a television series, it is too good to not be read by the children of today. It is about the love of a dog for its home and master. Lassie belongs to Joe and his family, and she is their pride and joy. Sam Caraclough, Joe's father, has had many offers for the dog from the Duke, but he always refuses to sell. One day, however, he does sell Lassie because he is out of work and needs money for his family. Joe is heartbroken but sure that he will get to keep Lassie when time after time, she breaks out of the Duke's kennels and returns to wait for Joe outside the school at four o'clock. Joe's father, an honest and honorable man, insists that Joe take Lassie back to the kennels and tell her to stay. Joe does and is sure that he will again see Lassie again. He is doubly sure when his father tells him that the Duke has taken Lassie 400 miles away to Scotland to groom her and train her for dog shows. Lassie is an obedient dog, but every day near four o'clock, her instinctive time sense tells her that it is time to go get Joe at school. She does not realize the distance involved, of course, and one day she manages to escape from the kennels and begin the long journey back to her home and Joe. The story of Lassie's trip, which takes her many more miles than the 400, is an enthralling one that makes it hard to put the book down. The story makes you cry, but unlike many other animal stories, it ends happily when Lassie does indeed come home!

6-8 *The Black Stallion* by Walter Farley (New York: Random House, 1941. 187 pages). Alec Ramsay is returning by ship from a visit to his uncle in Arabia when he first sees the beautiful black stallion. Although the horse is wild, Alec makes friends with him by taking sugar treats to him in his stall on the ship. A terrible storm at sea causes the ship to sink and Alec is thrown into the sea near the beautiful black horse who is struggling to swim nearby. Alec grabs on to a rope attached to the stallion's halter and he is miraculously pulled by the stallion to an island. They appear to be the only survivors of the shipwreak. Alec and the horse manage to survive on the bleak island, and Alec becomes enough of a friend to the stallion to ride him. However, the stallion, called The Black by Alec, is far from tame. A ship finally passes close enough to the island to see the smoke from an accidental fire in Alec's hut and sailors rescue Alec and The Black. At home, Alec and a neighbor, who was once a jockey, secretly work to tame and train the wild horse. At last Alec is able to ride The Black on a racetrack and finally gets the chance to race against the two best racehorses in the country. This is a fast-paced book that will be enjoyed by most young readers.

6-9 *Misty of Chincoteague* by Marguerite Henry (Chicago: Rand McNally, 1947. 173 pages). On Chincoteague Island, the people have a holiday called Pony Penning Day. On that day, the men drive the wild horses from Assateague Island across the water to Chincoteague. Besides having a happy holiday and a rodeo, the firemen sell some of the wild horses. Maureen and Paul set their hearts on the Phantom, an especially wild pony. For a year, the brother and sister work helping their grandfather break ponies so that they can earn money to buy the Phantom on the next Pony Penning Day. Paul gets to help herd the wild ponies over to Chincoteague. He is delighted when he sees that Phantom has a foal. Paul calls the foal Misty and he and Maureen determine to buy both Phantom and her foal Misty. At first they are disappointed because Misty has a "sold" rope around her neck, but the man who bought her changes his mind, so Paul and Maureen get both Misty and Phantom. They partially tame and train Phantom and she becomes a great racer, but they realize she is unhappy, so they release her to the wild. Misty is still theirs and she is truly their horse, Misty of Chincoteague.

6-10 *Incident at Hawk's Hill* by Allan W. Eckert (Boston: Little, Brown and Company, 1971. 173 pages). Ben is a different kind of little boy. Even his mother, who loves him deeply, realizes that a little boy who can imitate and almost seem to talk to the wild animals *is* different. The neighbors talk among themselves and decide that Ben is very strange and want to stay away from him. One stormy day, Ben disappears and the neighbors forget their distrust of him and begin a long search to find him. After several days, they give up the search, but Ben's family keeps looking. In the meantime, Ben has taken shelter in a female badger's den. When the badger returns, both the boy and the badger are wary, but Ben remembers the badger from a past encounter and they gradually begin to live together, with the badger providing wild game and other food for the boy to eat. After two months' time, he has become more like a badger than a boy. One day, Ben's big brother John is out searching— more for Ben's body than with any hope he is alive—when he sees Ben emerging from the badger den. When John grabs Ben, the boy at first fights and seems to not remember the rest of his family. But he soon remembers and is happy. He even seems to have changed and now talks to them more than he did before. The badger has followed Ben and comes into the house ready to fight for him. The family accepts the badger and it becomes a part of the family. This book has won many honors. It is readable and entertaining, even as it raises a lump in the reader's throat and brings tears to the eyes.

PROJECTS FOR
SASHA, MY FRIEND

Write a descriptive sentence about each of the following characters. Be sure you use complete sentences and that you use at least two adjectives in your sentences.

1. Hallie

_____

2. Birdie Penney

_____

3. John Penney

_____

4. Black Thunder

_____

5. Mrs. Penney

_____

CHOOSE ONE OF THE FOLLOWING PROJECTS:

1. Do you think the author could have had a different ending for the part of the story about Sasha? Could Sasha have lived rather than been killed by the trap set by John Penney? Write a new ending for the part about Sasha.
2. Research wolves and write a good report on them. Try to include any facts that you can learn about whether wolves can be tamed successfully. Read your report to the class. Illustrate it with drawings or with newspaper/magazine pictures.
3. Make a painting of Hallie and Sasha or of Sasha alone on the Christmas tree ranch. Show it to the class and talk about the story.
4. *Sasha, My Friend* doesn't tell us what happens to John Penney. Do you think he will end up in jail as the sheriff thinks he will or do you think something could happen to change him for the better? Write a story about what you think happens to John Penney.

6–1A

COMPARE THE TWO

Hallie Winthrop had to move from her home and friends in California to a new, very different home in Montana. Use your research skills to compare the state of Montana with the state of California.

1. a. What is the capital of Montana? _____

   b. What is the capital of California? _____

2. a. How many square miles are there in Montana? _____

   b. How many square miles are there in California? _____

3. a. How many acres of forested land are there in Montana? _____

   b. How many acres of forested land are there in California? _____

4. a. Name three principal industries of Montana: _____

   _____

   b. Name three principal industries of California: _____

   _____

5. a. Name three chief agricultural crops of Montana: _____

   _____

   b. Name three chief agricultural crops of California: _____

   _____

6. a. What is the state flower of Montana? _____

   b. What is the state flower of California? _____

7. a. What is the state nickname for Montana? _____

   b. What is the state nickname for California? _____

8. a. In what year did Montana become a state? _____

   b. In what year did California become a state? _____

9. a. On the back of this sheet, write what you would like to see if you visited Montana.

   b. On the back of this sheet, write what you would like to see if you visited California.

PROJECTS FOR
RUNAWAY STALLION

Match the characters to their descriptions. Write the letter on the appropriate line.

a. Jeff
b. Hank
c. Billy
d. Lem Decker
e. Fred Hunter
f. Goblin
g. Star
h. Harve

_____ 1. A tall man with black hair, he was friendly but not afraid of trouble.

_____ 2. A wealthy rancher, he won many races with his fast horse named Blackie.

_____ 3. This is a sleek red stallion who also is a famous race horse.

_____ 4. This is a colt who liked Jeff and his apples.

_____ 5. This is the man who trained Goblin.

_____ 6. The son of the blacksmith, he often said "Someday! Someday!" when he was angry.

_____ 7. This is the boy who called Jeff "Clodhopper."

_____ 8. He saved Goblin from the black muck and from Lem Decker's bullet.

CHOOSE ONE OF THE FOLLOWING PROJECTS:

1. Make a clay sculpture of Goblin. Perhaps your teacher or librarian will allow you to display the finished sculpture.
2. Make a painting of Goblin and show it to the class.
3. Write a different ending for *Runaway Stallion*. Could Jeff keep Goblin or find some way to see him often?
4. Write your own story about a boy or a girl and a horse.
5. Make a poster advertising Goblin for sale. Include all the necessary information.
6. Prepare a TV-style commercial to sell the class on reading the book.

ABOUT WALT MOREY

Part One

    1. Walt Morey was born on February 3, 1907. In what city and

       state was he born? _____

    2. What was the title of his first published book for children?

    _____

    3. Before becoming a writer, what other jobs did he have?

    _____

    _____

Part Two

Some of the awards Walt Morey has won have been for *Gentle Ben* and *Kavik the Wolf Dog*. Look in your library for books by Walt Morey. On the back of this sheet, list the titles and copyright dates of the Walt Morey books in your library. Who is the publisher for most of his

books? _____

Part Three

Many of Walt Morey's books are about Oregon and Alaska. Here are some questions about these two states.

    1. What is the population of Oregon? _____

    2. What is the population of Alaska? _____

    3. How many square miles are in Oregon? _____

    4. How many square miles are in Alaska? _____

    5. What is Oregon's state motto? _____

    6. What is Alaska's state motto? _____

PROJECTS FOR
RASCAL

1. Write a description of Rascal. Describe his appearance, his abilities, and the possible drawbacks of having him as a pet. _____

_____

_____

_____

_____

_____

2. Write a paragraph describing Sterling. What kind of a boy was he? Make your paragraph at least five or six sentences long. Use the back of this sheet for your description.

CHOOSE ONE OF THE FOLLOWING PROJECTS:

1. Make a clay model of a raccoon. If possible, use pottery clay and have your raccoon figure fired by an adult. Show your model to the class and talk about the book.
2. Use at least two sources to research raccoons and present your reports to the class. Talk about their habits, homes, and where they may be found. Try to include pictures in your report.
3. See if your teacher or librarian will allow you to promote and plan a Pet Day. If allowed, advertise the event and plan for it by deciding how children will show and tell about their pets, and where the pets will be kept or taken care of after the show. On the day of the event, be the master or mistress of ceremonies and introduce the students and their pets.
4. Make a large map of the United States and show where the native wildlife may be found. Use the animals mentioned in the wordsearch in Activity 6-3B. Use a key and color in the areas where the wildlife may be found or use a method of your own to show the animals' habitats.

A "RASCALLY" WORDSEARCH

Below are some wild animals found in the United States. After each animal, write where the animal can be found in the United States. Then circle the wild animals in the wordsearch.

1. raccoon _____

2. oppossum _____

3. grizzly bear _____

4. white-tailed deer _____

5. skunk _____

6. nutria _____

7. moose _____

8. elk _____

9. fox _____

10. buffalo _____

11. alligator _____

12. rattlesnake _____

© 1988 by The Center for Applied Research in Education, Inc.

U	C	R	T	H	I	B	E	R	A	M	Z	W	V	R	Q
V	O	E	D	G	T	K	O	D	N	L	K	Y	S	M	P
P	O	E	S	S	J	T	A	C	O	P	J	T	U	U	O
R	E	D	F	G	A	H	I	F	J	K	L	M	R	S	N
D	I	D	I	G	E	S	O	O	M	Q	I	A	A	S	C
C	N	E	I	E	I	L	B	X	R	J	E	B	T	O	D
B	M	L	L	E	F	A	K	Y	S	B	H	G	T	P	E
A	L	I	E	A	F	G	H	W	Y	T	U	F	L	P	O
A	U	A	B	U	F	F	A	L	O	S	V	P	E	O	N
D	O	T	I	F	E	W	Z	Z	R	H	C	O	S	K	M
I	I	E	L	I	I	Z	A	R	S	T	H	I	N	K	L
S	C	T	D	A	I	R	T	U	N	I	U	U	A	E	P
G	K	I	A	R	A	C	C	O	O	N	K	N	K	L	R
O	G	H	G	A	B	A	E	S	A	S	U	L	E	E	S
O	D	W	C	U	Y	I	Z	Z	T	W	V	M	O	O	T

PROJECTS FOR
WHERE THE RED FERN GROWS

1. Describe Billy's family. (Is the family rich or poor? How many children are in the family? What do the parents do? Is it a loving family?) _____

   _____

   _____

   _____

2. When do you think this story took place? (Before or after World War II? Before or during the 1920s?) _____

3. Did you like this book? _____ What would be another possible ending to the book?

   _____

   _____

   _____

4. Little Ann and Old Dan were very good friends, yet they were very different. On the back of this sheet, describe some of the ways in which they were different.

CHOOSE ONE OF THE FOLLOWING PROJECTS:

1. Make a clay model of Little Ann and Old Daniel. If possible, use clay that can be fired (by an adult) and display your models. Tell the class about the dogs.
2. Make a large painting illustrating something that happened in the book. Explain your illustration to the class.
3. Research hunting dogs. Write a report about the different breeds, how they are trained, etc. Give your report to the class and try to include pictures and/or charts, if possible.
4. Research the many different breeds of dogs. Make a crossword puzzle using the names of at least 15 different breeds. Be sure to make an answer key.

FIND THE BREEDS

There are many different breeds and types of dogs. Below are 14 different breeds. Try to find each one in the wordsearch. The words can be found horizontally, vertically, diagonally, forwards, and backwards.

GERMAN SHEPHERD   BULLDOG
POODLE   MASTIFF
COLLIE   MONGREL
DACHSHUND   COCKER SPANIEL
BLOODHOUND   BASSET HOUND
FOX TERRIER   WOLFHOUND
SCHNAUZER   BORZOI

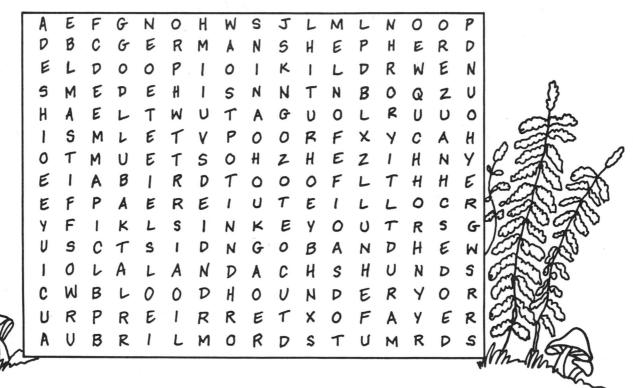

```
A E F G N O H W S J L M L N O O P
D B C G E R M A N S H E P H E R D
E L O O P I O I K I L D R W E N
S M E D E H I S N N T N B O Q Z U
H A E L T W U T A G U O L R U U O
I S M L E T V P O O R F X Y C A H
O T M U E T S O H Z H E Z I H N Y
E I A B I R D T O O O F L T H H E
E F P A E R E I U T E I L L O C R
Y F I K L S I N K E Y O U T R S G
U S C T S I D N G O B A N D H E W
I O L A L A N D A C H S H U N D S
C W B L O O D H O U N D E R Y O R
U R P R E I R R E T X O F A Y E R
A U B R I L M O R D S T U M R D S
```

PROJECTS FOR
A MORGAN FOR MELINDA

1. Why didn't Melinda tell her father that she was afraid of horses and did not want to learn to ride?

   _____

   _____

   _____

   _____

2. Did Melinda think Diana was a good friend? _____ Tell something from the book to support your answer. _____

   _____

   _____

3. Did Missy have any influence on how Melinda felt about horses and riding? _____

   Give evidence from the book to support your answer. _____

   _____

   _____

4. What would have been a good name for Melinda to give Merry Jo's foal?

   _____

CHOOSE ONE OF THE FOLLOWING PROJECTS:

1. Prepare a bibliography of horse books in your library. Make your bibliography more interesting by preparing it in the form of a book. You can cut the paper and the cover into the shape of a horse or horse's head, or put a picture of a horse on each page of the bibliography. Use the bibliography form recommended by your teacher or librarian and include at least ten books.
2. Make a clay model of Aranaway Ethan. Look at a book on horses to see what a Morgan horse looks like. Show your model to the class.
3. Research the Morgan horse and then give your report to the class. Try to include pictures, if possible. You might even draw your own pictures.
4. Prepare a report on the history of horses. Make a chart of the evolution of horses and show it to the class.

A NEW MORGAN FOR MELINDA

When *A Morgan for Melinda* ends, Melinda owns Missy's horse, Merry Jo. Merry Jo is soon to have a foal, and Melinda says she would have liked to include the foal's birth in the book. Finish the story for Melinda by telling about the new foal. Write the story as though Melinda is writing it and give the foal a name. Does Melinda train the horse? Does she keep it or sell it? Include anything else that will make the story interesting.

I couldn't believe that I, Melinda, who was afraid of horses and riding, would soon have not one but THREE horses! Soon Merry Jo will have her baby and I will have a tiny foal to take care of. I wonder if it will be a filly or a colt.

Then one day _____

_____

_____

_____

_____

_____

_____

_____

_____

_____

_____

_____

PROJECTS FOR
OLD YELLER

1. Describe Travis. Tell at least three things about him. _____

_____

_____

_____

2. Why didn't Travis want to keep Old Yeller at first? _____

_____

_____

3. Old Yeller saved Travis' life and Travis saved Old Yeller's life. On the back of this sheet, describe how these two things happened.

4. Do you think Travis will ever get another dog? ____ Give evidence from the book to

support your opinion. _____

_____

_____

_____

CHOOSE ONE OF THE FOLLOWING PROJECTS:

1. Make a clay model of Old Yeller. If possible, have your model fired (by an adult). Display your model and tell the class about Old Yeller.
2. Make a bibliography of at least 15 books about dogs that are in your library. Use the bibliography form recommended by your teacher or librarian. You might want to make your bibliography into a dog-shaped book (or a dog bone, dog dish, or dog house). Label your bibliography "Books about Dogs" and display it in the classroom or library with your teacher's or librarian's approval.
3. Make a 24″ x 30″ poster depicting the care of dogs. Use colorful construction paper, paints, and/or felt-tip pens.
4. Find a picture of a dog in a magazine. Cut it out and write a fictional story about the dog. Read your story to the class and then display it with the picture.

IT'S A DOG'S LIFE

Dogs have been friends and helpers to people for many, many years. They were the first animals to be tamed. Follow the directions below and use your research skills to solve the mystery message.

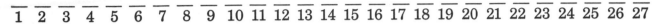

1̄ 2̄ 3̄ 4̄ 5̄ 6̄ 7̄ 8̄ 9̄ 1̄0̄ 1̄1̄ 1̄2̄ 1̄3̄ 1̄4̄ 1̄5̄ 1̄6̄ 1̄7̄ 1̄8̄ 1̄9̄ 2̄0̄ 2̄1̄ 2̄2̄ 2̄3̄ 2̄4̄ 2̄5̄ 2̄6̄ 2̄7̄

2̄8̄ 2̄9̄ 3̄0̄ 3̄1̄ 3̄2̄ 3̄3̄ 3̄4̄

1. If the chihuahua is the world's smallest breed of dogs, put an "A" in spaces 2, 4, 8, and 12. If it is not the smallest breed, put an "F" in those spaces.
2. If a samoyed is a working dog, put a "Y" in space 24. If it is a sporting dog, put an "E" in that space.
3. If a mongrel is a purebred hunting dog, put a "T" in space 31. If it is a dog of mixed breeds, put a "P" in that space.
4. If a weimaraner is a long-haired toy dog, put an "S" in space 3. If it is a short-haired sporting dog, put a "V" in that space.
5. If dogbane is a small dog, but an "A" in spaces 10 and 30. If it is not a dog but something else, put an "I" in those spaces.
6. If "dog days" are days of hot, sticky weather, put an "N" in spaces 13 and 34. If they are days when you are as "happy as dogs," put a "W" in those spaces.
7. If the dachshund originated in Scotland, put an "L" in spaces 5 and 29. If it originated in Germany, put a "G" in those spaces.
8. If a miniature schnauzer belongs to the terrier group, put a "T" in space 15. If it belongs to the hound group, put an "H" in that space.
9. If a dog's most highly developed sense is smell, put an "S" in spaces 1, 7, 11, and 32. If a dog's most highly developed sense is taste, put a "T" in those spaces.
10. If Eric Knight wrote *Lassie Come Home,* put an "E" in spaces 6, 17, and 27. If Katherine Paterson wrote *Lassie Come Home,* put a "K" in those spaces.
11. If Walt Morey wrote *Kavik the Wolf Dog,* put an "M" in space 9. If Scott O'Dell wrote *Kavik the Wolf Dog,* put an "O" in that space.
12. If Marguerite Henry wrote *Mishmash,* put a "B" in spaces 14, 20, 21, and 33. If Molly Cone wrote *Mishmash,* put an "O" in those spaces.
13. If Carol Brink wrote *Eddie, the Dog Holder,* put a "C" in space 16. If Carolyn Haywood wrote *Eddie, the Dog Holder,* put an "H" in that space.
14. If Jack London wrote *Call of the Wild,* put an "N" in spaces 13 and 34. If Joseph Krumgold wrote *Call of the Wild,* put a "J" in those spaces.
15. If Judy Blume wrote *Ribsy,* put an "L" in space 25. If Beverly Cleary wrote *Ribsy,* put an "F" in that space.
16. If Zachary Ball wrote *Bristle Face,* put a "B" in spaces 19 and 23. If Kate Seredy wrote it, put an "S" in those spaces.
17. If Wilson Rawls wrote *Where the Red Fern Grows,* put an "R" in spaces 18 and 26. If Ellen Raskin wrote it, put an "E" in those spaces.
18. If Jim Kjelgaard wrote *Big Red,* put a "K" in space 22. If William Pene de Bois wrote it, put a "W" in that space.

THE MESSAGE IS: _____

PROJECTS FOR
LASSIE COME HOME

1. Why was Joe's mother so cross with him when he begged to keep Lassie? _____
_____

2. List two occasions when humans were helpful to Lassie on her way home to Joe:

   a._____

   b._____

3. List two times when humans were cruel to Lassie:

   a._____

   b._____

4. Do you think the Duke was a mean man? _____ On the back of this sheet, tell why or why not.

CHOOSE ONE OF THE FOLLOWING PROJECTS:
1. Interview a dog breeder, a trainer, or a pet store owner. Ask about the person's work and about the dogs he/she deals with. If possible, invite the person to class to speak to your classmates. If not, tape your interview and play it for the class.
2. Read another dog book, such as *Lemon Meringue Dog* by Walt Morey. Compare that dog to Lassie and talk about the comparison to your class.
3. Make a painting of Lassie. Show your painting to the class and talk about Lassie.
4. Make a report about your own pet, if you have one. Include pictures, tell how you got the pet, what makes it a special pet, and any other interesting things about it.

HELP LASSIE GET HOME

Lassie has to cross many, many miles of Scotland and England to find her way home to the Carraclough family. Help Lassie get home by using your research skills to find out about the countries of Scotland and England.

1. If the capital of Scotland is Glasgow, go 5 spaces south. If the capital of Scotland is Edinburgh, go 3 spaces south.

2. If the most important river in Scotland is the Tay, go 2 spaces east. If the most important river is the River Clyde, go 5 spaces east.

3. If the official church of Scotland is the Roman Catholic Church, go 4 spaces south. If the official church is the Presbyterian Church, go 1 space south.

4. If English is the official language of Scotland, go 6 spaces west. If Gaelic is the official language, go 4 spaces west.

5. If Scotland's form of government is a democracy, go 7 spaces south. If its form of Government is a constitutional monarchy, go 4 spaces south.

6. Go as many spaces east as there are main land regions in Scotland.

7. If Scotland's flag is called "St. Andrew's Cross," go 2 spaces south. If it is called "Glorious Blue," go 5 spaces south.

8. If England's area is over 100,000 square miles, go 2 spaces west. If its area is just over 50,000 square miles, go 6 spaces west.

9. If England's basic monetary unit is the franc, go 4 spaces west. If the basic monetary unit of England is the pound, go 2 spaces north.

10. If England's official church is the Church of England, go 2 spaces west. If the official church is the Episcopalian Church, go 6 spaces west.

11. If England's longest river is the Trent, go 2 spaces south. If the longest river is the Thames, go 5 spaces south.

12. If England's capital is London, go 7 spaces east. If the capital is Manchester, go 5 spaces east.

13. If Queen Elizabeth II has four children, go 1 space south. If she has two children, go 3 spaces south.

14. If the main ruler of England is Queen Elizabeth II, go 1 space east. If the main ruler is the prime minister, go 4 spaces east.

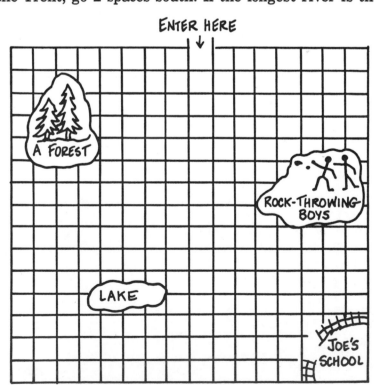

PROJECTS FOR
THE BLACK STALLION

1. Why were Alec and the Black Stallion able to survive on the deserted island? _____ _____

_____

2. Why did Alec sneak out every night to ride and train the Black Stallion instead of doing it during the day? _____

_____

3. Why did Henry know so much about training horses? _____

_____

4. Look in the card catalog of your library and find two other books by Walter Farley. On the back of this sheet, write their titles and copyright dates.

CHOOSE ONE OF THE FOLLOWING PROJECTS:

1. Write a diary of a week in Alec's life while he was on the deserted island with the Black Stallion. Tell what might happen each day of the week, pretending you are Alec.
2. Research Arabian horses and prepare a report on them. Use at least two references. Make your report at least 200 words long, and then read your report to the class. If possible, show pictures.
3. Make an illustration for something that happened in *The Black Stallion*. The shipwreck or Alec and the Black Stallion on the deserted island are two suggestions, or you may choose your own scene to illustrate. Show your illustration to the class and explain what the scene has to do with the book.
4. Research Walter Farley and his books. Consult a reference source such as *The Junior Book of Authors*. Read your report to the class and show several of his books.

SHIPWRECKED

In *The Black Stallion,* Alec and the Black Stallion are shipwrecked and find themselves on a deserted island, the only survivors of the wreck. Pretend you and a pet are on a deserted island and finish the story below.

The sailboat I had taken out on a clear sunny morning was now pitching and bobbing crazily in the rough sea. The sunshine and smooth sea had changed to black clouds and raging waves. I knew I had

taken the boat out too far. My pet dog, _____, whined and then barked.

Suddenly, the boat titled wildly and my dog and I found ourselves

in the raging sea. _____

_____

_____

_____

_____

_____

_____

_____

_____

_____

_____

_____

_____

_____

PROJECTS FOR
MISTY OF CHINCOTEAGUE

1. Describe Pony Penning Day. _____

_____

_____

_____

2. Grandma called Phantom and Misty the "topsy-turviest pair" she'd ever seen. Why?

_____

_____

3. Why did Maureen and Paul get to buy Phantom and Misty after Misty had already been

sold? _____

_____

4. Marguerite Henry won the Newbery Medal for one of her books. What was the book and

when did it win the Newbery Medal? _____

_____

CHOOSE OF OF THE FOLLOWING PROJECTS:

1. Research wild horses and make a report on them. The report should be at least 300 words long. Read your report to the class, and include pictures, if possible.
2. Make a clay model of Misty. Show it to the class and tell them about Misty.
3. Research Marguerite Henry. Write a report on her and her books. Give your report to the class and show them some of her many books.
4. Make a diorama of Assateague Island and include some of the wild horses that live there. Show your diorama to the class and tell them what the island has to do with the book. With the librarian's approval, display your diorama in the library along with Marguerite Henry's books.

SOME "HORSING" AROUND

Use the card catalog to help you figure out the message square below. Answer the questions about these books. Then cross off your answers on the grid. The remaining letters will spell a message.

1. Who is the author of *The Black Stallion?*

_____

2. What is the first name of the author of *King of the Wind?*

_____

3. Who is the illustrator of *Misty of Chincoteague?*

_____

4. Who is the author of *Black Beauty?*

_____

5. Who is the author of *A Morgan for Melinda* and *Little Vic?*

_____

6. Who is the author of *Runaway Stallion?*

_____

7. Who is the author of *National Velvet?*

_____

8. Who is the author of *The Horse Catcher?*

_____

9. Who is the author of *Keeping Barney?*

_____

10. Who is the author of *A Horse Called Dragon?*

_____

© 1988 by The Center for Applied Research in Education, Inc.

H	W	O	A	L	T	R	E	R	F	A	R	S	L	E	Y
E	M	A	S	R	G	U	E	T	R	I	O	T	R	E	I
W	E	E	S	L	E	S	Y	D	E	N	A	N	I	R	S
E	A	N	A	N	A	S	E	L	W	E	L	W	L	A	Y
D	S	O	F	R	I	S	G	A	A	V	T	O	R	E	S
W	A	I	L	T	M	T	E	O	R	B	E	O	O	Y	K
S	E	N	F	I	D	B	O	A	G	R	N	O	B	L	D
M	O	A	Y	R	S	I	E	A	S	A	N	N	D	O	Z
D	J	E	S	G	S	I	E	H	I	A	R	A	L	S	S
L	T	Y	O	N	N	R	H	E	A	A	L	D	L		

THE MESSAGE IS: _____

_____

PROJECTS FOR
INCIDENT AT HAWK'S HILL

1. Describe Ben. Be sure to use complete sentences. _____

   _____

   _____

2. Why do you think Ben acted the way he did? _____

   _____

   _____

3. What kind of work do you think Ben should go into when he grows up? _____

   _____

4. Use *Reader's Guide to Periodical Literature* or *Children's Magazine Guide* and find two articles about wildlife native to the United States. On the back of this sheet, write the title of the article, name of the magazine, the date of the magazine, and the page on which the article may be found.

CHOOSE ONE OF THE FOLLOWING PROJECTS:

1. Research badgers and write at least a 300-word report. Read your report to the class, and include pictures, if possible.
2. Make a clay model of a badger. Show your model to the class and talk about the book.
3. Not many people can imitate animal sounds as Ben did, but many people can imitate bird sounds. If you know anyone who can imitate bird calls, invite that person to class to demonstrate their bird calls. Introduce your guest to the class and then send a thank-you letter later to the guest.
4. Write a radio or television commercial for *Incident at Hawk's Hill*. Make your commercial as exciting and dramatic as possible. Give an idea of what the book is about and don't forget the sales pitch!

THE FINAL CHAPTER

Incident at Hawk's Hill ends with the reader not knowing if the badger who saves Ben's life lives or dies. Add a chapter to the book telling what happens to the badger and Ben. Use complete sentences and as many descriptive words as possible. Make your chapter at least 200 words long.

_____

_____

_____

_____

_____

_____

_____

_____

_____

_____

_____

_____

_____

_____

_____

_____

_____

_____

_____

PROJECTS FOR
YOUR CHOICE OF AN ANIMAL IN FICTION BOOK

1. What is the title of your book? _____

_____

2. Who is the author of the book? _____

_____

3. What is the name of the main animal character in

your book? _____

What kind of animal is it? _____

4. Are there any human characters in the book? _____ What is one of their names?

_____

5. On the back of this sheet, briefly tell the plot of the book.

CHOOSE ONE OF THE FOLLOWING PROJECTS:

1. Make an animal wordsearch. Use at least 12 animals and make your wordsearch as neat and attractive as possible. Be sure to prepare an answer key, too.
2. Make a television commercial for the book you just read. Your commercial should be as exciting and as visual as possible. Tell or act out a scene from the book and be sure to tell the title, author, price, and where it can be found or purchased.
3. Research the type of animal that was the main character in the book. Include information about the animal's history, habitate, food needs, enemies, and so on. Present your report to the class and include pictures and charts.
4. Make a clay model of the main animal character in your book. Show it to the class and tell about the character.

MYSTERY TITLES OF BOOKS ABOUT ANIMALS

Try to figure out these titles of books about animals.

1. antonym for "white" + antonym for "ugly" =

_____

2. antonym for "queen" + a preposition rhyming with "dove" + THE + a strong breeze =

_____

3. fluffy frozen rain + a canine = _____

4. antonym for "laddie" + antonym for "go" + where you live =

_____

5. what you wear on your feet "inside" your shoes = _____

6. THE + a yellow citrus fruit + a topping for pie + a canine =

_____

7. rhymes with "hall" + a preposition rhyming with "dove" + THE + antonym for "tame" =

_____

8. rhymes with "now" + THE + a pachyderm + past tense of "get" + a possessive pronoun + something you pack things in =

_____

9. THE + a feline + what an owl says + past tense of "go" + homonym of "two" + paradise =

_____

10. a hare + a small mountain = _____

ANSWER KEYS

Unit 1 FANTASY AND SCIENCE FICTION

1-1A Projects for *The Lion, the Witch, and the Wardrobe*

1. Belfast is in Ireland.
2. C stands for Clive and S stand for Staples.
3. A theologian is a person who studies God and man's relation to God. *(Students' wording may vary.)*
4. *The Lion, the Witch, and the Wardrobe*
5. 1952

1-1B Save Lucy

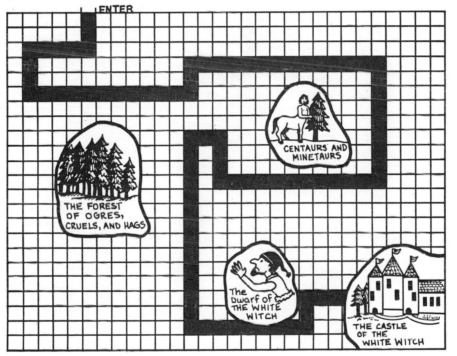

1-2A Projects for *The Indian in the Cupboard*

1. Answers will vary.
2. Answers will vary.
3. Answers will vary.

1-2B The Magic Box

Stories will vary.

1-3A Projects for *The White Mountains*

1. Liverpool, England
2. 1922
3. Samuel Youd
4. Answers may vary, but most students should say the Alps.

5. The White Mountains in eastern California, southwest Nevada, and in the Appalachian Range

6. The "Ancients" were probably the people of our present civilization. (Students' wording may vary.)

1-3B Can You Find the White Mountains?

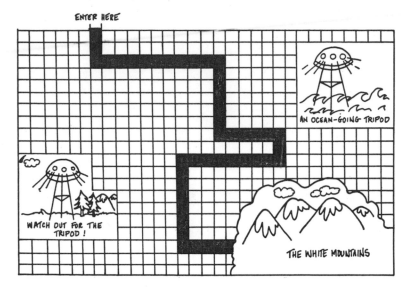

1-4A Projects for *The Great Rescue Operation*

1. Marvin
2. Raymond
3. Marvin
4. Fats

5. Fats
6. Raymond
7. Marvin
8. Marvin

1-4B Can You Rescue Fats?

1-5A Projects for *The Book of Three*

4, 11, 15, 14, 5, 1, 2, 6, 3, 10, 8, 13, 12, 9, 7

1-5B A Real Puzzler

1. Eilonwy
2. Spiral Castle
3. Fflewddur
4. Cair Dathyl
5. pigkeeper
6. gwythaint
7. Lord Gwydion
8. Cair Dallben
9. enchantress

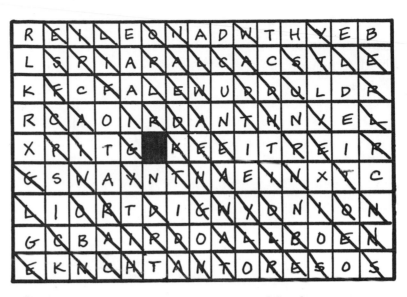

THE MESSAGE IS: Read The Black Cauldron next. It is a good book too.

1-6A Projects for *The House with a Clock in Its Walls*

1. 1938
2. Marshall, Michigan
3. *The House with a Clock in Its Walls*
4. Answers will vary.
5. Answers will vary.
6. Answers will vary according to your collection.

1-6B Find the Words

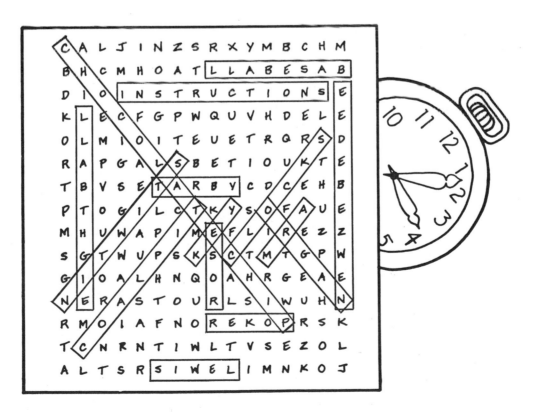

1-7A Projects for *Omega Station*

1. July 20, 1969
2. Neil Armstrong and Edwin Aldrin, Jr.
3. Eagle
4. (Any four) Charles Conrad, Jr.; Alan Bean; Alan Shepherd, Jr.; Edgar Mitchell; David Scott; James Irwin; John Young; Charles Duke, Jr.; Eugene Cernan; Harrison Schmitt
5. The first in orbit was Yuri Gagarin from Russia in Vostok I. The flight was on April 12, 1961, and it lasted for one hour and 48 minutes.

1-7B How to Reach Omega Station

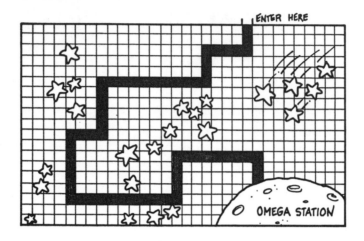

1-8A Projects for *The Wonderful Flight to the Mushroom Planet*

1. Cookies, bread, celery, carrots, lettuce, wienerwurst, sliced ham, a package of cheese, oranges, bananas, apples, dates, raisins, shelled nuts, cooking chocolate, candy, peanut butter, Mrs. Pennyfeather, and a bag of chicken feed
2. Answers will vary.
3. F, D, A, E, C, B

1-8B Read All About It!

Stories will vary.

1-9A Projects for *In the Keep of Time*

3, 6, 5, 2, 4, 1

1-9B A "Timeless" Wordsearch

1. Andrew
2. Smailholm
3. rabbit hole
4. Cedric
5. Ollie
6. Kelso
7. Muckle-Mooth Meg
8. Vianah
9. Aunt Grace
10. Ian

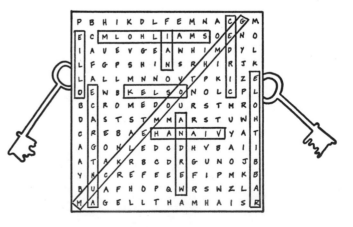

1-10A Projects for *The Forgotten Door*

1. Answers will vary.
2. Answers will vary.
3. Answers will vary depending on your collection.

1-10B If You Found Little Jon

Stories will vary.

1-11A Projects for Your Choice of Fantasy or Science Fiction

All answers will vary.

1-11B Fantasy and Science Fiction Wordsearch

1. Christopher
2. Cameron
3. John Bellairs
4. Alexander Key
5. Lynne Banks
6. Alfred Slote
7. Van Leeuwen
8. Lloyd Alexander
9. Madeleine
10. Lewis Carroll
11. George Seldon
12. Juster

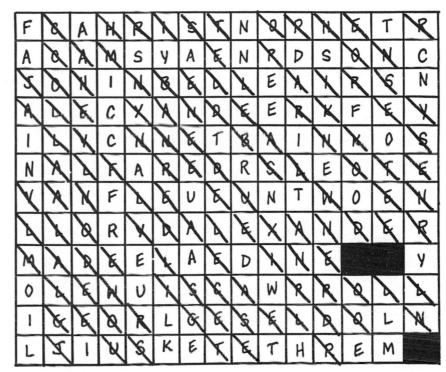

THE MESSAGE IS: Fantasy and Science Fiction are fun to read. You will like them.

Unit 2 MYSTERY AND ADVENTURE

2-1A Projects for *The One-Hundredth Thing about Caroline*

Answers may vary, but possible answers include:

1. J.P.'s wiring of Mr. Fiske's chair so that he would get a shock
2. J.P. going into Mr. Fiske's apartment to find evidence that he was planning to murder Caroline and him
3. Caroline reading Mr. Fiske's discarded mail
4. J.P. removing things from Mr. Fiske's apartment as evidence

2-1B Do You Remember?

1. Three spines should be colored red.
2. Three spines should be colored blue.
3. The number 3 should be written on the dinosaur's back.

4. Three spines should be colored orange.

5. "Doing the laundry" should be written on the tail.

6. "Investigative reporter" should be written on the neck.

7. "Stegosaurus" should be written under the number 3.

8. Two book titles by Lois Lowry should be written under the dinosaur.

9. Answer may vary depending on the edition of the book. Subtract the number of pages in the edition used from 1983. Put that number on the front right leg.

10. The student's name should be written in the lower left-hand corner of the sheet.

2-2A Projects for *The Curse of Camp Gray Owl*

1. Roy was unable to get a football scholarship because of his leg injury. He was also fearful that one teacher would be too difficult.

2. If Roy did some original research on Camp Gray Owl, he would get a good grade from the teacher he thought would be too difficult.

3. Answers will vary.

4. Longbow wanted to keep his presence a secret so that no one would interfere with his work. He also was trying to scare them away because Camp Gray Owl was dangerous.

2-2B Researching Other Camps

Part One

Books by Patricia Clyne will vary according to your collection.

Part Two

1. Virginia
2. North Carolina
3. New Jersey
4. Georgia
5. Arizona
6. South Carolina
7. Virginia
8. Oklahoma

Part Three

Answers may vary, but might include that southern states have more suitable weather for outdoor training.

Part Four

Answers will vary.

2-3A Projects for *The Adventures of Tom Sawyer*

All answers will vary.

2-3B Remembering and Categorizing

Answers may vary, but possible answers include:

1. The time Tom fed his cat the cough medicine Aunt Polly wanted Tom to take. He claimed to have helped the cat.

2. The time Tom saved Becky Thatcher's life by finding a way out of the cave.

3. The time Tom took the blame for tearing the teacher's book and then took the whipping that Becky deserved.

4. The time Tom and Huck found the treasure in the cave.

5. The time Tom told about the murder he and Huck witnessed and so saved Muff Potter.

6. The time Tom "conned" the boys into white-washing the fence or when he "conned" them out of their Bible-verse tickets.

7. The time Tom, Huck, and Joe went to Jackson Island on a raft and pretended to be pirates for several days.

2-4A Projects for *The Ghost Next Door*

1. It did not have love behind the eyes.
2. She wanted Miss Judith to love her more than Miranda.
3. He was too grief stricken to talk about it at first, and then he felt he had waited too long and his wife and daughter would not understand.
4. She found out from Miranda's diary.
5. Answers will vary.

2-4B A "Ghostly" Crossword Puzzle

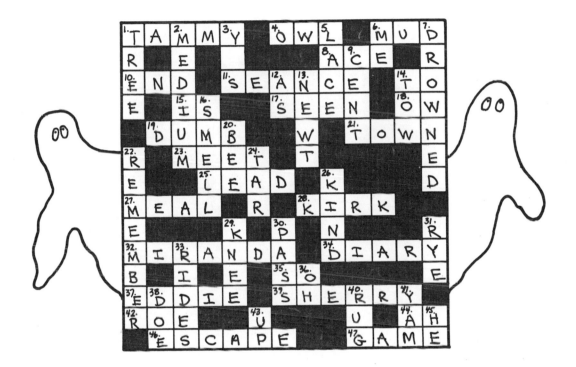

2-5A Projects for *My Side of the Mountain*

1.a. Daniel Defoe; copyright date varies according to the edition
  b. Walt Morey; 1972
  c. Johann Wyss; copyright date varies according to the edition
  d. Lilith Norton; 1970
  e. Jean Craighead George; 1972
2. Answers will vary.
3. Answers will vary.

2-5B On Your Own

Stories will vary.

2-6A Projects for *The Red Room Riddle*

All answers will vary according to your collection.

2-6B Find Your Way Out of the Haunted House

2-7A Projects for *The Dollhouse Murders*

All answers will vary.

2-7B The Secret Message

1. Claiborne
2. Ellen
3. puppet
4. tulip
5. eleven
6. pizza

7. thirteen
8. Treloar
9. newspaper
10. dolls
11. *A Doll's House*
12. Reuben

THE MESSAGE IS: The note said Reuben did it.

2-8A Projects for *The Egypt Game*

1. May 11, 1928
2. rural southern California
3. Books and animals
4. At age 8
5. *Season of Ponies*
6. *The Egypt Game*
7. Answers will vary according to your collection.

2-8B Find Out about Egypt

1. Queen of Egypt and wife of the pharaoh Anhenaton, whose reign was around 1367-1350 B.C.
2. 1372-1350 B.C.
3. We remember Nefertiti because of the preserved sculptures of her.
4. Isis was the most important female goddess of ancient Egypt. She was both the sister and wife of Osiris and was the mother of Horus. She was called "the mother of all things, lady of all elements, the beginning of time."
5. A pharaoh was a king of Egypt.
6. The word "pharaoh" means "great house."

2-9A Projects for *The Callender Papers*

All answers may vary.

2-9B A Callender Crossword Puzzle

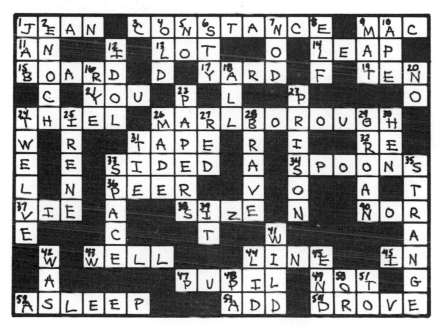

2-10A Projects for *The Case of the Baker Street Irregulars*

1. Sarah Wiggins
2. She had been ordered to get Sherlock Holmes out of the country.
3. Answers will vary.
4. Answers will vary.

2-10B Be a Sherlock Holmes

1. G	9. N
2. L	10. S
3. F	11. U
4. D	12. W
5. C	13. I
6. T	14. E
7. R	15. O
8. V	

THE MESSAGE IS:
Good detectives use reference sources well.

2-11A Projects for Your Choice of Mystery or Adventure

All answers will vary.

2-11B Title Riddles

1. *My Side of the Mountain* (by Jean George)
2. *The Haunted House* (by Peggy Parish)
3. *The Ghost Next Door* (by Wylly Folk St. John)
4. *The Dollhouse Murders* (by Betty Ren Wright)
5. *Encyclopedia Brown, Boy Detective* (by Donald Sobol)
6. *Treasure Island* (by Robert Louis Stevenson)
7. *Kidnapped* (by Robert Louis Stevenson)
8. *Old Yeller* (by Fred Gipson)
9. *The Red Room Riddle* (by Scott Corbett)
10. *Island of the Blue Dolphin* (by Scott O'Dell)

Unit 3 BOYS AND GIRLS OF TODAY

3-1A Projects for *The Unmaking of Rabbit*

All answers will vary.

3-1B A Constance Greene Wordsearch

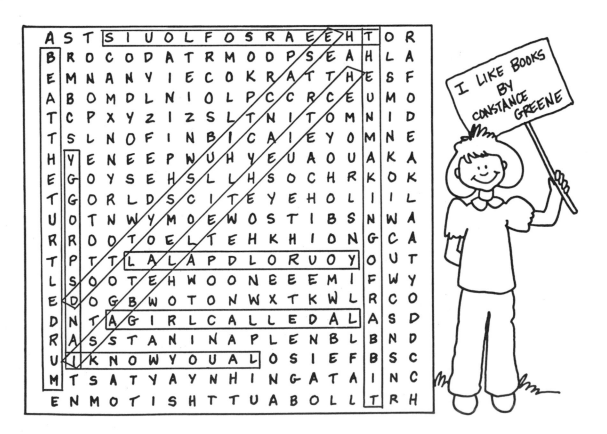

3-2A Projects for *Don't Hurt Laurie*

Answers will vary.

3-2B What's the Message?

1. Jack
2. George
3. Nell
4. Shelly
5. Tim
6. Annabelle
7. Amigo
8. Laurie
9. Mrs. Gerrold
10. ravine

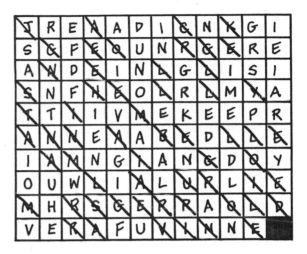

THE MESSAGE IS: Reading is fun. Reading is informative. Keep reading and you will have fun.

3-3A Projects for *Nothing's Fair in Fifth Grade*

The following answers are based on the 1984 *World Almanac:*

1. 15,538 school districts
2. 2,129,697 teachers
3. 423,062 teachers in 1900
4. $325 in 1900
5. $19,100 in 1981

3-3B Good Books to Read about Kids and School

1. Jamie Gilson
2. Patricia Giff
3. Barthe DeClements
4. Meindert DeJong
5. John Fitzgerald
6. Jan Greenberg
7. Judy Blume
8. Harry Allard
9. Lilian Moore
10. Rebecca Caudill
11. Gertrude Warner
12. William Hooks

THE MESSAGE IS: There are many good books about kids and schools. Use the card catalog to find one. Check it out and then have fun reading it.

3-4A Projects for *The Iceberg and Its Shadow*

All answers will vary.

3-4B A "Fishy" Puzzle

1. Mindy Gottfried
2. Jill Blair
3. Carl Gottfried
4. Mrs. Trilling
5. Anabeth Blair
6. Carolyn Turner
7. Skokie
8. Rachel Horwitz
9. Goldy
10. Neil Bennet

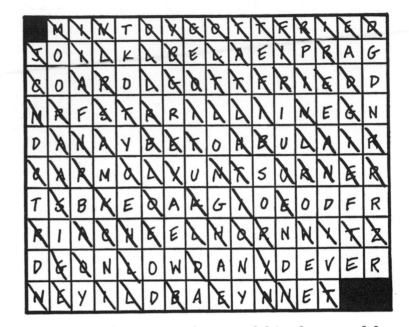

THE MESSAGE IS: To keep a good friend, you must be a good friend now and forever.

3-5A Projects for *Hideaway*

1. Answers will vary.
2. Jerry's mother thought he was with his father and so did the stepchildren's Aunt Carol. Jerry's father had forgotten that he was supposed to pick up Jerry and keep him for a week.
3. Answers will vary.
4. Answers will vary, but may include that Hanna, after agreeing to go to California with Jerry, made him realize the hard, drab, and lonesome life they faced it they went.

3-5B Jerry's Missing

Posters will vary, but should include Jerry's name, his description, and that he was last seen in Portland, Oregon (on a made-up date), in September.

3-6A Projects for *Philip Hall Likes Me. I Reckon Maybe*

1. a. 2,349,000 people (as of 1984)
   b. *Regnat Populus* (The People Rule)
   c. Little Rock
   d. 72201
2. 10.8 in 1982; 11.4 in 1984
3. They picketed his store.
4. Answers will vary.

3-6B Do You Remember?

1. Beth Lambert
2. Baby Benjamin
3. Annie Lambert
4. Calvin Cook
5. Putterham
6. Bonnie Blake
7. Gordon
8. Philip Hall
9. Luther Lambert
10. Reverend Ross
11. Tiger Hunters
12. Pretty Pennies
13. Leonard
14. Madeline

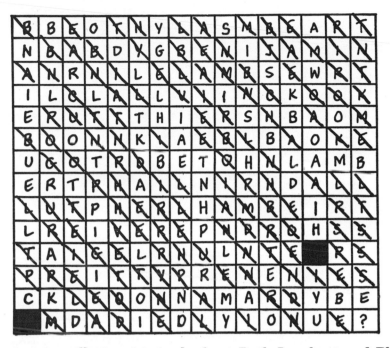

THE MESSAGE IS: Boys and girls will like this book about Beth Lambert and Philip Hall. I reckon maybe. Did you?

3-7A Projects for *Cracker Jackson*

1. Answers will vary.
2. Answers will vary.
3. *Summer of the Swans* in 1971
4. Answers will vary depending on your collection.

3-7B Mixed-Up Nursery Rhymes

(The words to the nursery rhymes may vary slightly according to the edition used.)

1. Mary, Mary quite contrary,
   How does your garden grow?
   With silverbells and cockleshells,
   And pretty maids all in a row.

2. Little Jack Horner
   Sat in a corner
   Eating his Christmas pie.
   He stuck in his thumb,
   And pulled out a plum,
   And said, "What a good boy am I."

3. Old Mother Goose when she wanted to wander,
   Would ride through the air on a very fine gander.

4. I had a little pony,
   His name was Dapple-grey.
   I lent him to a lady,
   To ride a mile away.

> She whipped him and she slashed him,
> She rode him through the mire;
> I would not lend my pony now,
> For all that lady's hire.

5. Diddle, diddle dumpling, my son John,
   Went to bed with his stockings on,
   One shoe off and one shoe on.
   Diddle, diddle dumpling, my son John.

3-8A Projects for *What Do You Do When Your Mouth Won't Open?*

3, 7, 10, 9, 1, 2, 6, 5, 8, 4

3-8B Our Fears

1. Franklin Delano Roosevelt
2. Arthur Wellesley, Duke of Wellington
3. Benedict (Baruch) Spinoza
4. Thomas Carlyle

3-9A Projects for *Will the Real Gertrude Hollings Please Stand Up?*

All answers will vary.

3-9B North, South, East, West

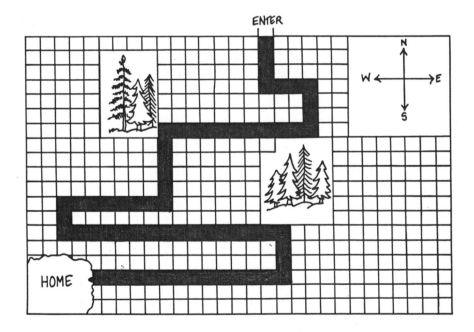

3-10A Projects for *Hello, My Name Is Scrambled Eggs*

All answers will vary.

3-10B Your Own Story

Stories will vary.

3-11A Projects for Your Choice of a Book about Boys and Girls of Today

All answers will vary.

3-11B Book Title Riddles

1. *Ginger Pye* by Eleanor Estes
2. *The TV Kid* by Betsy Byars
3. *Do Bananas Chew Gum?* by Jamie Gilson
4. *The Noonday Friends* by Mary Stolz
5. *The Real Me* by Betty Miles
6. *Diary of a Frantic Kid Sister* by Hila Colman
7. *Dear Mr. Henshaw* by Beverly Cleary
8. *Beat the Turtle Drum* by Constance Greene
9. *Up a Road Slowly* by Irene Hunt
10. *A Summer to Die* by Lois Lowry

Unit 4 HUMOROUS STORIES

4-1A Projects for *Thirteen Ways to Sink a Sub*

4-1B Can You Sink the Sub?

1. $44,070 + 97,128 = 141,198$
2. $141,198 - 301 = 140,897$
3. $140,897 - 1767 = 139,130$
4. $139,130 \div 2 = 69,565$
5. $69,565 \div 5 = 13,913$
6. $13,913 - 21 = 13,892$
7. $13,892 \div 4 = 3,473$
8. $3,473 - 58 = 3,415$
9. $3,415 \div 5 = 683$
10. $683 + 32 = 715$
11. $715 \div 55 = 13$

4-2A Projects for *Me and the Terrible Two*

1. Answers will vary according to your collection.
2. Answers will vary.
3. Answers will vary.
4. a. March 20, 1942
   b. New York
   c. Ellen Conford believed it when told that her writing was good. She also read a lot as a child.

4-2B Headlines from Literature

1. "Jack and Jill Went Up the Hill"
2. *Tales of a Fourth Grade Nothing*
3. "The Three Little Pigs"

4. "There Was an Old Woman Who Swallowed a Fly"

5. *The Three Bears*

6. *The Boxcar Children*

7. *Charlie and the Chocolate Factory*

8. *Curious George Rides a Bike*

9. *Jack and the Beanstalk*

10. "Ding Dong Bell, Pussy's in the Well"

4-3A Projects for *The Great Brain*

1. They put liver on the soles of their shoes so that Brownie would be able to find the scent back to the cave's opening.

2. He got even with the teacher by planting bottles in the room so that the school board would think the teacher was a drinker and fire him. He did confess in time, however, so that the teacher was not fired.

3. Answers will vary.

4. a. 1,461,037 (according to the 1980 census)

   b. "Industry"

   c. Salt Lake City

4-3B A Message for Great Brains

1. U	9. R
2. D	10. A
3. F	11. N
4. A	12. O
5. I	13. A
6. B	14. E
7. S	15. R
8. G	16. T

THE MESSAGE IS: A Great Brain is not great if it is not used.

4-4A Projects for *The Kid's Candidate*

1. Theodore Roosevelt at age 42

2. John F. Kennedy at age 43

3. Dorothy Straight; *How the World Began;* at age 4 (as of 1985)

4. Tracy Austin; at age 16 (as of 1985)

5. Cody Locke; at age 9 (as of 1985)

4-4B Who Said What?

Part One

1. Barnaby Brome

2. Billy White

3. Frank Feldman

4. Winifred Nobber

5. Lester Wagner

Part Two

Answers will include three of the following:

1. All bathrooms in schools are to remain unlocked.
2. All schools must offer some food that kids like to eat.
3. All schools must offer at least a few courses that kids really want to take.
4. No new teacher can become a permanent teacher unless two-thirds of the class vote for him/her.
5. No homework for elementary children. No more than one hour of homework for junior high students. No more than necessary in senior high school and no homework for anyone in the spring when the weather is nice.

Part Three

Articles will vary.

4-5A Projects for *The Cybil War*

All answers will vary.

4-5B True or False?

1. False (The tallest building in the world is the Sears Tower in Chicago.)
2. False (Whales are mammals, not fish.)
3. False (The capital of West Germany is Bonn.)
4. True
5. False (The capital of Oregon is Salem.)
6. False (Alaska is the largest state in the United States.)
7. True
8. True
9. True
10. False (A calorie is a measure of heat.)
11. False (*Ramona the Pest* is by Beverly Cleary.)
12. True
13. False (Canines are in the dog family; felines are in the cat family.)
14. True
15. True
16. False (A biography is a book about a real person.)
17. True
18. False (Antipasto is an Italian course of appetizers, etc.)
19. True
20. False (Indigo is a deep blue dye used to color clothing, etc.)

4-6A Projects for *Anastasia on Her Own*

All answers will vary.

4-6B Anastasia's Wordsearch

1. Purple
2. Illustrator
3. Steve Harvey
4. Sonya Isaacson
5. California
6. Frank
7. Katherine
8. Myron
9. Electric blanket
10. Ralph

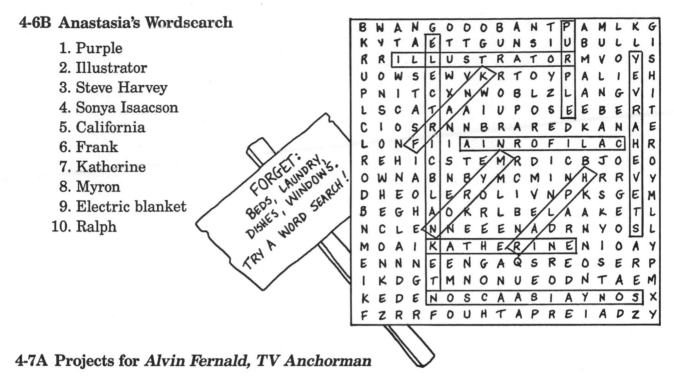

4-7A Projects for *Alvin Fernald, TV Anchorman*

1. Answers will vary.
2. Answers will vary.
3. Alvin advised the president to invite a big delegation of kids to come to this country to visit and send a big delegation of kids from this country to the Middle East. The adults should then watch the kids play together and learn from them that kids are the "key to peace."
4. It was becoming boring. He could only stand doing one thing for any length of time before wanting to try something new.

4-7B Watch Those Numbers!

1. 1962
2. 19,901 + 1962 = 21,863
3. 21,863 − 12,010 = 9853
4. 9853 − 701 = 9152
5. 9152 ÷ 2 = 4576
6. 4576 − 1971 = 2605
7. 2605 − 1797 = 808
8. 808 × 2 = 1616
9. 1616 + 1835 = 3451
10. 3451 − 1956 = 1495
11. 1495 + 503 = 1998
12. 1998 − 18 = 1980

4-8A Projects for *Mysteriously Yours, Maggie Marmelstein*

1. Answers will vary, but might include that the article about Ellen dealt chiefly with her good points, while the article about Dipsey dealt with her problems.
2. Thad and Henry were suspicious of Maggie. When Henry found a column handwritten by the mystery person and noticed the wiggly "w's," Thad and Henry decided to trap Maggie into writing a "w."

3. Answers will vary.

4. Answers will vary according to your collection.

4-8B "Creatively" Yours, Maggie Marmelstein

Stories will vary.

4-9A Projects for *Buddies*

All answers will vary.

4-9B Camping with a Buddy

1. South Dakota
2. Nevada
3. Georgia
4. Colorado
5. Wisconsin
6. Arizona
7. New Mexico
8. Oregon
9. California
10. Washington
11. Illinois
12. Kentucky

4-10A Projects for *Soup on Wheels*

1. Answers will vary.

2. Answers will vary.

3. a. "Freedom and Unity"
   b. Red clover
   c. Hermit thrush

4-10B Find the Mistakes

Soup and Robert <u>dicided</u> to give a party. It would be a <u>realy grate</u> one. <u>Their</u> would be prizes for the best <u>custume</u> and the food would be <u>terific</u>!

They <u>planed</u> to have <u>barbaqued</u> chicken, <u>potatoe</u> salad, <u>crossants</u> and, for <u>desert</u>—an ice cream <u>sunday</u>!

The party was to be on <u>Wensday</u> and the boys were <u>reddy</u> an hour early. They waited and waited but <u>noboddy</u> came.

"Where is everyone?" Soup asked.

"<u>There</u> not coming, I think," said Soup with aggravation.

"They should have <u>recieved there</u> invitations a long time ago," Soup said. "You mailed them last <u>weak,</u> didn't you?"

"Why <u>know</u>! I thought you mailed them," Robert gasped in <u>surprize.</u> "No wonder <u>they're</u> no guests coming!"

"Oh, well," sighed Soup, "there's a <u>barel</u> of food, so let's eat!"

decided	potato	received
really	croissants	their
great	dessert	week
there	sundae	no
costume	Wednesday	surprise
terrific	ready	there are
planned	nobody	barrel
barbecued	they're	

4-11A Projects for Your Choice of a Humorous Story

All answers will vary.

5-5B Words of the American Revolution

1. Alexander Hamilton
2. George Washington
3. Nathan Hale
4. Patrick Henry
5. John Adams
6. John Quincy Adams
7. Thomas Paine
8. Thomas Jefferson
9. Benjamin Franklin

5-6A Projects for *An Orphan for Nebraska*

1. Kevin knew how to read because his father had been a schoolteacher and had taught him.
2. Uncle Michael was in jail because he had thrown a spade at a foreman for calling him Paddy "once too often" and the foreman had died of a heart attack.
3. Kevin was not picked because they said he was too little and too fair skinned.
4. His real name was Euclid Smith, and he was editor of the town newspaper.

5-6B All about Nebraska

1. True
2. False (689 deaths on March 18, 1925)
3. True
4. True
5. False (March 1, 1867)
6. True
7. True
8. True
9. False (The cottonwood)
10. True
11. False (Lincoln)
12. True
13. True
14. False (Omaha)
15. False ("Flat water")

16. False

17. True

TOTAL: 37 points

5-7A Projects for *Snow Treasure*

1. Children were used because they would not be suspected, so there would be a better chance for success.

2. At first, Uncle Victor suspected Jan, but Jan proved himself by saving Peter from the German camp.

3. Peter was taken because he was in trouble with the Germans for the snowball incident and was known to them. If Peter stayed in Norway, Uncle Victor did not know what the Germans would do to him.

4. The villagers kept the schools closed by pretending there was a serious epidemic among the young children that might spread if schools were open.

5-7B A Snowy Wordsearch

1. James Russell Lowell
2. Christina Rossetti
3. Silver Lake, Colorado
4. Five
5. Oslo
6. Canada
7. Austria
8. Gunde Svan
9. Olga Pall
10. Stein Eriksen
11. Sonja Henie

5-8A Projects for *Fire in the Wind*

1. Answers will vary.

2. Answers will vary.

3. Mr. Arnold could not save his home because the water mains were broken and he could not get water.

4. Jeff and his father managed to save their home because Jeff's father had stored up as much water as possible and then they kept the roof wet by covering it with wet blankets and rewetting the blankets as they dried. They also burned all the wooden material (fences, etc.), shrubs, etc., around the house so that there was no fuel for the fire near the house.

4-11B Figure Out the Humorous Titles

1. *Thirteen Ways to Sink a Sub* (Jamie Gilson)
2. *Superfudge* (Judy Blume)
3. *Soup for President* (Robert Newton Peck)
4. *I Know You Al* (Constance Greene)
5. *Homer Price* (Robert McCloskey)
6. *The Last Guru* (Daniel Pinkwater)
7. *The Great Brain* (John Fitzgerald)
8. *Skinnybones* (Barbara Park)
9. *Me and the Terrible Two* (Ellen Conford)
10. *Hello, My Name Is Scrambled Eggs* (Jamie Gilson)
11. *Nothing's Fair in Fifth Grade* (Barthe De Clements)
12. *Tales of a Fourth Grade Nothing* (Judy Blume)

Unit 5 HISTORICAL FICTION

5-1A Projects for *The Sign of the Beaver*

1. Massachusetts became a state on February 6, 1788; Maine, on March 15, 1820.
2. Passamaquoddy, Penobscot, Maliseet; the Penobscot Indians were mentioned in the story.
3. Answers will vary.

5-1B Lost in the Wilderness

Stories will vary.

5-2A Projects for *The Terrible Wave*

1. 2,200 (according to 1984 *World Almanac*)
2. Yellow River (Hwang-ho) in China (according to 1985 *Guinness Book of World Records*)
3. October 1877
4. 900,000
5. 15901
6. 35,496 (according to 1984 *World Almanac*)

5-2B Help Megan Escape the Flood

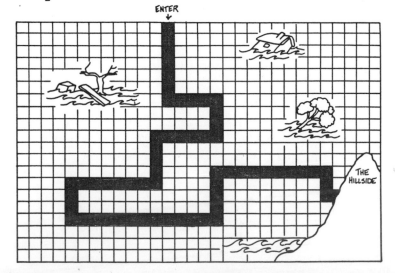

5-3A Projects for *Wait for Me, Watch for Me, Eula Bee*

1. Grass Woman, Cabral, Martin Quinero, and Tomas
2. Answers will vary.
3. The Comanches took children because they did not have many children of their own.
4. Answers will vary.

5-3B Eula Bee's Wordsearch

1. Many Horses
2. Grass Woman
3. Quintero
4. Small Buffalo
5. Lewallen
6. Eula Bee
7. Tomas
8. Cabral
9. Angelita
10. Comanche
11. Kiowa
12. Lorena

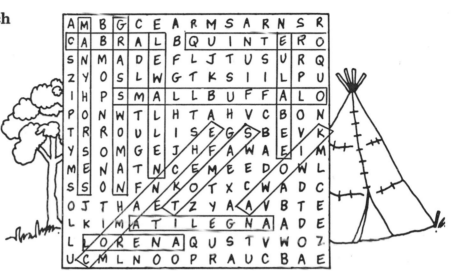

5-4A Projects for *Journey to Topaz*

1. Answers will vary, but will probably include the fact that the Japanese-Americans could be more readily identified than the German-Americans or Italian-Americans.
2. Mrs. Jamieson, Mimi Nelson, and the entire Nelson family.
3. *Issei* were Japanese immigrants to the United States and *Nissei* were children born to Japanese immigrants, so they were natural born citizens of the United States.
4. Modern drugs have made tuberculosis hospitals a thing of the past in most cases.

5-4B What Does It Say?

1. O
2. A
3. R
4. P
5. L
6. M
7. G
8. T
9. S
10. K
11. I
12. F
13. C
14. E

THE MESSAGE IS: People of all races make America great.

5-5A Projects for *My Brother Sam Is Dead*

1. Answers will vary, but might include that Tim admired Sam, wanted to show off to him, loved him, was sometimes angry with him, and often felt a sibling rivalry with him.
2. The cowboys were men who robbed on the excuse that they were working for the Rebels, but were really criminals working only for themselves.
3. The general wanted to show the townspeople that the soldiers would not steal from them and also to make an example of Sam to the other soldiers.
4. Answers will vary.

5-8B A Firey Puzzle

1. October
2. Kenya, Africa (1985 *Guinness Book of World Records*)
3. Meteor
4. Firefly
5. Fireworks
6. Fireproof
7. Volunteer
8. Extinguisher
9. Smokey the Bear
10. Oxygen

THE MESSAGE IS: It is not smart to play with fire. Fire is not a toy. Learn the rules of fire prevention today.

5-9A Projects for *Three Knocks on the Wall*

1. Answers will vary.
2. Boxed handkerchiefs; answers will vary.
3. She put up a high wall to keep the existence of Sinette (Antoinette) a secret.
4. Answers will vary.

5-9B Help Antoinette

ENTER

5-10A Projects for *When Hitler Stole Pink Rabbit*

1. Anna and her family have to leave because they are afraid that if the Nazi party comes into power, they will be persecuted not only because they are Jews, but also because their father has written things against the Nazi party.
2. Onkel Julius is at first skeptical that anything will happen to the Jews. He thinks that everything will be normal in Germany in a few months and Anna's family will be able

to come home. He begins to witness the persecution of the Jews and, through a code, tells the family that they were right to escape. He is not allowed to leave and is fired from his job. Even his pass to his beloved zoo is taken from him solely because he has a Jewish grandmother. He eventually kills himself by taking sleeping pills.

3. Answers will vary.

5-10B An Historical Fiction Puzzle

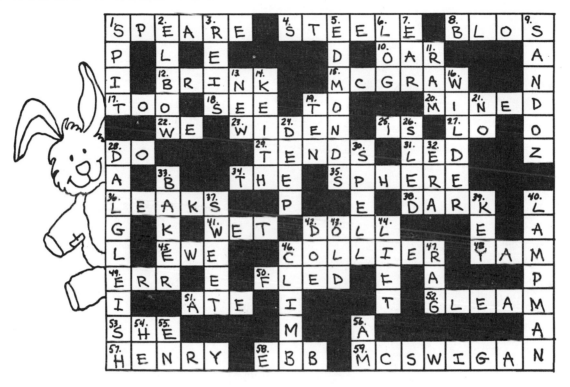

5-11A Projects for Your Choice of an Historical Fiction Book

All answers will vary.

5-11B An "Historical" Message

1. Joan Blos
2. Joanna Reis
3. Carrie Brink
4. Collier
5. Edmonds
6. Dalgleish
7. Esther Forbes
8. Harold Keith
9. Irene Hunt
10. Eloise McGraw
11. Mari Sandoz
12. Charles Hawes

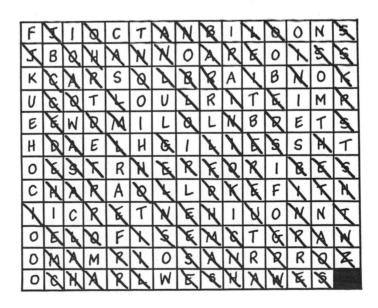

THE MESSAGE IS: Fiction books about our time will be the historical fiction of tomorrow.

Unit 6 ANIMALS IN FICTION

6-1A Projects for *Sasha, My Friend*

All answers will vary.

6-1B Compare the Two

1. a. Helena
   b. Sacramento
2. a. 147,138 square miles (1984 *World Almanac*)
   b. 158,693 square miles (1984 *World Almanac*)
3. a. 22,559,300 acres
   b. 40,152,100 acres
4. a. Agriculture, mining, manufacturing, and tourism
   b. Agriculture, aerospace, manufacturing, construction, and recreation
5. a. Wheat, cattle, barley, sheep, sugar beets, hay, flax, and oats
   b. Cotton, grapes, dairy products, nuts, apricots, avocados, citrus fruits, barley, rice, and olives
6. a. Bitterroot
   b. Golden poppy
7. a. Treasure State
   b. Golden State
8. a. November 8, 1889
   b. September 9, 1850
9. a. Answers will vary.
   b. Answers will vary.

6-2A Projects for *Runaway Stallion*

1. e
2. d
3. f
4. g
5. h
6. b
7. c
8. a

6-2B About Walt Morey

Part One

1. Hoquiam, Washington
2. *Gentle Ben*
3. Answers will vary, but may include working at sawmills, working at veneer plants, and construction.

Part Two

Answers will vary according to your collection. E. P. Dutton is the publisher of most of his books.

Part Three

The following answers are according to the 1980 census and the 1986 *World Almanac:*

1. 174,768
2. 33,426

3. 96,184 square miles

4. 570,833 square miles

5. "The Union"

6. "North to the Future"

6-3A Projects for *Rascal*

All answers will vary.

6-3B A "Rascally" Wordsearch

1. All of continental U.S.
2. All of continental U.S.
3. Alaska, Rocky Mountains
4. All of U.S.
5. All of continental U.S.
6. Southeastern U.S.
7. Northern U.S., Alaska
8. Mostly west of the Rocky Mountains, but being brought back to other states
9. Grey fox in most of U.S.; Red fox in northern U.S.
10. In wild game preserves or parks in most of U.S.
11. Southeastern and south central U.S.
12. Southwestern U.S. and in northern U.S. west of the Rocky Mountains

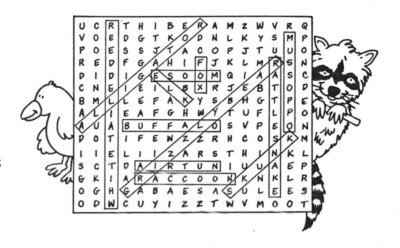

6-4A Projects for *Where the Red Fern Grows*

1. Answers will vary, but might include that Billy's family was a loving but poor family. There were three children—two girls and one boy.
2. Answers will vary, but should be before 1920.
3. Answers will vary.
4. Answers will vary, but might include that Little Ann was more intelligent and careful, while Dan was more aggressive, impulsive, and excitable.

6-4B Find the Breeds

6-5A Projects for *A Morgan for Melinda*

1. Melinda wanted her father to be proud of her and she hoped to make up for the death of his son, her brother.
2. Answers will vary.
3. Yes. Evidence will vary.
4. Answers will vary.

6-5B A New Morgan for Melinda

Stories will vary.

6-6A Projects for *Old Yeller*

1. Answers will vary.
2. Old Yeller had stolen a side of meat. Travis also did not want a dog because his old dog had died. (Answers may vary slightly.)
3. Old Yeller saved Travis from the wild hogs. Travis saved the dog from death by risking his own life to carry the dog back home after the dog was badly injured by the wild hogs when he was defending Travis. (Other instances also may be given.)
4. Answers will vary.

6-6B It's a Dog's Life

1. A	7. G	13. H
2. Y	8. T	14. N
3. P	9. S	15. F
4. V	10. E	16. B
5. I	11. M	17. R
6. N	12. O	18. K

THE MESSAGE IS: *Savage Sam* is another book by Fred Gipson.

6-7A Projects for *Lassie Come Home*

1. She felt badly that they could not afford to keep Lassie. (Answers may vary slightly.)
2. Answers will vary, but may include the time the young couple saved Lassie from being brutally treated by the dog catchers and the time the old couple saved Lassie from starvation and exhaustion.
3. Answers will vary, but may include the time the boys threw stones at Lassie and the men shot at her, and the time the dog catchers were brutal to her.
4. Answers will vary.

6-7B Help Lassie Get Home

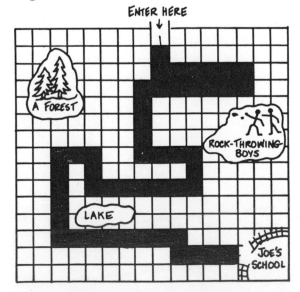

6-8A Projects for *The Black Stallion*

1. The island offered water and edible moss.
2. Alec knew his mother would not let him ride if she knew.
3. Henry had been a jockey and then a trainer of horses.
4. Answers will vary according to your collection.

6-8B Shipwrecked

Stories will vary.

6-9A Projects for *Misty of Chincoteague*

1. Pony Penning Day is a festive day with a rodeo, wild horse sale, food, etc.
2. They were "topsy-turvy" because Misty, the colt, was teaching her mother how to react to humans rather than the other way around.
3. They were able to buy Misty because the original buyer backed out when his son won a pony in the drawing and he preferred that pony.
4. *King of the Wind* in 1949

6-9B Some "Horsing" Around

1. Walt Morey
2. Marguerite (Henry)
3. Wesley Dennis
4. Anna Sewell
5. Doris Gates
6. Walt Morey
7. Enid Bagnold
8. Marie Sandoz
9. Jessie Haas
10. Lynn Hall

THE MESSAGE IS: Horse stories are always favorite books for boys and girls to read.

6-10A Projects for *Incident at Hawk's Hill*

1. Answers will vary, but should include that Ben was very small for his age and that he did not talk much. He liked to observe all animals, to imitate them, and mimic their sounds.
2. Answers will vary.
3. Answers will vary, but might include being a zoologist, an animal trainer, a zookeeper, etc.
4. Answers will vary.

6-10B The Final Chapter

Stories will vary.

6-11A Projects for Your Choice of an Animal in Fiction Book

All answers will vary.

6-11B Mystery Titles of Books about Animals

1. *Black Beauty* (by Helen Sewell)
2. *King of the Wind* (by Marguerite Henry)
3. *Snow Dog* (by Jim Kjelgaard)

4. *Lassie Come Home* (by Eric Knight)
5. *Socks* (by Beverly Cleary)
6. *The Lemon Meringue Dog* (by Walt Morey)
7. *Call of the Wild* (by Jack London)
8. *How the Elephant Got Its Trunk* (by Rudyard Kipling)
9. *The Cat Who Went to Heaven* (by Elizabeth Coatsworth)
10. *Rabbit Hill* (by Robert Lawson)